FREE FONTS SOURCE BOOK
JEUX DE POLICES GRATUITES
FAMILIAS DE TIPOGRAFÍAS GRATUITAS

D1407090

FREE FONTS SOURCE BOOK
JEUX DE POLICES GRATUITES
FAMILIAS DE TIPOGRAFÍAS GRATUITAS

MAIA FRANCISCO

FONTOLOGY:
FREE FONTS SOURCE BOOK / JEUX DE POLICES GRATUITES / FAMILIAS DE TIPOGRAFÍAS GRATUITAS

Original Project: **maomao** publications

Editorial coordination: Anja Llorella Oriol

Editing & text: Maia Francisco

English translation: Cillero & de Motta

French translation: Cillero & de Motta

Art director: Emma Termes Parera

Layout: Esperanza Escudero Pino

Cover design: zona

Copyright @ 2010 English/French/Spanish language edition by Promopress

PROMOPRESS is a brand of:
PROMOTORA DE PRENSA INTERNACIONAL SA
Ausias March, 124
08013 Barcelona, Spain
T: + 34 932 451 464
F: + 34 932 654 883
E-mail: info@promopress.es
www.promopress.info

First Published in 2010 by Promopress

ISBN 978-84-92810-09-3
Printed in Spain

All rights reserved. It is strictly prohibited, without the written authorisation of the copyright holders, under the established legal sanctions, to reproduce this work, completely or partially, by any means or procedure, including reprographics, computer treatment and the distribution of copies through public rental or loan.

Tous droits réservés. Il est formellement interdit, sauf consentement écrit des titulaires du copyright, sous peine des sanctions prévues par la loi, de procéder à une reproduction totale ou partielle de cette œuvre, quel que soit le moyen ou procédé utilisé, y compris la reprographie, le traitement informatique et la distribution d'exemplaires par location ou prêt public.

Reservados todos los derechos. Queda rigurosamente prohibida, sin la autorización escrita de los titulares del copyright, bajo las sanciones establecidas en las leyes, la reproducción, total o parcial, de esta obra por cualquier medio o procedimiento, comprendidos la reprografía, el tratamiento informático y la distribución de ejemplares mediante alquiler o préstamo público.

Summary /

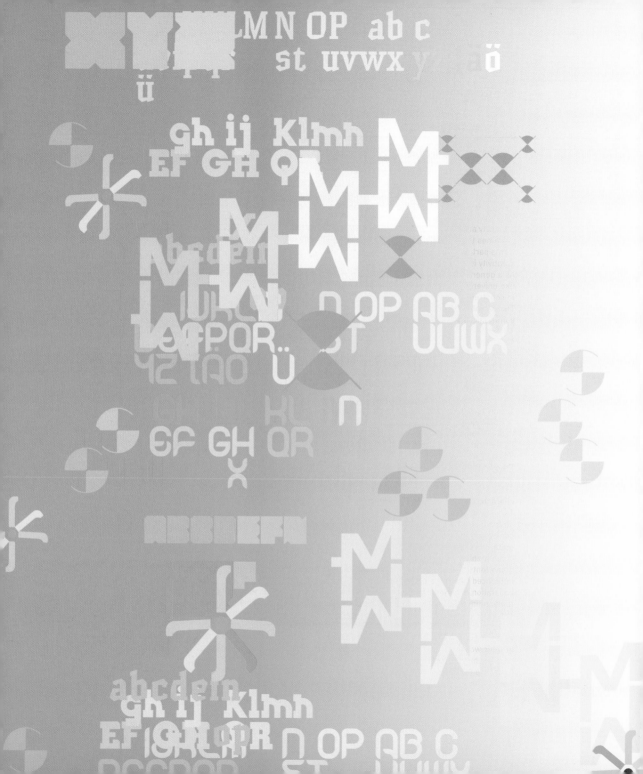

Introduction /

The printing trade was established around the year 1450 in Germany as a result of Johannes Gutenberg's important invention of mechanical movable type printing. However, the Japanese are thought to have already used a basic printing process known as xylography centuries earlier. Xylography entails working with the text on a block of wood, then covering it with ink and transferring it to paper by applying pressure on it.

Today, the printer's trade carried out in a studio crammed full of cases of movable metal type, bottles of ink and stacks of paper has become obsolescent. The technological revolution has generated digital tools that are as functional and complete as the computer. Today software abounds in the field of typographic design, opening the door to total creativity and inviting the typographer to experiment with the design of characters to extremes that really stretch our imagination. The Free Font Phenomenon, which in turn forms part of the free culture movement, is the result of this explosion of freedom and creativity in typographic design.

As a general rule, Free Fonts have been designed to serve small linguistic communities like university environments or developing countries, whose graphic designers endeavor to construct a typographic culture and thus stem the tide of those resorting to pirate fonts. This social intent using this type of font offers the world a means of keeping literacy and communication within a specific community.

This book, however, alludes to the parallel trend dealing with the less traditional facet of typographic design: a selection of the more experimental and creative designs – those that generate fonts with an informal, decorative style. Fonts that are not well suited to running text but more appropriate for headings or exhibition work. Fonts generated for the purpose of stimulating the creative process for any piece of graphic work.

The free culture movement is on the rise, defending the view of culture promoted by a heterogeneous social movement believing in the freedom to disseminate and modify creative work, it seeks a a way to mesh with the widespread movement fronted by Copyleft and Opensource. In all cases, the free nature of the fonts will always be set out explicitly in the details of the license. For this reason, some Free Fonts maintain standard license agreements while others are distributed under Creative Commons licenses.

The designs inspired by the graffiti and skateboard culture are common fixtures in the Free Font world. These are usually decorative stencil-like fonts with the letters divided into several parts to create templates which can be reproduced on another surface. There is also another trend to simulate the script of old computers like Commodore 64 or the ASCII characters used in programming functions.

The appearance of some fonts in this selection are reminiscent of construction techniques or design tools such as: nibs, paintbrushes of various thicknesses, and felt-tip pens. Others consist of letters made up of loose individual elements that are formed from organic materials such as potatoes, jello or beans. The letter or physical object is digitalized so that it can then be refined by computer.

Some fonts belong to the group known as "faux foreign fonts". These are fonts that are influenced by writing systems that do not use the Roman or Latin alphabet, such as the adaptation of cuneiform script (used by the Sumerians towards the end of the fourth millennium BC), Sanskrit (the classical language of India), or the adaptation of the Kana characters from Japanese writing.

The pages of this book illustrate the standard repertoire of characters for each font, shown in various sizes so that they can be displayed properly. Each typeface is accompanied by a graphic work including the application of the font in question. Thus, there is an immediate relationship between the conceptual or visual context of the font, albeit in the form of a fanzine, a road sign, or the names of dishes on the menu in a bar. The CD accompanying the book includes the folders of the font ready for installation on the computer.

Leabharlanna Poiblí Chathair Bhaile Átha Cliath
Dublin City Public Libraries

Introduction /

La typographie est née aux alentours de 1450, en Allemagne, avec la grande invention de Johannes Gutenberg : l'imprimerie moderne à caractères métalliques mobiles. On suppose cependant que, des siècles auparavant, les Japonais utilisaient déjà une impression rudimentaire, appelée impression par xylographie. La xylographie consistait à travailler le texte sur une tablette en bois, puis à encrer celle-ci et à la transférer sur le papier par pression.

Actuellement, le métier de typographe dans un atelier rempli de caisses de caractères métalliques mobiles, de bidons d'encre et de piles de papier est devenu obsolète. La révolution technologique a produit des outils numériques aussi fonctionnels et complets que l'ordinateur. Il existe de nombreux logiciels pour le design typographique, qui laissent libre cours à la créativité et invitent à faire des expériences dans le design de caractères jusqu'à des limites inimaginables. Le fruit de cette explosion de liberté et de créativité dans le design typographique est le phénomène Free Font, qui fait partie à son tour du mouvement Culture Libre.

Plus généralement, les Free Fonts ont été conçues pour servir des petites communautés linguistiques, comme des environnements universitaires ou des pays en voie de développement, où les designers graphiques essayent de construire une culture typographique tout en évitant d'utiliser des typographies piratées. Ce type de polices à intention sociale propose au monde le maintien d'un alphabétisme et la communication dans une communauté.

Ce livre se réfère cependant au courant parallèle qui accueille la facette moins traditionnelle du design graphique. Une sélection des designs les plus expérimentaux et créatifs, ceux qui génèrent des polices avec une esthétique informelle et décorative. Des polices peu adaptées à du texte mais utiles pour des titres ou des typographies d'exposition. Des polices créées dans le but de favoriser le processus créatif de n'importe quel projet graphique.

Le mouvement Culture Libre s'étend et défend la vision de la culture promue par un mouvement hétérogène social, basé sur la liberté de distribuer et modifier des travaux et des œuvres de création, tout en recherchant la convergence avec le vaste mouvement Copyleft et Opensource. Dans tous les cas, la liberté des polices devient toujours explicite grâce à leur licence. C'est la raison pour laquelle, quelques Free Fonts ont des accords de licence standard, tandis que d'autres sont distribuées avec des licences Creative Commons. Les designs inspirés de la culture du graffiti et du skateboard sont très communes dans le domaine des Free Fonts. Ce sont généralement des polices décoratives, de style stencil, caractérisées par leurs lettres divisées en plusieurs parties afin de créer des modèles et de les reproduire sur d'autres surfaces. Il existe aussi une tendance à imiter l'écriture des anciens ordinateurs, comme le Commodore 64, ou les caractères ASCII de programmation. L'aspect de certaines polices de la sélection présente font référence à des techniques de construction ou à des outils de design comme la plume, le rouleau, le pinceau et le feutre. D'autres consistent en des lettres composées d'éléments individuels isolés, formés à partir de matériaux organiques comme la pomme de terre, la gélatine ou les haricots. La lettre, ou objet physique, est numérisée afin d'être affinée ensuite par ordinateur.

Certaines polices appartiennent au groupe « faux foreign fonts », ce sont celles influencées par des systèmes d'écriture en dehors de l'alphabet romain ou latin. Comme l'adaptation de l'écriture cunéiforme (utilisée par les sumériens à la fin du quatrième millénaire avant J-.C), le sanscrit (la langue classique de l'Inde) ou l'adaptation des caractères *kana* de l'écriture japonaise.

Les pages de ce livre présentent le répertoire standard de caractères pour chaque police, dans différentes tailles, pour une meilleure visualisation. Chaque typographie est accompagnée d'une œuvre graphique utilisant la police. Le contexte conceptuel ou visuel de la police est ainsi immédiatement relié, fanzine, panneau de signalisation ou titres d'un menu de bar. Le CD fourni avec le livre inclut les dossiers de la police prêts à l'emploi pour les installer sur l'ordinateur.

Introducción /

El oficio de la tipografía nace alrededor de 1450 en Alemania gracias al gran invento de Johannes Gutenberg: la imprenta moderna de caracteres móviles metálicos. Sin embargo, se cree que siglos antes los japoneses ya utilizaban una imprenta rudimentaria denominada imprenta por xilografía. La xilografía consistía en trabajar el texto sobre una tablilla de madera, para luego entintarla y transferirla al papel por presión.

Actualmente, el oficio de tipógrafo llevado a cabo en un taller repleto de cajas de tipos móviles metálicos, botes de tinta y pilas de papel ha quedado obsoleto. La revolución tecnológica ha generado herramientas digitales tan funcionales y completas como el ordenador. Existen multitud de programas informáticos para el diseño tipográfico que dejan vía libre a la creatividad total e invitan a experimentar con el diseño de caracteres hasta límites inimaginables. Fruto de esta explosión de libertad y creatividad en el diseño de tipografía es el fenómeno Free Font, el cual, a su vez, forma parte del movimiento Cultura Libre.

A nivel general, las Free Fonts han sido diseñadas para servir a comunidades lingüísticas pequeñas, como entornos universitarios o países en vías de desarrollo, cuyos diseñadores gráficos tratan de construir una cultura tipográfica evitando recurrir a tipografías pirateadas. Con una intención social, este tipo de fuentes ofrecen al mundo el mantenimiento de un alfabetismo y comunicación dentro de una comunidad.

Sin embargo, este libro se refiere a la corriente paralela que acoge la faceta menos tradicional del diseño tipográfico. Una selección de los diseños más experimentales y creativos, los que generan fuentes de estética informal y decorativa. Tipografías poco apropiadas para texto corrido pero ideales para titulares o material de muestra, creadas con la intención de favorecer el proceso creativo de cualquier proyecto gráfico.

El movimiento Cultura Libre se expande, defiende la visión de la cultura promovida por un heterogéneo movimiento social basada en la libertad de distribuir y modificar trabajos y obras creativas, buscando la manera de encajar con el amplio movimiento Copyleft y Opensource. En todo caso, la libertad de las fuentes siempre se hará explícita a través de su licencia. Por ello, algunas Free Fonts mantienen acuerdos de licencia estándar, mientras que otras se distribuyen bajo licencias Creative Commons.

Los diseños inspirados en la cultura del grafiti y el *skateboarding* resultan muy comunes en el campo de las Free Fonts. Suelen ser fuentes decorativas de estilo stencil caracterizadas por sus letras divididas en varias partes para crear plantillas y reproducirlas en otras superficies. También existe la tendencia a simular la escritura de los ordenadores antiguos como Commodore 64 o los caracteres ASCII en programación.

El aspecto de algunas fuentes en la presente selección hace referencia a técnicas de construcción o herramientas de diseño como la plumilla, la brocha, el pincel o el rotulador. Otras consisten en letras compuestas por elementos individuales sueltos que se forman a partir de materiales orgánicos como la patata, la gelatina o las judías. La letra u objeto físico se digitaliza para posteriormente ser retocada en el ordenador.

Algunas fuentes pertenecen al grupo «faux foreign fonts». Se trata de fuentes influenciadas por sistemas de escritura fuera del alfabeto romano o latino, como la adaptación de la escritura cuneiforme (utilizada por los sumerios a finales del siglo ıv a.C.), el sánscrito (lengua clásica de la India), o la adaptación de los caracteres *kana* de la escritura japonesa. Las páginas de este libro muestran el repertorio estándar de caracteres para cada fuente, en diversos tamaños para una mejor visualización. Cada tipografía va acompañada de una obra gráfica donde se ha aplicado la fuente. De este modo, se relaciona de forma inmediata el contexto conceptual o visual de la fuente, ya sea un fanzine, una señal de tráfico o los títulos del menú de un bar. El CD que acompaña el libro incluye las carpetas de las fuentes listas para instalar en el ordenador.

ACTION OF THE TIME

Galdino Otten | galdinoottenbr.blogspot.com

ACTION OF THE TIME

1234567890
ABCDEFGHIJ
KLMNOPQR
STUVWXYZ
ABCDEFGHI
JKLMNOPQR
STUVWXYZ
{$?!%@}(&#+:)Ç

ABCDEFGHIJKLMNOPQRSTUVWXYZ[ÄÖÜÅÇÑ]
ABCDEFGHIJKLMNOPQRSTUVWXYZ
1234567890(.,:;?$&-){ÄÖÜÅÇÑ}

8/10 pt

ABCDEFGHIJKLMNOPQRSTUVWXYZ[ÄÖÜÅÇÑ]
ABCDEFGHIJKLMNOPQRSTUVWXYZ
1234567890(.,:;?$&-){ÄÖÜÅÇÑ}

10/12 pt

ABCDEFGHIJKLMN
OPQRSTUVWXYZ[ÄÖÜÅÇÑ]
ABCDEFGHIJKLMN
OPQRSTUVWXYZ
1234567890(.,:;?$&-){ÄÖÜÅÇÑ}

18/18 pt

ABCDEFGHIJKLMN
OPQRSTUVWXYZ[ÄÖÜÅÇÑ]
ABCDEFGHIJKLMN
OPQRSTUVWXYZ
1234567890
(.,:;?$&-){ÄÖÜÅÇÑ}

24/24 pt

Designed for use in projects that have Pop Art or artistic connotations, while conjuring up the sensation of action and emotion. The font's name comes from its eroded appearance, suggesting the effect of the passing of time. The very black and bold stroke has scratches running through it in all directions. This trait lends the font a very informal appearance. The letters and numbers appear to be misplaced with respect to the baseline, giving them a more dynamic effect. The result is a decorative sans serif font, built up continuously with parallel edge stems.

Conçue pour des projets à connotation artistique et avec un style Pop Art qui impliquent à la fois une sensation d'action et d'émotion. Le nom de cette police de caractères provient de son apparence érodée qui reflète l'effet du temps. Le trait très noir et gras est marqué par une multitude de rayures qui vont dans tous les sens. Cette particularité en fait une police de caractères à l'aspect très informel. Les lettres et les chiffres ne semblent pas alignés sur la ligne de base ce qui leur donne un effet plus dynamique. Le résultat est une police décorative sans serif, avec une construction continue et des bords parallèles.

Diseñada para proyectos de connotaciones artísticas o de estilo Pop Art, que implican al mismo tiempo una sensación de acción y de emoción. El nombre de la fuente proviene de su apariencia erosionada, que denota el efecto del paso del tiempo. El trazo grueso y muy negro queda marcado por multitud de rasguños en todas direcciones. Esta particularidad le da un carácter muy informal. Las letras y números aparecen descolocados respecto a la línea base para un efecto más dinámico. El resultado es una fuente decorativa de palo seco, de construcción continua, con astas de bordes paralelos.

Alhambra Regular/ Alhambra Deep

tales of the alhambra to the traveller imbued with a feeling for the historical and poetical, so inseparably inter twined in the annals of romantic spain, the alhambra is as much an object of devotion as is the kaaba to all true muslims. how many legends and traditions, true and fabulous; how many songs and ballads, arabian and spanish, of love and war and chivalry, are associated with this oriental pile!

abcdefghijklmnopqrstuvwxyz[áöúáœœęñ]
abcdefghijklmnopqrstuvwxyz
1234567890(.,;:?¿$£¥ę-*)[áöúáœœęñ]

8/10 pt

abcdefghijklmnopqrstuvwxyz[áöúáœœęñ]
abcdefghijklmnopqrstuvwxyz
1234567890(.,;:?¿$£¥ę-*)[áöúáœœęñ]

8/10 pt

abcdefghijklmn
opqrstuvwxyz[áöúáœœęñ]
abcdefghijklmn
opqrstuvwxyz
1234567890
(.,;:?¿$£¥ę-*)[áöúáœœęñ]

18/18 pt

abcdefghijklmn
opqrstuvwxyz[áöúáœœęñ]
abcdefghijklmn
opqrstuvwxyz
1234567890
(.,;:?¿$£¥ę-*)[áöúáœœęñ]

18/18 pt

The Alhambra font family is based on Kufi Arabic calligraphy, which is the oldest style of Arabic script. It belongs to the group of "faux foreign fonts": fonts influenced by writing systems not included in the Roman or Latin alphabet. In, for example, the Arabic alphabet, there are a great many complex ligatures. Alhambra includes extras to create a more authentic look. The orthographic symbols such as the circumflex accent or the bracket include decorative elements at the ends, while the hyphen is lengthened. Alhambra includes the Regular and Deep variants.

La famille typographique Alhambra s'inspire de la calligraphie arabe *koufi*, la forme la plus ancienne de calligraphie arabe. Elle appartient au groupe de « faux foreign fonts » : des sources influencées par des systèmes d'écriture qui n'appartiennent ni à l'alphabet romain ni à l'alphabet latin. Pour des alphabets comme l'arabe les ligatures sont nombreuses et complexes. L'Alhambra inclut des extras afin de lui donner un aspect plus authentique. Les signes diacritiques, comme l'accent circonflexe, ou les signes graphiques doubles, comme l'accolade, incluent des éléments décoratifs aux extrémités alors que la partie du milieu se prolonge. L'Alhambra comporte des variantes Regular et Deep.

La familia tipográfica Alhambra se inspira en la caligrafía *kufi*, la forma más antigua de caligrafía árabe. Pertenece al grupo de «faux foreign fonts»: fuentes influidas por sistemas de escritura que no son el alfabeto romano o latino. En alfabetos como el arábigo las ligaduras son muy numerosas y complejas. Alhambra incluye extras para crear un aspecto más auténtico. Algunos signos ortográficos, como el acento circunflejo o la llave, presentan elementos decorativos en sus extremos, mientras que el guión medio se prolonga. Alhambra incluye las variantes Regular y Deep.

Almost Sanskrit Taj

Galdino Otten | galdinoottenbr.blogspot.com

abcdefghijklmnopqrstuvwxyz
1234567890

8/10 pt

abcdefghijklmnopqrstuvwxyz
1234567890

10/12 pt

abcdefghijklmn
opqrstuvwxyz
1234567890

18/18 pt

abcdefghijklm
nopqrstuvwxyz
1234567890

24/24 pt

abcdefghijklm
nopqrstuvwxyz
1234567890

32/34 pt

Sanskrit is a classical Indian language, while traditional also being one of the oldest Indo-European languages. Nowadays it is mainly used as a ceremonial language in Hindu and Buddhist liturgy, in the form of hymns and mantras. Almost Sanskrit Taj refers to Indian or Indo-Aryan languages, a subgroup of languages spoken in the countries on the Indian subcontinent forming part of the principle modern languages that evolved from Sanskrit. This exotic font is ideal for magazines, newspapers or any other publication with content associated with India or its religions.

Le sanscrit est une langue classique indienne, une des langues indo-européennes les plus anciennes. De nos jours il est principalement utilisé comme langue de cérémonie dans la liturgie hindoue et bouddhiste, sous la forme d'hymnes et de mantras. Almost Sanskrit Taj fait référence aux langues indo-aryennes ou indiques, un sous-groupe de langues parlées dans les pays du sous-continent indien, qui font partie des principales langues modernes qui ont évolué à partir du sanscrit. Cette police de caractères exotique est idéale pour les revues, les journaux ou n'importe quel moyen de communication dont le contenu a un rapport avec l'Inde ou ses religions.

El sánscrito es una lengua clásica de la India, además de una de las lenguas indoeuropeas más antiguas. En la actualidad se utiliza principalmente como lenguaje ceremonial en la liturgia hinduista y el budismo, en la forma de himnos y mantras. Almost Sanskrit Taj hace referencia a las lenguas indoarias o índicas, un subgrupo de idiomas que se hablan en los países del subcontinente indio y que forman parte de las principales lenguas modernas que evolucionaron del sánscrito. Esta fuente exótica resulta muy adecuada para aplicar en revistas, periódicos o en cualquier medio de comunicación cuyo contenido esté relacionado con la India o sus religiones.

Barco

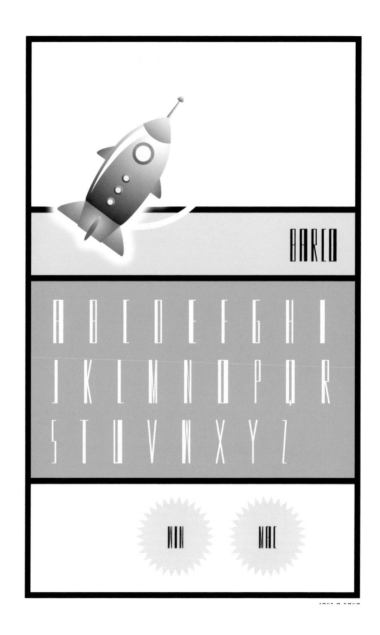

8/10 pt

10/12 pt

ABCDEFGHIJKLMNOPQRSTUVWXYZ
ÀÁÂÃÄÅÇ

18/18 pt

ABCDEFGHIJKLMNOPQRSTUVWXYZ
ÀÁÂÃÄÅÇ

24/24 pt

ABCDEFGHIJKLMNOPQRSTUVWXYZ
ÀÁÂÃÄÅÇ

32/34 pt

The design mimics the shape of a bar code. Each letter is inscribed within a vertical stylized rectangle, giving it a more condensed aspect. It is a monospace font, constructed continuously, with angular and square curves. The treatment of the stems is exaggerated, with parallel edges and changeable width. The crossbars occupy a central position and the arcs are left completely open. There is an extremely marked contrast, with a vertical axis and instant transition. This medium-weight sans serif font has uppercase characters only.

Le design imite la forme des codes-barres. Chaque lettre s'inscrit dans un rectangle stylisé dans le sens vertical ce qui lui donne un aspect condensé. Il s'agit d'une police à chasse fixe. La construction est continue, les courbes sont angulaires et ont un aspect carré. Les fûts sont exagérés, avec les bords parallèles et une largeur variable. Les fûts sont placés au milieu et les boucles semblent totalement ouvertes. Cela met en avant un contraste exagéré avec un axe vertical et une transition instantanée. Cette police sans serif de poids moyen propose uniquement des caractères en forme de carrés en hauteur.

El diseño imita la forma de los códigos de barras. Cada letra se inscribe en un rectángulo estilizado vertical, generando un aspecto condensado. Se trata de una fuente monoespaciada. De construcción continua, el tratamiento de las curvas es angular y de aspecto cuadrado. El aspecto de las astas verticales es exagerado, con bordes paralelos y anchura variable. Las astas transversales se sitúan en posición central y los arcos aparecen totalmente abiertos. Muestra un contraste exagerado, con eje vertical y transición instantánea. Esta fuente de palo seco y peso medio solamente ofrece caracteres de caja alta.

BD Algebra minus/plus

Lopetz, Büro Destruct | www.typedifferent.com | www.burodestruct.net

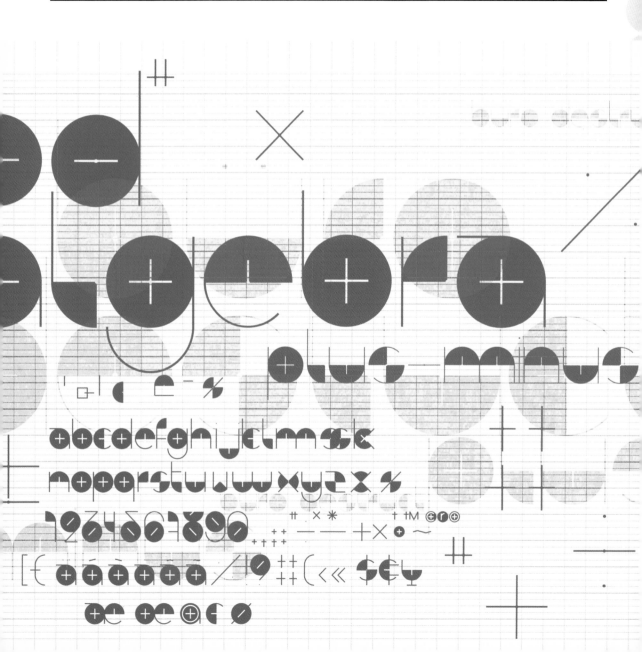

abcdefghijklmnopqrstuvwxyz[æœøßøøøøøœ(^)]
abcdefghijklmnopqrstuvwxyz
'?¿!¡%&$§@(.,;:•¸%,¢£€¥+-*)(æœøøøøøœ(^)]

8/10 pt

abcdefghijklmnopqrstuvwxyz[æœøøøøøøœ(^)]
abcdefghijklmnopqrstuvwxyz
'?¿!¡%&$§@(.,;:•¸%,¢£€¥+-*)(æœøøøøøœ(^)]

8/10 pt

abcdefghijklmnopqrstuvwxyz[æœøøøøøøœ(^)]
abcdefghijklmnopqrstuvwxyz
'?¿!¡%&$§@(.,;:•¸%,¢£€¥+-*)(æœøøøøøœ(^)]

10/12 pt

abcdefghijklmnopqrstuvwxyz[æœøøøøøøœ(^)]
abcdefghijklmnopqrstuvwxyz
'?¿!¡%&$§@(.,;:•¸%,¢£€¥+-*)(æœøøøøøœ(^)]

10/12 pt

abcdefghijklmn
opqrstuvwxyz[æœøøøøøøœ(^)]
abcdefghijklmnopqrstuvwxyz
'?¿!¡%&$§@(.,;:•¸%,¢£€¥+-*)
(æœøøøøøœ(^)]

18/18 pt

abcdefghijklmn
opqrstuvwxyz[æœøøøøøøœ(^)]
abcdefghijklmnopqrstuvwxyz
'?¿!¡%&$§@(.,;:•¸%,¢£€¥+-*)
(æœøøøøøœ(^)]

18/18 pt

Broadly speaking, the font combines an ample or full counter with hairline upward and downward stems. There is no obvious exaggeration in the treatment of the stem, which has parallel edges. There are no emphatic or exceptional transition points between the strokes or breaks between the various elements. The curves are drawn as a continuous stroke with a circular appearance. The crossbars or cross strokes occupy a central position. The font is of medium width with a small x-height. The contrast is exaggerated, with medium color or weight. BD Algebra is a font lacking any of the decorative elements offered in the minus and plus versions.

De manière générale, cette police allie une boucle pleine avec des hampes ascendantes et descendantes très maigres. La hampe verticale est exagérée avec des contours parallèles. Il n'existe pas de points emphatiques ou singuliers de transition entre les traits ou les ruptures entre les éléments. Les boucles sont continues et ont un aspect arrondi. La position des traverses ou barres horizontales est centrale. Il s'agit d'une police d'une largeur moyenne avec une petite hauteur d'œil. Le contraste est exagéré et la couleur ou le poids sont moyens. BD Algebra est une police sans serif qui existe en version minus et plus.

A grandes rasgos, la fuente combina el ojal relleno con astas verticales ascendentes y descendentes de líneas muy finas. Se aprecia un tratamiento exagerado del asta vertical, cuyos bordes son paralelos. No existen puntos enfáticos o singulares de transición entre trazos o rupturas entre elementos. El tratamiento de las curvas es continuo y de aspecto circular. La posición de las barras o astas transversales es central. Se trata de una fuente de anchura media con altura de la x pequeña, de contraste exagerado y color o peso medio. BD Algebra es una fuente sin remate que ofrece las versiones minus y plus.

BD AsciiMax

Lopetz, Büro Destruct | www.typedifferent.com | www.burodestruct.net

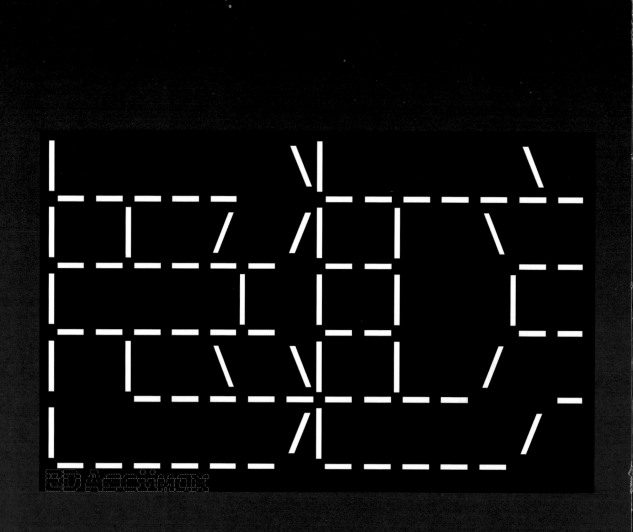

abcdefghijklmnopqrstuvwxyzàçéèùï
ABCDEFGHIJKLMNOPQRSTUVWXYZ
1234567890(.,;:!?&$£€)-%#ÀÇÉÈÙÏ+/÷

8/10 pt

abcdefghijklmnopqrstuvwxyzàçéèùïï
ABCDEFGHIJKLMNOPQRSTUVWXYZ
1234567890(.,;:!?&$£€)-%#ÀÇÉÈÙÏ+/÷

10/12 pt

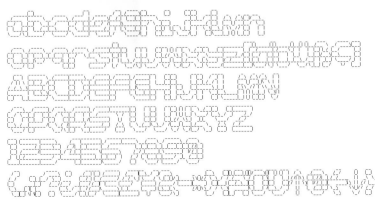

abcdefghijklmn
opqrstuvwxyzàçéèùï
ABCDEFGHIJKLMN
OPQRSTUVWXYZ
1234567890
(.,;:!?&$£€)-%#ÀÇÉÈÙÏ+/÷

18/18 pt

abcdefghijklmn
opqrstuvwxyzàçéèùï
ABCDEFGHIJKLMN
OPQRSTUVWXYZ
1234567890
(.,;:!?&$£€)-%#ÀÇÉÈÙÏ+/÷

24/24 pt

The ASCII character code is used in the programming of virtually all current computer systems. It is also the support favored by a minority art discipline: ASCII art, which involves the creation of images using printable ASCII characters. BD AsciiMax is based on ASCII-Art that was at its height during the era of the postal service, just before the onset of the age of email and the Internet. It uses monospace typeface, with all characters being allocated a standard width. The letters on traditional typewriters and the Courier or Monaco fonts on computers are examples of monospace typeface.

La norme de codage de caractères ASCII s'utilise pour la programmation de presque tous les systèmes informatiques actuels. Elle est également le support d'une discipline artistique minoritaire : l'art ASCII, qui consiste à réaliser des images à l'aide de caractères spéciaux contenus dans ASCII. BD AsciiMax s'inspire de la scène ASCII-Art qui fut particulièrement active à l'époque du courrier postal, juste avant l'ère du mail et d'Internet. Cette police utilise des typographies à chasse fixe dans lesquelles tous les caractères ont la même largeur. Les lettres traditionnelles des machines à écrire ainsi que les polices d'écriture comme Courier ou Monaco sont des exemples de caractères à chasse fixe.

El código de caracteres ASCII se utiliza en programación para casi todos los sistemas informáticos actuales. También es el soporte de una disciplina artística minoritaria: el arte ASCII, que consiste en la composición de imágenes mediante caracteres imprimibles ASCII. BD AsciiMax se inspira en esta disciplina, principalmente activa durante la época del correo postal, justo antes del email e Internet. Utiliza tipografías monoespaciadas donde todos los caracteres tienen asignado el mismo ancho de composición. Las letras de las máquinas de escribir tradicionales y las fuentes de ordenador Courier o Monaco son ejemplos de tipos monoespaciados.

BD Beans

Lopetz, Büro Destruct | www.typedifferent.com | www.burodestruct.net

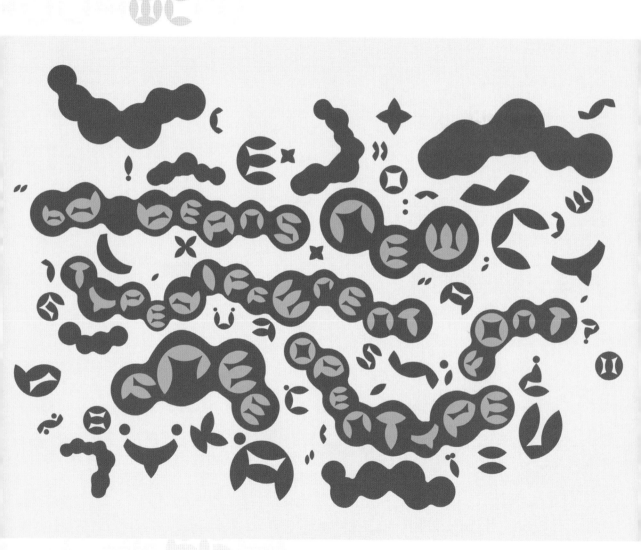

AbCdEFGHIJKLMNOPQRSTUUWXYZ
1234567890(.,:?¿+-×)(ÄÖÜÄ①ℂℳ)

8/10 pt

AbCdEFGHIJKLMNOPQRSTUUWXYZ
1234567890(.,:?¿+-×)(ÄÖÜÄ①ℂℳ)

10/12 pt

AbCdEFGHIJKLMNOPQRSTUUWXYZ
1234567890(.,:?¿+-×)(ÄÖÜÄ①ℂℳ)

18/18 pt

AbCdEFGHIJKLMN
OPQRSTUUWXYZ
1234567890
(.,:?¿+-×)(ÄÖÜÄ①ℂℳ)

24/24 pt

AbCdEFGHIJKLMN
OPQRSTUUWXYZ
1234567890
(.,:?¿+-×)(ÄÖÜÄ①ℂℳ)

32/34 pt

Edamame is a snack that is prepared with green soybeans in the pod, and are either steamed or boiled in salted water. It is generally consumed in Japanese, Chinese, Hawaian or Korean restaurants. BD Beans is based on this delicious Japanese appetizer. The upward and downward stems and the arms of the letters in this font mimic the pods of soybeans. The result is a sans serif font, constructed continuously with circular curves. This clearly decorative font is only available in uppercase and therefore it is not very suitable for running text.

L'édamame est un aliment souvent servi en apéritif, à base de haricots de soja verts en gousse, que l'on peut bouillir dans de l'eau avec du sel ou cuire à la vapeur. Il est généralement consommé dans les restaurants au Japon, en Chine, à Hawaii et en Corée. BD Beans s'inspire de ce délicieux amuse-bouche japonais Edamame. Les hampes ascendantes et descendantes de cette police ainsi que les traverses des lettres imitent les gousses des haricots de soja. Le résultat est une police sans serif, de construction homogène avec des lignes arrondies. Cette police, manifestement décorative, ne propose que des caractères haut de casse. Elle est peu appropriée pour un texte continu.

Edamame es un aperitivo que consiste en una preparación a base de habas de soja verdes en vaina que se hierven en agua con sal o se cocinan al vapor, y que se consume generalmente en los restaurantes de Japón, China, Hawaii y Corea. BD Beans se inspira en este delicioso aperitivo. Las astas ascendentes y descendentes de esta tipografía, así como los brazos de las letras, imitan las vainas de las habas de soja. El resultado es una fuente de palo seco, de construcción continua con aspecto de las curvas circular. Esta fuente claramente decorativa solo ofrece caracteres de caja alta, por lo que resulta poco apropiada para texto corrido.

BD BillDing

Heiwid, Büro Destruct | www.typedifferent.com | www.burodestruct.net

abcdefghijklmnopqrstuvwxyz[yöüñ]
ABCDEFGHIJKLMNOPQRSTUVWXYZ
1234567890[.,;:?$£¥+--][AOÜ]

8/10 pt

abcdefghijklmnopqrstuvwxyz[yöüñ]
ABCDEFGHIJKLMNOPQRSTUVWXYZ
1234567890[.,;:?$£¥+--][AOÜ]

10/12 pt

abcdefghijklmn
opqrstuvwxyz[yöüñ]
ABCDEFGHIJKLMN
OPQRSTUVWXYZ
1234567890
[.,;:?$£¥+--][AOÜ]

18/18 pt

abcdefghijklmn
opqrstuvwxyz[yöüñ]
ABCDEFGHIJKLMN
OPQRSTUVWXYZ
1234567890
[.,;:?$£¥+--][AOÜ]

24/24 pt

Created to erect buildings using typeface, the logo of a Swiss building company Bill Baut is the source of inspiration for this font. It has condensed proportions that are broad and square, with thick stems and parallel edges, and heavy sans serif terminals. The font is constructed continuously and has a dark and thick appearance. An extreme contrast can be seen with the vertical constructive axis and instant transition. Replacing the curves with straight lines creates a squarish appearance. The width of the capital letters is regular with a single-space and a small x-height.

Créée pour la construction de bâtiments fondée sur la typographie, cette police s'inspire d'un logotype d'une société suisse de construction dénommée Bill Baut. Il s'agit d'une lettre condensée, large et carrée dont les fûts sont gras, les bords parallèles, et les traits des traverses gras et sans serif. La police est obscure et épaisse avec une construction homogène. On dénote un fort contraste avec l'axe de construction vertical et la transition instantanée. Des lignes droites remplacent les courbes produisant un aspect carré. La largeur des capitales est régulière, à chasse fixe, avec une petite hauteur d'œil.

Creada para erigir edificios a base de tipografía, esta fuente se inspira en el logotipo de la empresa de construcción suiza Bill Baut. De proporciones condensadas, anchas y cuadradas, presenta astas verticales gruesas y de bordes paralelos, y trazos terminales pesados y sin remates. La fuente resulta oscura y espesa, de construcción continua. Se aprecia un contraste extremo con eje constructivo vertical y de transición instantánea. Las curvas sustituidas por rectas generan un aspecto de las curvas cuadrado. La anchura de las capitales es regular, monoespaciada, con altura de la x pequeña.

BD Bonbon

Heiwid, Büro Destruct | www.typedifferent.com | www.burodestruct.net

ABCDEFGHIJKLMNOPQRSTUVWXYZ
1234567890O.,;:?!i---)(

8/10 pt

ABCDEFGHIJKLMNOPQRSTUVWXYZ
1234567890O.,;:?!i---)(

10/12 pt

ABCDEFGHIJKLMNOPQRSTUVWXYZ
1234567890O.,;:?!i---)(

18/18 pt

ABCDEFGHIJKLMN
OPQRSTUVWXYZ
1234567890
O.,;:?!i---)(

24/24 pt

ABCDEFGHIJKLMN
OPQRSTUVWXYZ
1234567890
O.,;:?!i---)(

32/34 pt

The sign in the window of an Italian sweetshop provided the inspiration for this typeface. This discontinuous font generates modular letters composed of separate individual elements. The curves have been given an angular treatment, resulting in a squarish appearance. The stems have parallel edges with a sans serif design and rounded corners. The contrast is exaggerated, with a vertical axis and instant transition. This typeface is only available in standard width. The capital letters have a generally even width and reach the same height as the ascenders.

L'enseigne d'une pâtisserie italienne est à l'origine de cette police d'écriture. Sa construction non homogène produit des lettres modulaires composées d'éléments individuels isolés. Les courbes sont angulaires et donnent aux lettres un aspect carré. Les hampes sont parallèles, les lettres sans serif et les angles arrondis. Cela met en avant un contraste exagéré avec un axe vertical et une transition instantanée. Cette typographie n'est disponible qu'en chasse large. La chasse des capitales est généralement régulière et les hampes ascendantes sont de la même hauteur que les capitales.

El letrero del escaparate de una tienda de dulces italiana ha servido de inspiración para esta tipografía. Esta fuente de construcción discontinua genera letras modulares compuestas por elementos individuales sueltos. El tratamiento de las curvas es angular, por lo que les da un aspecto cuadrado. Las astas son de bordes paralelos sin remates, con las esquinas redondeadas. Presenta un contraste exagerado, con eje vertical y transición instantánea. Este tipografía sólo está disponible en anchura media. La anchura de las capitales es regular y los ascendentes tienen la misma altura que las mayúsculas.

BD Elautobus

Heiwid, Büro Destruct | www.typedifferent.com | www.burodestruct.net

abcdefghijklmnopqrstuuwxyz(äöüàœçñ)
ABCDEFGHIJKLMNOPQRSTUUWXYZ
1234567890(.,;?¿$£¥&-*)(ÄÖÜÀ.ŒÇÑ)

8/10 pt

abcdefghijklmnopqrstuuwxyz(äöüàœçñ)
ABCDEFGHIJKLMNOPQRSTUUWXYZ
1234567890(.,;?¿$£¥&-*)(ÄÖÜÀ.ŒÇÑ)

10/12 pt

abcdefghijklmn
opqrstuuwxyz(äöüàœçñ)
ABCDEFGHIJKLMN
OPQRSTUUWXYZ
1234567890
(.,;?¿$£¥&-*)(ÄÖÜÀ.ŒÇÑ)

18/18 pt

abcdefghijklmn
opqrstuuwxyz(äöüàœçñ)
ABCDEFGHIJKLMN
OPQRSTUUWXYZ
1234567890
(.,;?¿$£¥&-*)
(ÄÖÜÀ.ŒÇÑ)

24/24 pt

The outlying districts of Ecuador, where children entertain themselves playing simple games such as rolling a tire with their hands, is the inspiration for this font. This font therefore conveys the idea of a simple and unaffected style, by means of its clean lines. The characters are built up without any breaks between the various elements. The curves are continuous and circular in form while the bowls and stems do not quite connect up with one another. The vertical stems have parallel edges and the crossbars occupy a central position. The ends of the strokes do not have serifs, although they have rounded tips.

Cette typographie s'inspire de l'Équateur, des quartiers en périphérie, observant comment les enfants s'amusent avec des jeux très simples, comme entourer un pneu avec les bras. Pour cela, cette police transmet simplicité et clarté, à partir de lignes bien définies. La construction des caractères ne présente aucune rupture entre les éléments. Les courbes sont homogènes et arrondies. Les boucles et les fûts ne se touchent pas. Les hampes verticales sont parallèles et les traverses se situent au milieu. Les lettres finales sont sans serif mais présentent toutefois des angles arrondis.

Los barrios periféricos de Ecuador, donde los niños se divierten con juegos muy simples, tales como rodar un neumático con las manos, han servido de inspiración para esta fuente, que transmite simplicidad y sencillez, a través de líneas limpias. La construcción de los caracteres no presenta rupturas entre elementos. Las curvas son continuas y de aspecto circular mientras que los anillos y astas no llegan a tocarse. Las astas verticales son de bordes paralelos y las transversales se sitúan en el medio. Los trazos de los terminales no tienen remates, aunque presentan los ángulos redondeados.

BD Equipment

Lopetz, Büro Destruct | www.typedifferent.com | www.burodestruct.net

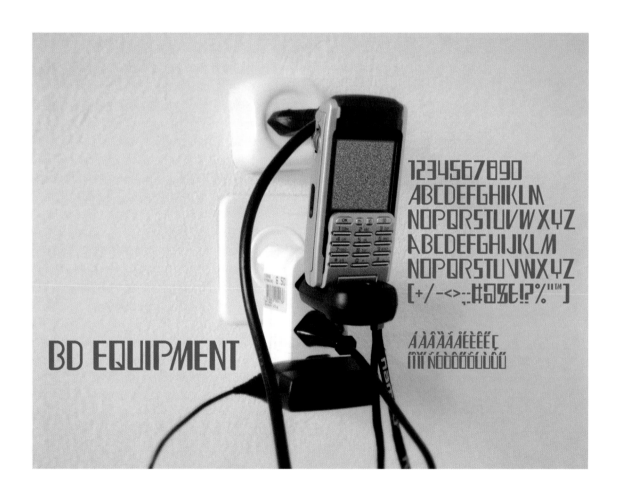

ABCDEFGHIJKLMNOPQRSTUVWXYZ[ÄÖÜÅÇÑ]
ABCDEFGHIJKLMNOPQRSTUVWXYZ
1234567890[.,;:?¿%&] [€¥+-*][ÁÖÜÅ0ÇÑ]

8/10 pt

ABCDEFGHIJKLMNOPQRSTUVWXYZ[ÄÖÜÅÇÑ]
ABCDEFGHIJKLMNOPQRSTUVWXYZ
1234567890[.,;:?¿%&] [€¥+-*][ÁÖÜÅ0ÇÑ]

10/12 pt

ABCDEFGHIJKLMN
OPQRSTUVWXYZ[ÄÖÜÅÇÑ]
ABCDEFGHIJKLMN
OPQRSTUVWXYZ
1234567890[.,;:?¿%&] [€¥+-*][ÁÖÜÅ0ÇÑ]

18/18 pt

ABCDEFGHIJKLMN
OPQRSTUVWXYZ[ÄÖÜÅÇÑ]
ABCDEFGHIJKLMN
OPQRSTUVWXYZ
1234567890
[.,;:?¿%&] [€¥+-*][ÁÖÜÅ0 ÇÑ]

24/24 pt

The technical aspect of the font makes it very suitable for use in the headings of manuals for electronic equipment. The characters are built up continuously, without any breaks between the various elements and the curves are sharp and angular. The stems are not connected and the arcs are left wide open. This sans serif font has a medium weight and width and a high contrast with a vertical axis and instant transition. The letters with slanting stems such as the A or V are offered either leaning to the right or to the left. The design includes uppercase characters, along with numbers, punctuation marks and symbols.

Grâce à son apparence technique cette police est idéale pour les titres des modes d'emplois des appareils électriques. La forme des caractères est homogène, sans rupture entre les éléments et les courbes sont angulaires. Les hampes ne se touchent pas et les arches sont très ouvertes. Cette lettre sans serif présente une chasse étroite et un poids moyen, ainsi qu'un contraste exagéré avec un axe vertical et une transition instantanée. Les diagonales des lettres comme la A ou la V peuvent être inclinées soit vers la droite soit vers la gauche. Cette typographie propose des caractères haut de casse, des chiffres, des signes de ponctuation et des symboles.

Su aspecto técnico la convierte en una fuente ideal para titulares de manuales de aparatos electrónicos. La construcción de los caracteres es continua, sin rupturas entre elementos, y el tratamiento de las curvas es angular. Las astas no llegan a tocarse y los arcos son muy abiertos. Esta fuente de palo seco presenta una anchura y peso medio, y un contraste alto con eje vertical y transición instantánea. Las letras con astas verticales inclinadas como A o V se ofrecen con ambas inclinaciones a la derecha y a la izquierda. El diseño incluye los caracteres para caja alta junto con números, signos de puntuación y símbolos.

BD Geminis

H1reber, Büro Destruct | www.typedifferent.com | www.burodestruct.net

ABCDEFGHIJKLMNOPQRSTUVWXYZ(AOUACN)
ABCDEFGHIJKLMNOPQRSTUVWXYZ
1234567890[.,;:?)(AOUAØCN)

08/10 pt

ABCDEFGHIJKLMNOPQRSTUVWXYZ(AOUACN)
ABCDEFGHIJKLMNOPQRSTUVWXYZ
1234567890[.,;:?)(AOUAØCN)

10/12 pt

ABCDEFGHIJKLMN
OPQRSTUVWXYZ(AOUACN)
ABCDEFGHIJKLMN
OPQRSTUVWXYZ
1234567890[.,;:?)(AOUAØCN)

18/18 pt

ABCDEFGHIJKLMN
OPQRSTUVWXYZ(AOUACN)
ABCDEFGHIJKLMN
OPQRSTUVWXYZ
1234567890[.,;:?)(AOUAØCN)

24/24 pt

This is an interpretation of the retro-sci-fi stylestyle. It is a style of art based on the classic science fiction of the nineteen seventies and eighties (*War Games*, *Blade Runner*, *West World*, etc.) The font is characterized by the angular treatment of the curves, which also have a rounded appearance. The letters are of medium width and the widths of the capitals are generally even. The font has medium contrast with a horizontal axis and two different thicknesses. There is also a gradual transition. The font alternates serif and sans serif elements. There are thick stroke endings on the feet of some letters, whereas on others the stem, drawn with a very thin line, is sans serif.

Il s'agit d'une interprétation du style rétro-SF, une conception et un art inspiré de la science fiction classique des années 70 et 80 (*Jeux de guerre*, *Blade Runner*, *Mondwest*...). Cette police se caractérise par l'aspect angulaire des courbes qui sont à la fois arrondies. La chasse des lettres est moyenne ; les chasses des capitales sont généralement régulières. Elle offre un contraste moyen avec un axe horizontal et deux épaisseurs différentes, la transition est progressive. La police alterne entre empattements et lettres sans serif. Les traits gras à la base apparaissent aux extrémités de certaines lettres, tandis que pour d'autres, le fût est très fin et sans serif.

Esta fuente es el resultado de una interpretación del *retro-sci-fi*, un estilo artístico inspirado en la ciencia ficción clásica de los años 70 y 80 (*Juegos de guerra*, *Blade Runner*, *West World*, etc.). Se caracteriza por el tratamiento angular de las curvas, que son redondeadas. La anchura de la letra es media y las anchuras de las capitales son regulares. Presenta un contraste medio con eje horizontal y dos grosores diferentes, y la transición es gradual. Esta fuente alterna el remate con el palo seco. Los trazos terminales gruesos aparecen en los pies de algunas letras, mientras que, en otras, el asta vertical de línea muy fina no lleva remate.

BD Ramen

Lopetz, Büro Destruct | www.typedifferent.com | www.burodestruct.net

BD Ramen

1 4 14 40
SET SPEED   MUTE

AABCDEFFGHIJKLM
NOPQRSTUVWXYZ
0123456789£¥$?!/
abcdefghijklmnop
qrrstuvwxyzäöüæ

abcdefghijklmnopqrstuvwxyzäöüç
ABCDEFGHIJKLITINOPQRSTUUWXYZ
1234567890(.,;:?$£¥+-"')ÄÖÜÑÇ

8/10 pt

abcdefghijklmnopqrstuvwxyzäöüç
ABCDEFGHIJKLITINOPQRSTUUWXYZ
1234567890(.,;:?$£¥+-"')ÄÖÜÑÇ

10/12 pt

abcdefghijklmnopqrstuvwxyzäöüç
ABCDEFGHIJKLITINOPQRSTUUWXYZ
1234567890(.,;:?$£¥+-"')ÄÖÜÑÇ

18/18 pt

abcdefghijklmn
opqrstuvwxyzäöüç
ABCDEFGHIJKLITIN
OPQRSTUUWXYZ
1234567890
(.,;:?$£¥+-"')ÄÖÜÑÇ

24/24 pt

This typeface draws its inspiration from the taste and enjoyment of a bowl of hot ramen noodle soup (Japanese version of Chinese noodle soup) by the font designer while on a trip to Japan. The font is characterized by modular letters consisting of individual elements with breaks between them suggestive of the shape of noodles. The letters have continuous curves but no serifs, with the arms and stems ending in rounded tips. The descender of the lowercase g has no bowl. It does however have an ear as a slight prolongation of the stem. The swashes are inserted in the stem as an individual element.

Le typographe s'est inspiré d'une soupe de vermicelles ramen (version japonaise des vermicelles chinois) bien chaude, qu'il a savourée lors d'un voyage au Japon, pour élaborer cette police. Cette police d'écriture se caractérise par des lettres modulaires composées d'éléments individuels en rupture les uns avec les autres ce qui fait ressortir la forme des vermicelles. Les courbes sont homogènes, les lettres sont sans serif, les traverses et les hampes ont les angles arrondis. La lettre « g » n'a pas de boucle dans son jambage inférieur mais une oreille, c'est-à-dire un prolongement de la hampe verticale. Les panses s'insèrent à la hampe en tant qu'élément individuel.

El tipógrafo se inspira en un momento de un viaje a Japón, en el que saboreó y disfrutó de una sopa de fideos ramen (versión japonesa de la sopa de fideos chinos) bien caliente. Esta fuente se caracteriza por las letras modulares compuestas por elementos individuales con rupturas entre sí que hacen referencia a la forma de los fideos. De curvas continuas, la fuente no presenta remate y los extremos de brazos y astas son de ángulos redondeados. No existe ojal en el descendente de la letra g de caja baja, pero sí oreja como una corta prolongación del asta vertical. Los bucles se insertan en el asta como un elemento individual.

BD Tinyfont

Bataais, Büro Destruct | www.typedifferent.com | www.burodestruct.net

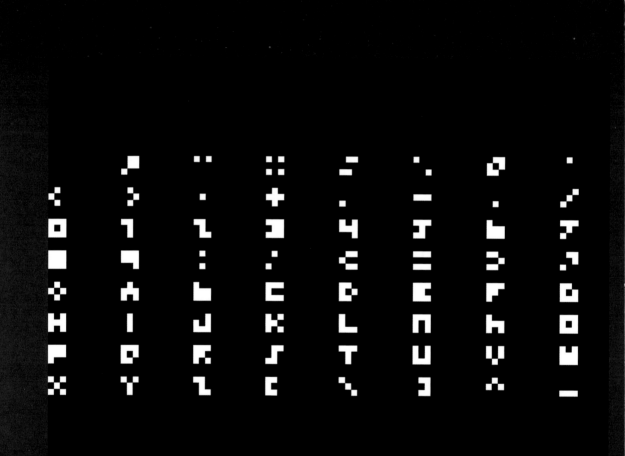

A B C D E F G H I J K L N H O P Q R S T U V W X Y Z E J
1 2 3 4 5 6 7 8 9 0 ...

8/10 pt

A B C D E F G H I J K L N H O P Q R S T U V W X Y Z E J
1 2 3 4 5 6 7 8 9 0 ...

10/12 pt

A B C D E F G H I J K L N H
O P Q R S T U V W X Y Z E J
1 2 3 4 5 6 7 8 9 0
...

18/18 pt

This is a pixelated font with characters strictly designed from a 3 × 3 pixel grid. The design of each character involves the representation of the formal attributes by using the six squares of the 3 × 3 pixel grid since it is imperative that the glyph be readable. The result is a font without any serifs. It is constructed continuously and features angular curves giving it a square appearance, and stems with parallel edges. Since it is not possible to generate certain forms in the 3 × 3 grid, upper or lowercase letters are used depending on the morphology of each character.

Il s'agit d'une police pixélisée dont les caractères ont été conçus à partir d'un quadrillage de 3 × 3 pixels. Le dessin de chaque lettre envisage la représentation des attributs formels en utilisant les six carrés de la réticule de 3 × 3 pixels, le glyphe doit être intelligible. Le résultat est une police sans serif, de forme homogène, des courbes angulaires dont l'aspect est carré et les hampes verticales sont parallèles. Face à l'impossibilité de créer certaines formes carrées 3 × 3, plusieurs lettres sont représentées en bas de casse ou en haut de casse en fonction de la morphologie de chaque caractère.

Es una fuente pixelada cuyos caracteres han sido estrictamente diseñados a partir de una cuadrícula de 3 × 3 píxeles. El diseño de cada carácter contempla la representación de los atributos formales utilizando los seis cuadrados de la retícula de 3 × 3 píxeles, formando un glifo inteligible. El resultado es una fuente sin remates, de construcción continua, con tratamiento de la curva angular y aspecto de la curva cuadrado, con astas verticales de bordes paralelos. Ante la imposibilidad de generar ciertas formas en la cuadrícula 3 × 3, se utiliza la caja alta o la caja baja dependiendo de la morfología de cada carácter.

A B C D E F G H I J K L
N H O P Q R S T
U V W X Y Z E J
1 2 3 4 5 6 7 8 9 0
...

24/24 pt

BD Wakarimasu

Lopetz, Büro Destruct | www.typedifferent.com | www.burodestruct.net

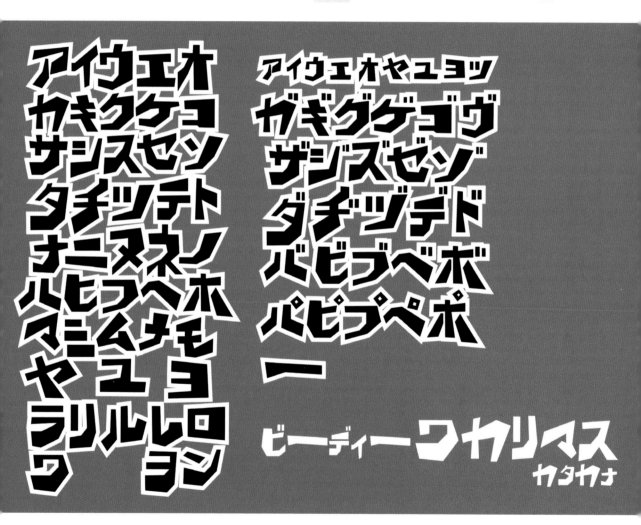

ﾁｺﾝｿﾝｲﾊﾐｷｸﾆｲﾉﾘﾓﾐﾗｾﾀｽﾄｶｫﾋﾃﾃﾝﾂ.ﾑ
ﾁｺﾞﾝｿﾞｨｲﾊﾞﾐﾞｸﾞﾊﾟﾋﾟﾌﾟﾍﾟﾎﾟｰｰｾﾞﾀﾞｽﾞﾄﾞｶﾞﾞ ﾋﾞﾃﾞｻﾞｯﾂﾂ
ﾇﾌｱｳｴｵﾔﾕﾖﾜﾞｭﾙﾈﾚﾚﾞ?ｳｷｫ ﾎｹﾞｮ(ｱｲｴ)

8/10 pt

ﾁｺﾝｿﾝｲﾊﾐｷｸﾆｲﾉﾘﾓﾐﾗｾﾀｽﾄｶｫﾋﾃﾃﾝﾂ.ﾑ
ﾁｺﾞﾝｿﾞｨｲﾊﾞﾐﾞｸﾞﾊﾟﾋﾟﾌﾟﾍﾟﾎﾟｰｰｾﾞﾀﾞｽﾞﾄﾞｶﾞﾞ ﾋﾞﾃﾞｻﾞｯﾂﾂ
ﾇﾌｱｳｴｵﾔﾕﾖﾜﾞｭﾙﾈﾚﾚﾞ?ｳｷｫ ﾎｹﾞｮ(ｱｲｴ)

10/12 pt

ﾁｺﾝｿﾝｲﾊﾐｷｸﾆｲﾉﾘﾓﾐ
ﾗｾﾀｽﾄｶｫﾋﾃﾃﾝﾂ.ﾑ
ﾁｺﾞﾝｿﾞｨｲﾊﾞﾐﾞｸﾞﾊﾟﾋﾟﾌﾟﾍﾟﾎﾟｰ
ｰｾﾞﾀﾞｽﾞﾄﾞｶﾞﾞ ﾋﾞﾃﾞｻﾞｯﾂ
ﾇﾌｱｳｴｵﾔﾕﾖﾜ
ｭﾙﾈﾚﾚﾞ?ｳｷｫ ﾎｹﾞｮ(ｱｲｴ)

18/18 pt

ﾁｺﾝｿﾝｲﾊﾐｷｸﾆｲﾉﾘﾓﾐ
ﾗｾﾀｽﾄｶｫﾋﾃﾃﾝﾂ.ﾑ
ﾁｺﾞﾝｿﾞｨｲﾊﾞﾐﾞｸﾞﾊﾟﾋﾟﾌﾟﾍﾟﾎﾟｰ
ｰｾﾞﾀﾞｽﾞﾄﾞｶﾞﾞ ﾋﾞﾃﾞｻﾞｯﾂ
ﾇﾌｱｳｴｵﾔﾕﾖﾜ
ｭﾙﾈﾚﾚﾞ?ｳｷｫ ﾎｹﾞｮ(ｱｲｴ)

24/24 pt

Originally, some of the letters were used as characters to design a collection of T-shirts. This typeface is derived from a Japanese *katakana* font. In modern Japanese, it is customary to use this script to transcribe words from foreign languages. It corresponds to a Japanese syllabary, a writing system in which the characters represent syllables. This is a component of the Japanese writing system, along with *haragana*, *kanji* and, in some cases, the Latin alphabet. *Katakana* is characterized by short, straight strokes with angular corners, and is the simplest form of all Japanese scripts.

Au début, certaines lettres étaient utilisées en tant que caractères pour la conception d'une collection de t-shirts. Cette typographie correspond à une police d'écriture japonaise *katakana*, dans la langue japonaise moderne elle est le plus souvent utilisée pour transcrire des mots d'origine étrangère. Elle correspond à un syllabaire japonais, système d'écriture dans lequel les caractères représentent des syllabes. Il s'agit d'une des écritures du japonais avec le *harigana*, le *kanji* et parfois l'alphabet latin. Le *katakana* se caractérise par des petits traits droits avec des angles accusés ; parmi les écritures japonaises celle-ci est la plus simple.

Inicialmente, algunas de las letras se utilizaron como caracteres para el diseño de una colección de camisetas. Esta tipografía corresponde a una fuente japonesa *katakana*, que en el lenguaje japonés moderno se utiliza habitualmente para transcribir palabras de lenguas extranjeras. Corresponde a un silabario japonés, sistema de escritura en la que los caracteres representan sílabas. Se trata de un componente del sistema de la escritura japonesa, junto con el *haragana*, el *kanji* y, en algunos casos, el alfabeto latino. El *katakana* se caracteriza por los trazos cortos y rectos con esquinas anguladas, es la más simple de todas las escrituras japonesas.

Be Cross

Brain Eaters Font Company (BEFCo) | www.braineaters.com

ABCDEFGHIJKLMNOPQRSTUVWXYZ

..::¯

8/10 pt

ABCDEFGHIJKLMNOPQRSTUVWXYZ

..::¯

10/12 pt

ABCDEFGHIJKLMNOPQRSTUVWXYZ

...::¯

18/18 pt

ABCDEFGHIJKLMN
OPQRSTUVWXYZ

..::¯

24/24 pt

ABCDEFGHIJKLMN
OPQRSTUVWXYZ

.::¯

32/34 pt

This cross is reminiscent both of the medieval dagger and the Presbyterian cross used in protestant religion. The design of Be Cross is based on the cross with the foot being larger than the other arms, with flourishes that are thicker than the main strokes of the letters. It is a highly decorative font, only available in uppercase, along with a basic set of punctuation marks. It is therefore not suitable for running text but can be useful for brief titles, headers or isolated characters.

Cette typographie rappelle la dague médiévale mais aussi la croix presbytérienne, utilisée dans la religion protestante. Chaque lettre est conçue à partir de la forme de la croix : le fût est plus long que le reste des traverses et les empattements plus épais que les principaux traits des lettres. Il s'agit d'une police totalement décorative qui ne présente que des caractères haut de casse ainsi qu'un ensemble de signes de ponctuation de base. Elle ne convient donc pas pour un texte long mais elle peut être très utile pour des titres brefs, des en-têtes ou des caractères isolés.

Recuerda la forma de la daga medieval y la de la cruz presbiteriana utilizada en la religión protestante. Cada una de las letras de Be Cross se ha diseñado a partir de la forma de cruz, con el pie mayor que el resto de los brazos y con los remates más gruesos que los trazos principales de las letras. Se trata de una fuente totalmente decorativa que solamente ofrece el set de caracteres de caja alta, junto con una selección de signos de puntuación básicos. De este modo, no resulta apta para texto corrido pero puede llegar a convertirse en un recurso muy útil para títulos breves, encabezamientos o para caracteres aislados.

Bead Chain/Marquee

GLASS, PLASTIC, AND STONE ARE PROBABLY THE MOST COMMON MATERIALS, BUT BEADS ARE ALSO MADE FROM BONE, HORN, IVORY, METAL, SHELL, PEARL, CORAL, GEMSTONES, POLYMER CLAY, METAL CLAY, RESIN, SYNTHETIC MINERALS, WOOD, CERAMIC, FIBER, PAPER, AND SEEDS.

ABCDEFGHIJKLMNOPQRSTUVWXYZ
1234567890(.,;:?¿$¢£€¥&-*){ÄÖÜÅØÆŒÇÑ}

8/10 pt

ABCDEFGHIJKLMNOPQRSTUVWXYZ
1234567890(.,;:?¿$¢£€¥&-*){ÄÖÜÅØÆŒÇÑ}

8/10 pt

ABCDEFGHIJKLMNOPQRSTUVWXYZ
1234567890(.,;:?¿$¢£€¥&-*){ÄÖÜÅØÆŒÇÑ}

10/12 pt

ABCDEFGHIJKLMNOPQRSTUVWXYZ
1234567890(.,;:?¿$¢£€¥&-*){ÄÖÜÅØÆŒÇÑ}

10/12 pt

ABCDEFGHIJKLMNOPQRSTUVWXYZ
1234567890
(.,;:?¿$¢£€¥&-*){ÄÖÜÅØÆŒÇÑ}

18/18 pt

ABCDEFGHIJKLMNOPQRSTUVWXYZ
1234567890
(.,;:?¿$¢£€¥&-*){ÄÖÜÅØÆŒÇÑ}

18/18 pt

This set includes two fonts: Bead Chain/Marquee. The basic structure for the shape of each Bead Chain letter starts with the classic Gill Sans typeface. It is very simple to build: loose elements in the form of tiny dots have been used, as though they formed part of a string of beads. Marquee is the font's other half – forming a mirror image. It looks a bit like those bright posters from yesteryear, appearing on theater awnings, made with a cluster of small light bulbs. It is a sans serif font that reduces the characters to their essential outline and is characterized by the barely noticeable thickness of the stroke and contrast.

Voici deux types de polices d'écriture : Bead Chain et Marquee. La structure de base pour chaque lettre de Bead Chain s'inspire de la typographie classique Gill Sans. La réalisation est très simple, il s'agit d'éléments isolés en forme de petits points, comme s'il s'agissait d'une chaîne de boules en métal. Marquee est son âme sœur mais en négatif. Son aspect rappelle les pancartes lumineuses démodées, situées dans les marquises des théâtres, faits avec des petites ampoules. Cette police sans serif, qui réduit les caractères à un schéma basique, se caractérise par l'épaisseur du trait et le contraste peu visible.

Este set incluye dos fuentes: Bead Chain y Marquee. La estructura básica para la forma de cada letra de Bead Chain parte de la clásica tipografía Gill Sans. La construcción es muy simple: utiliza elementos sueltos en forma de pequeños puntos, como si se tratara de un collar de cuentas. Marquee es su alma gemela pero en negativo. Su aspecto recuerda los carteles luminosos pasados de moda, situados en las marquesinas de los teatros, hechos con pequeñas bombillas. Es una fuente de palo seco que reduce los caracteres a su esquema esencial y se caracteriza por un grosor del trazo y un contraste poco perceptibles.

Benny Blanco

Popdog Fonts | popdog_fonts.tripod.com

abcdefghijklmnopqrstuvwxyzδθφόιεψζηρ
ABCDEFGHIJKLMNOPQRSTUVWXYZ
1234567890(,.?Ω✳A✳–✳)ΔΦαΕΨΖΗΡ

8/10 pt

abcdefghijklmnopqrstuvwxyzδθφόιεψζηρ
ABCDEFGHIJKLMNOPQRSTUVWXYZ
1234567890(,.?Ω✳A✳–✳)ΔΦαΕΨΖΗΡ

10/12 pt

abcdefghijklmn
opqrstuvwxyzδθφόιεψζηρ
ABCDEFGHIJKLMN
OPQRSTUVWXYZ
1234567890
(,.?Ω✳A✳–✳)ΔΦαΕΨΖΗΡ

18/18 pt

abcdefghijklmn
opqrstuvwxyzδθφόιεψζηρ
ABCDEFGHIJKLMN
OPQRSTUVWXYZ
1234567890
(,.?Ω✳A✳–✳)
ΔΦαΕΨΖΗΡ

24/24 pt

A decorative edged font that is suggestive of a paintbrush as the creative tool, offering the appearance of a stroke traced with white correction fluid. This is a sans serif font without any contrast. It has continuous curves, which give it a circular appearance. The font has Latin and Greek characters for upper and lowercase letters, along with numbers, punctuation marks and basic symbols. The list of the most important lowercase key characters includes: a with a single story; e with a cross stroke; g without a link or counter. Furthermore, the description of the key uppercase characters includes: A with a straight apex; Q with a tail cutting through the bowl; and R with a straight tail.

Cette police d'écriture décorative qui fait référence au pinceau en tant qu'outil de création, a un tracé dont l'aspect rappelle un dessin au correcteur liquide blanc. Sans serif, elle n'a pas de contraste. Ses courbes sont homogènes et circulaires. Elle propose des caractères latins et grecs bas de casse et haut de casse, ainsi que des chiffres, des signes de ponctuation et des symboles de base. Parmi les caractères bas de casse les plus remarqués : le « a » en cursive, le « e » avec une barre horizontale, le « g » dans queue ni oreille. Cependant, les caractères haut de casse incluent : le « A » avec une pointe droite, le « Q » avec la queue qui coupe l'anneau, le « R » avec la queue droite.

Fuente decorativa perfilada que hace referencia al pincel como herramienta de creación, proporcionando un aspecto de trazo dibujado con fluido corrector blanco. Es una fuente de palo seco sin contraste. Muestra curvas de construcción continua y de aspecto circular. Ofrece caracteres latinos y griegos para caja alta y baja, con números, signos de puntuación y símbolos básicos. Los caracteres clave destacados de caja baja son la a de un piso, la e con barra horizontal y la g sin cuello ni ojal. Los caracteres clave de caja alta son la A con vértice recto, Q con cola que corta el anillo, R con cola recta.

Bigfish

Felix Braden | www.floodfonts.com

Zur Feier meines
60.
Geburtstags
lade ich Euch ganz
herzlich
am **Freitag,**
den **25. April** 2008
um 19 Uhr
zum 1-A-Treff
ins Tennishaus
Rübenach ein.

60
Geburtstag in
Rübenach

1-A-TREFF

ABCDEFGHIJKLMNOPQRSTUVWYXZ
abcdefghijklmnopqrstuvwyxz
1234567890!@★$%&()?

8/10 pt

ABCDEFGHIJKLMNOPQRSTUVWYXZ
abcdefghijklmnopqrstuvwyxz
1234567890!@★$%&()?

10/12 pt

ABCDEFGHIJKLM
NOPQRSTUVWYXZ
abcdefghijklmnopqrs
tuvwyxz
1234567890!@★$%&()?

18/18 pt

ABCDEFGHIJKLMN
OPQRSTUVWYXZ
abcdefghijklmn
opqrstuvwyxz
1234567890!@★$%&()?

24/24 pt

Bigfish is a straight style of font rather like the Comic typeface. The upper part of each character is much heavier in proportion to the lower part. The font is reminiscent of the design of old circus posters but with a modern touch thanks to the computer-generated curve. The creative process is mainly based on the idea of designing a font by hand but on the screen, without pencil or paper. After setting the marks for the corners, the typographer uses the pixelated font as a template and draws the outline with Bézier curves in Freehand.

Bigfish est une police droite similaire à la typographie Comic. La partie supérieure de chaque caractère est proportionnellement plus grande que la partie inférieure. Cette police rappelle la typographie des anciennes affiches de cirque avec une touche moderne grâce au style courbé produit sur l'ordinateur. Le processus créatif se fonde principalement sur l'idée de concevoir une police imitant l'écriture manuscrite mais uniquement à l'écran, sans utiliser aucune feuille ni aucun crayon. Après avoir fixé les points sur les angles, le typographe utilise une police pixélisée comme un modèle et il dessine le contour des courbes de Bézier en Freehand.

Bigfish es una fuente de gracia recta similar a la tipografía Comic. La parte superior de cada carácter es proporcionalmente más pesada que la inferior. La fuente recuerda el diseño de los carteles de circo antiguos pero con un toque moderno gracias al estilo de curva generada por ordenador. El proceso creativo se basa principalmente en la idea de diseñar una fuente de forma manual pero únicamente sobre la pantalla, sin utilizar papel ni lápiz. Después de fijar los puntos de las esquinas, el tipógrafo utiliza la fuente pixelada como una plantilla y dibuja el contorno con las curvas de Bézier en Freehand.

BP Diet

George Triantafyllakos | www.backpacker.gr

abcdefghijklmnopqrstuvwxyz[]
ABCDEFGHIJKLMNOPQRSTUVWXYZ
1234567890(.,;:?$£€¥&-*){}

8/10 pt

abcdefghijklmnopqrstuvwxyz[]
ABCDEFGHIJKLMNOPQRSTUVWXYZ
1234567890(.,;:?$£€¥&-*){}

8/10 pt

abcdefghijklmnopqrstuvwxyz[]
ABCDEFGHIJKLMNOPQRSTUVWXYZ
1234567890(.,;:?$£€¥&-*){}

10/12 pt

abcdefghijklmnopqrstuvwxyz[]
ABCDEFGHIJKLMNOPQRSTUVWXYZ
1234567890(.,;:?$£€¥&-*){}

10/12 pt

abcdefghijklmn
opqrstuvwxyz[]
ABCDEFGHIJKLMN
OPQRSTUVWXYZ
1234567890
(.,;:?$£€¥&-*){}

18/18 pt

abcdefghijklmn
opqrstuvwxyz[]
ABCDEFGHIJKLMN
OPQRSTUVWXYZ
1234567890
(.,;:?$£€¥&-*){}

18/18 pt

BP Diet, an extremely thick and heavy font, plays on the irony in its name and proposes a metaphorical diet so that the font loses weight. This font is ideal for titles and really short texts. The typographer proposes experimenting with the spacing and kerning in between the letters in several ways until achieving the best result. This is a sans serif font with very wide parallel edge stems. The set comes in two variations: Regular and Italics for the Latin and Greek alphabets. This font includes upper and lowercase characters with numbers, orthographic accents, punctuation marks and a wide range of symbols.

Extrêmement épaisse et grande, BP Diet utilise l'ironie pour son nom et de façon métaphorique il propose un régime afin que la police perde du poids. Elle convient parfaitement aux titres et aux textes très courts. Le typographe propose de tester l'espace entre les lettres et le crénage de plusieurs manières, afin d'obtenir le meilleur résultat possible. Cette police est sans serif avec des contours parallèles très larges. Elle propose plusieurs variantes : Regular et Italics pour l'alphabet latin et grec. Cette police d'écriture inclut des caractères bas de casse et haut de casse, des accents orthographiques, des signes de ponctuation et une grande variété de symboles.

Extremadamente gruesa y pesada, BP Diet utiliza la ironía en su nombre y metafóricamente aconseja una dieta para que la fuente pierda peso. Resulta muy apropiada para títulos y textos realmente cortos. El tipógrafo propone ensayar el espaciado entre letras y el kerning de varias maneras, hasta conseguir el resultado óptimo. Se trata de una fuente de palo seco con astas de bordes paralelos muy anchas. El set ofrece dos variantes: Regular e Italics para el alfabeto latino y griego. Esta fuente incluye caracteres de caja alta y baja con números, acentos ortográficos, signos de puntuación y una gran variedad de símbolos.

BPmono Regular/Italics/Bold

George Triantafyllakos | www.backpacker.gr

knowledge and appreciation of what was //
Tradition is not merely a dead and sterile state. It is a set of well-established working rules and procedures that triumphed over time and diverse socio-technical contexts. Learn to love the past. Learn from the past. Learn the past.

and insight of what will be //
There is no future. The future is now. Learn to live now and you will build a great future. Learn to appreciate what was and change will smoothly glide in.

So, like any other kind of design, type design is just

abcdefghijklmnopqrstuvwxyz[]
ABCDEFGHIJKLMNOPQRSTUVWXYZ
1234567890(.,;:?$£€¥&-*){}

8/10 pt

abcdefghijklmnopqrstuvwxyz[]
ABCDEFGHIJKLMNOPQRSTUVWXYZ
1234567890(.,;:?$£€¥&-){}*

8/10 pt

abcdefghijklmnopqrstuvwxyz[]
ABCDEFGHIJKLMNOPQRSTUVWXYZ
1234567890(.,;:?$£€¥&-*){}

8/10 pt

abcdefghijklmnopqrstuvwxyz[]
ABCDEFGHIJKLMNOPQRSTUVWXYZ
1234567890(.,;:?$£€¥&-*){}

18/18 pt

abcdefghijklmnopqrstuvwxyz[]
ABCDEFGHIJKLMNOPQRSTUVWXYZ
1234567890(.,;:?$£€¥&-){}*

18/18 pt

abcdefghijklmnopqrstuvwxyz[]
ABCDEFGHIJKLMNOPQRSTUVWXYZ
1234567890(.,;:?$£€¥&-*){}

18/18 pt

This is a monospaced font suitable for programming and/or technical texts. BPmono and BPmono Bold have been designed using a special process of manual adjustment known as "hinting". Hinting enables each character to be specifically optimized by means of specific instructions for its appearance on the screen. The font has been adapted from 9 px to 16 px so that it can be used in a range of advanced programming and text editors such as: Visual Studio.net, Visual Web Developer, MS Word. A monospaced font should always be aligned to the left (or, where necessary, to the right) but never centered or justified.

Il s'agit d'une police d'écriture à chasse fixe qui convient aux textes techniques et aux programmations. BPmono et BPmono Bold ont été conçues en utilisant un processus spécial d'ajustement manuel appelé « hinting ». Le hinting permet d'optimiser de manière spécifique chaque caractère à l'aide d'instructions concrètes pour définir son aspect à l'écran. La police s'est adaptée de 9 px à 16 px afin d'être utilisée pour plusieurs éditeurs de texte et de programmation avancée comme : Visual Studio.net, Visual Web Developer, MS Word. Un texte avec une police à chasse fixe devrait toujours être aligné à gauche (ou à droite si nécessaire) mais ne devrait jamais être centré ou justifié.

Se trata de una fuente monoespaciada apropiada para textos técnicos o de programación. BPmono y BPmono Bold han sido diseñadas a través del proceso especial de ajuste manual llamado *hinting*, que permite la optimización específica de cada carácter mediante instrucciones concretas para el aspecto en pantalla. La fuente se ha adaptado de 9 px hasta 16 px para ser utilizada en varios editores de texto y programación avanzados como Visual Studio.net, Visual Web Developer y MS Word. Una fuente monoespaciada debería siempre alinearse a la izquierda (o a la derecha, si necesario) pero nunca ser centrada o justificada.

BPreplay Regular/Italics/Bold

George Triantafyllakos | www.backpacker.gr

EUROPEAN DESIGN
all questions and no answers

Is there actually such a thing as **EUROPEAN** DESIGN or merely an assembly of diverse frameworks and approaches (eg. **Polish, French, German** or **Swiss**)? Do we really need to think in such holistic terms? Do we really want to? Is such an attempt feasible? Assuming that we follow the holistic approach of **EUROPEAN** DESIGN, what are the aesthetic interrelations, influences and interactions between the former and well established, non-European approaches, such as those of **North American, Japanese** and **Iranian** design? What are their differences? Are there any differences? Do we wish for them to exist (or disappear all the same)?

abcdefghijklmnopqrstuvwxyz[]
ABCDEFGHIJKLMNOPQRSTUVWXYZ
1234567890(.,;:?$£€¥&-*){}

8/10 pt

abcdefghijklmnopqrstuvwxyz[]
ABCDEFGHIJKLMNOPQRSTUVWXYZ
1234567890(.,;:?$£€¥&-){}*

8/10 pt

abcdefghijklmnopqrstuvwxyz[]
ABCDEFGHIJKLMNOPQRSTUVWXYZ
1234567890(.,;:?$£€¥&-*){}

8/10 pt

abcdefghijklmnopqrstuvwxyz[]
ABCDEFGHIJKLMNOPQRSTUVWXYZ
1234567890(.,;:?$£€¥&-*){}

18/18 pt

abcdefghijklmnopqrstuvwxyz[]
ABCDEFGHIJKLMNOPQRSTUVWXYZ
1234567890(.,;:?$£€¥&-){}*

18/18 pt

abcdefghijklmnopqrstuvwxyz[]
ABCDEFGHIJKLMNOPQRSTUVWXYZ
1234567890(.,;:?$£€¥&-*){}

18/18 pt

BPreplay emerged from the need to improve MgOpenModata, a rounded typeface made recently available as an open source font from its owner Magenta Ltd. The redesigning process used MgOpenModata's Regular variant as a starting point, with a number of glyph corrections and complete alterations in the characters alpha, epsilon, zeta, xi, omega, BPreplay emerged as a result of this process. BPreplay Italics, Bold and Bold Italics, together with lowercase letters and old-style numerals were redesigned on the basis of BPreplay Regular. It is interesting to use the Greek letter Alfa as an alternative to the A used in Latin text.

Cette police provient du besoin d'améliorer MgOpenModata, une typographie aux formes arrondies que son propriétaire Magenta Ltd a récemment transformé en une police open source. Le processus de nouvelle conception de la variante Regular de MgOpenModata qui a subi une série de corrections en ce qui concerne les glyphes ainsi que des modifications complètes de la représentation des caractères : alpha, epsilon, zêta, xi, oméga. C'est à travers ce processus qu'est né BPreplay. BPreplay Italics, Bold et Bold Italics, ainsi que les minuscules et les chiffres à l'ancienne, ont été conçus à partir de BPreplay Regular. Il est intéressant d'utiliser la lettre grecque alpha à la place du « a » dans les textes avec une écriture latine.

Surgió de la necesidad de mejorar la MgOpenModata, una tipografía redondeada recientemente convertida en Open Source por Magenta Ltd. El rediseño partió de la variante Regular, que sufrió una serie de correcciones en los glifos y alteraciones completas en los caracteres a, épsilon, xeta, xi y omega. A través de este proceso nació BPreplay Regular. A partir de ella se rediseñaron BPreplay Italics, Bold y Bold Italics, junto con las minúsculas y cifras a la antigua. Es interesante utilizar la letra alfa como alternativa a la a en textos latinos.

BP Script

George Triantafyllakos | www.backpacker.gr

backpacker.gr
A retrospective
Or: how to label a button
on your website
to prevent prospective
users from using it_____*

abcdefghijklmnopqrstuvwxyz[ ]
ABCDEFGHIJKLMNOPQRSTUVWXYZ
1234567890(.,¡:?$£€¥&-*)}}

8/10 pt

abcdefghijklmnopqrstuvwxyz[ ]
ABCDEFGHIJKLMNOPQRSTUVWXYZ
1234567890(.,¡:?$£€¥&-*)}}

10/12 pt

abcdefghijklmnopqrstuvwxyz[ ]
ABCDEFGHIJKLMNOPQRSTUVWXYZ
1234567890(.,¡:?$£€¥&-*)}}

18/18 pt

abcdefghijklmn
opqrstuvwxyz[ ]
ABCDEFGHIJKLMN
OPQRSTUVWXYZ
1234567890(.,¡:?$£€¥&-*)}}

24/24 pt

This sans serif font with its clean, smooth stokes is ideal for headings and short texts. One attribute worthy of special note with respect to this font is the joined-up nature of the lowercase characters. The uppercase characters incorporate a decorative element in the form of a swash emerging from the top of the main stem. Some characters are also prolonged at the bottom of the stem generating an exaggerated tail. It is recommended that uppercase letters be used to accompany lowercase characters so as to avoid running a number of uppercase letters together. One key character that stands out is the lowercase g with a loop but no link or ear.

Convenant parfaitement aux en-têtes et aux textes courts, cette police aux traits doux et propres est sans serif. Une de ses caractéristiques est l'existence d'union entre les caractères bas de casse. Les caractères haut de casse comportent un ornement de forme arrondie qui provient de la partie supérieure de la hampe principale. Pour certains caractères, la partie inférieure de la hampe est prolongée créant une queue exagérée. Il est conseillé d'utiliser les caractères haut de casse pour accompagner les bas de casse, évitant d'écrire uniquement en haut de casse. Une des lettres qui se distingue est le « g » bas de casse, sans boucles, ni délié de jonction, ni oreille.

Muy adecuada para encabezamientos y textos cortos, esta fuente de trazos suaves y limpios no tiene remates. Como atributo especial cabe destacar la existencia de unión entre los caracteres de caja baja. Los caracteres de caja alta incorporan un adorno en forma de trazo curvo que nace en la parte superior del asta principal. Algunos caracteres también añaden una prolongación en la parte inferior del asta, generando una cola exagerada. Se aconseja utilizar los caracteres de caja alta en combinación con los de caja baja. Como carácter clave destaca la g de caja baja con ojal pero sin cuello y sin oreja.

Brüll

André Rösler, Boris Kahl | www.volcano-type.de

abcdefghijklmnopqrstuvwxyzäöüßæç
ABCDEFGHIJKLMNOPQRSTUVWXYZ
1234567890(.,;:?$£&-*)(ÄÖÜÆŒÇ)

8/10 pt

abcdefghijklmnopqrstuvwxyzäöüßæç
ABCDEFGHIJKLMNOPQRSTUVWXYZ
1234567890(.,;:?$£&-*)(ÄÖÜÆŒÇ)

10/12 pt

abcdefghijklmnopqrstuvwxyzäöüßæç
ABCDEFGHIJKLMNOPQRSTUVWXYZ
1234567890(.,;:?$£&-*)(ÄÖÜÆŒÇ)

18/18 pt

abcdefghijklmnopqrstuvwxyzäöüßæç
ABCDEFGHIJKLMNOPQRSTUVWXYZ
1234567890(.,;:?$£&-*)(ÄÖÜÆŒÇ)

24/24 pt

abcdefghijklmn

opqrstuvwxyzäöüßæç

ABCDEFGHIJKLMNOPQRSTUVWXYZ

1234567890(.,;:?$£&-*)(ÄÖÜÆŒÇ)

32/34 pt

This font came into being as the result of a design for the book *Can you shout?* by Andre Rösler and Karin Koch, published by Peter Hammler. Brüll is a sans serif hand-designed font that includes two variants: Brüll Aussen and Brüll Innen. In the first only the outline has been drawn leaving the inside of the bowl hollow. On the other hand, Brüll Innen maintains the dimensions and shape of the design but the outline is filled in. Due to the fact that the characters are not resting on the baseline and the edges and dimensions are uneven, it is more appropriate for an informal environment – for billboards or headers – avoiding running text.

Elle provient du design du livre *Can you shout ?* de Andre Rösler et Karin Koch, publié par la maison d'édition Peter Hammler. Brüll est une police sans serif dessinée à la main qui propose deux variantes : Brüll Aussen et Brüll Innen. La première ne montre que le contour des caractères laissant l'intérieur vide. En revanche, Brüll Innen conserve les dimensions et la forme des caractères mais l'intérieur est plein. Étant donné que les caractères ne sont pas alignés sur la ligne de base et que les bords et les dimensions sont irréguliers, elle convient davantage à un environnement informel, comme des publicités ou des titres, en évitant des textes longs.

Surge del diseño para el libro *Can you shout?* de Andre Rösler y Karin Koch, publicado por la editorial Peter Hammler. Brüll es una fuente de palo seco diseñada a mano que incluye dos variantes: Brüll Aussen y Brüll Innen. La primera tan sólo muestra el contorno perfilado dejando hueco el interior del trazo. Al contrario, Brüll Innen conserva las dimensiones y la forma del diseño pero el trazo queda relleno. Debido a que los caracteres no se apoyan en la línea base y los bordes y dimensiones son irregulares, resulta más apropiada para un entorno de carácter informal, para carteles publicitarios o titulares que no para el texto corrido.

BubbleMan

Brain Eaters Font Company (BEFCo) | www.braineaters.com

ABCDEFGHIJKLMNOPQRSTUVWXYZ[ß]
ABCDEFGHIJKLMNOPQRSTUVWXYZ
1234567890(.,;:?$¢£¥&-*){}

8/10 pt

ABCDEFGHIJKLMNOPQRSTUVWXYZ[ß]
ABCDEFGHIJKLMNOPQRSTUVWXYZ
1234567890(.,;:?$¢£¥&-*){}

10/12 pt

ABCDEFGHIJKLMNOPQRSTUVWXYZ[ß]
ABCDEFGHIJKLMN
OPQRSTUVWXYZ
1234567890(.,;:?$¢£¥&-*){}

18/18 pt

ABCDEFGHIJKLMN
OPQRSTUVWXYZ[ß]
ABCDEFGHIJKLMN
OPQRSTUVWXYZ
1234567890(.,;:?$¢£¥&-*){}

24/24 pt

The name refers to the classic *BubbleMan* science-fiction movie. This font is just as dangerous as the bubble machine used by this monster robot to wipe out the human race. The letters are full of bubbles, and for this reason it was nearly called Swiss Cheese, however, the name had already been reserved for the famous cheese. This decorative font is ideal for headings with a message that contains holed or perforated connotations. It never occurred to the typographer what a crazy idea it was to try to perforate all the letters one by one. Despite the time spent on the rough draft of all the bubbles, the effect worked.

Il s'agit d'une référence au film classique de science fiction *Bubbleman*. Cette police d'écriture est aussi dangereuse que la machine à bulles que ce robot-monstre utilise pour en finir avec la race humaine. Les lettres sont pleines de bulles, pour cela elles ont été sur le point de s'appeler Swiss Cheese, mais le nom était déjà réservé pour le fameux fromage. Cette police d'écriture convient parfaitement aux gros titres dont le message fait référence à des trous ou au perforage. Le typographe ne pouvait imaginer le délire qu'impliquerait le fait de perforer les lettres une à une. En dépit du temps passé à créer toutes les bulles au brouillon, l'effet a porté ses fruits.

Hace referencia a la película clásica de ciencia ficción *Bubbleman*. Esta fuente resulta igual de peligrosa que la máquina de burbujas que utiliza este robot-monstruo para acabar con la raza humana. Las letras están repletas de burbujas, por ese motivo estuvo a punto de llamarse Swiss Cheese, pero el nombre ya estaba reservado para el famoso queso. Esta fuente decorativa resulta ideal para titulares cuyo mensaje posee connotaciones de agujereado o perforado. El tipógrafo no podía imaginarse la chifladura que supondría ir perforando las letras una a una. A pesar del tiempo empleado en diseñar todas las burbujas, el efecto funcionó.

Leabharlanna Poibli Chathair Bhaile Átha Cliath
Dublin City Public Libraries

Bunker

Ewen Prigent | www.laboitegraphique.fr

ABCDEFGHIJKLMNOPQRSTUVWXYZ
1234567890(.,:?-)ÄÖ

8/10 pt

ABCDEFGHIJKLMNOPQRSTUVWXYZ
1234567890(.,:?-)ÄÖ

10/12 pt

ABCDEFGHIJKLMNOPQRSTUVWXYZ
1234567890(.,:?-)ÄÖ

18/18 pt

ABCDEFGHIJKLMN
OPQRSTUVWXYZ
1234567890(.,:?-)ÄÖ

24/24 pt

ABCDEFGHIJKLMN
OPQRSTUVWXYZ
1234567890(.,:?-)ÄÖ

32/34 pt

The highly polished treatment of this form gives this font a thick, heavy appearance. The base of each glyph is formed by a rectangle that seems to be minimally carved, revealing the essence of each letter. This is a sans serif font without any stems, bars, arms, loops, counters or bowls. The only prominent element is the tail of the Q, which cuts straight through the center. has a range of characters adapted to the French language, including vowels with an acute or grave accent, circumflex or dieresis. It also includes numbers and basic punctuation marks, along with the adaptation of the at symbol.

La forme hautement dépurée donne une apparence massive et lourde. La base de chaque glyphe se compose d'un rectangle qui semble taillé de forme minime, qui permet de révéler l'essence de chaque lettre. Il s'agit d'une police sans serif, ni hampes, ni traverses, ni boucles, ni panses. Le seul élément proéminent est la queue du « Q » au milieu de la lettre. Cette police propose des caractères adaptés au français, avec des accents aigus, graves, circonflexes et des trémas. Elle comporte également des chiffres et les signes de ponctuation de base ainsi que le symbole arobase.

El tratamiento altamente depurado de la forma ofrece a esta fuente un aspecto macizo y pesado. La base constitutiva de cada glifo está formada por un rectángulo que aparece tallado de forma mínima, logrando revelar la esencia de cada letra. Se trata de una fuente de palo seco que carece de astas, barras horizontales, brazos, bucles, ojales o anillos. El único elemento prominente es la cola de la Q que corta por el centro. La fuente ofrece caracteres adaptados a la lengua francesa, incluyendo vocales con acentos agudo y grave, acento circunflejo y diéresis. También incluye números y los signos de puntuación básicos, así como la adaptación del símbolo arroba.

CA Nihil Superstar

Stefan Claudius | www.cape-arcona.com

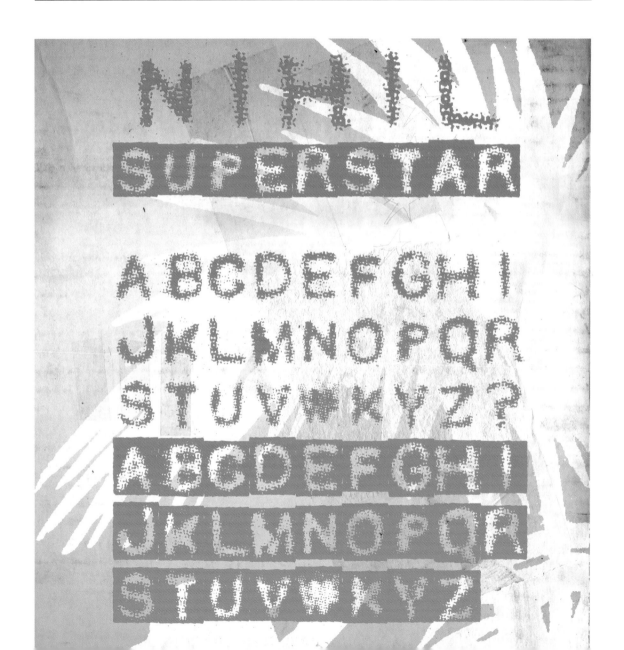

ABCDEFGHIJKLMNOPQRSTUVWKYZ
ABCDEFGHIJKLMNOPQRSTUVWKYZ
1234567890(.,;:?¿-*)ÄÖÜ

8/10 pt

ABCDEFGHIJKLMNOPQRSTUVWKYZ
ABCDEFGHIJKLMNOPQRSTUVWKYZ
1234567890(.,;:?¿-*)ÄÖÜ

10/12 pt

ABCDEFGHIJKLMNOPQRSTUVWKYZ
ABCDEFGHIJKLMNOPQRSTUVWKYZ
1234567890(.,;:?¿-*)ÄÖÜ

18/18 pt

ABCDEFGHIJKLMN
OPQRSTUVWKYZ
ABCDEFGHIJKLM
NOPQRSTUVWKYZ
1234567890
(.,;:?¿-*)ÄÖÜ

24/24 pt

This font is derived from the typeface of the typewriter belonging to Friedrich Nietzsche. The model used by the German philosopher was one of the first typewriters in history and also boasted a very modern typographic style. However, it did not include numbers, and so Nietzsche had to write them by hand. The current result is a monospaced sans serif text with a jagged, uneven outline, uniformly constructed, with rounded and slightly square-shaped curves, without contrast. The stroke is created by clustering a number of small dots together.

Cette typographie est issue de la police intégrée dans la machine à écrire de Friedrich Nietzsche. Le modèle qui appartenait au philosophe allemand était une des premières machines à écrire de l'histoire qui disposait d'un style typographique très moderne. Cependant, elle ne comportait pas les chiffres et Nietzsche devait les écrire à la main. Le résultat actuel est une police de caractères sans serif et à chasse fixe, aux contours rugueux et irréguliers. Sa forme est homogène, avec des courbes arrondies légèrement carrées et sans contrastes. Le trait est obtenu à partir de petites taches accolées les unes aux autres.

Deriva de la fuente incorporada en la máquina de escribir de Friedrich Nietzsche. El modelo perteneciente al filósofo alemán fue una de las primeras máquinas en la historia que a la vez incorporaba un estilo tipográfico muy moderno. Sin embargo, no incluía números, por lo que Nietzsche tenía que escribirlos a mano. El resultado actual es una fuente sin remates y monoespaciada, de contorno rugoso e irregular, de construcción continua, con curvas redondas ligeramente cuadradas y sin contraste. El trazo se ha generado a partir de la aglutinación de pequeñas manchas.

CA Plushy

Stefan Claudius | www.cape-arcona.com

abcdefghijklmnopqrstuvwxyzäöüß
abcdef ghijklmnopqr-sthvwxyz
. , ? - ä öü

8/10 pt

abcdefghijklmnopqrstuvwxyzäöüß
abcdef ghijklmnopqr-sthvwxyz
. , ? - ä öü

10/12 pt

abcdefghijklmn
opqrstuvwxyzäöüß
abcdef ghijklmn
opqr-sthvwxyz
. , ? - ä öü

18/18 pt

abcdefghijklmn
opqrstuvwxyzäöüß
abcdef ghijklmn
opqr-sthvwxyz
. , ? - ä öü

24/24 pt

This is an informal font that simulates writing with a paintbrush. The letters are traced with vigorous strokes using a brush loaded with ink. The upper and lowercase letters differ in terms of style but not in height. For this reason, the user has the opportunity to modify the design by alternating between upper and lowercase characters in accordance with their own criteria. It does not look as monotonous as other similar typefaces on account of its spontaneous strokes, which are deliberately uneven and seem to dance on the base line. It works particularly well with informal designs for logos, menus, correspondence or exhibition work such as posters.

Typographie qui relève de la calligraphie, imitant une écriture au pinceau. Les lettres sont tracées avec des coups énergiques de pinceau imbibé de peinture. Les caractères bas de casse et haut de casse ont un style différent mais la même hauteur. L'usager a donc la possibilité d'alterner entre minuscules et majuscules selon son bon vouloir. Son apparence n'est pas aussi monotone que celle d'autres typographies du même genre grâce à ses traits spontanés, volontairement irréguliers qui dansent sur la ligne de base. Elle convient particulièrement pour des designs non formels comme des logotypes, des menus, une correspondance ou des projets d'exposition comme des affiches.

Tipografía caligráfica informal que simula la escritura con pincel. Las letras quedan plasmadas a través de los trazos enérgicos de la brocha cargada de tinta. Los caracteres de caja alta y caja baja difieren en estilo pero no en altura. Por este motivo, el usuario tiene la oportunidad de diseñar alternando caja alta y caja baja según su criterio. No resulta tan monótona como otras tipografías similares gracias a sus trazos espontáneos, deliberadamente irregulares que bailan sobre la línea base. Funciona especialmente bien en diseños informales de logotipos, menús, correspondencia o material de muestra como pósters.

Chango

Setemeia | www.studiosetemeia.com/blog

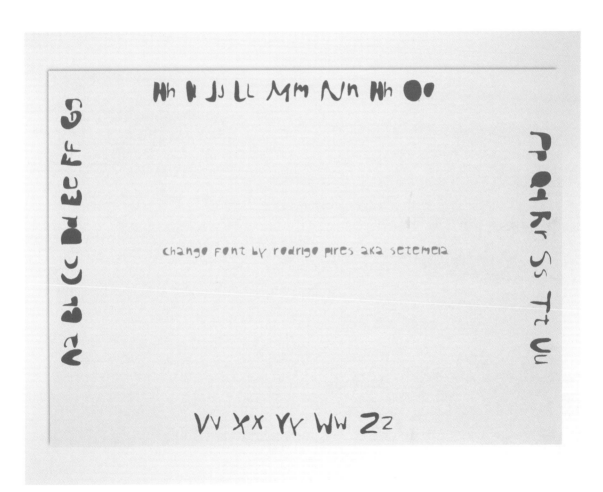

abcdefghijklmnopqrstuvwxyz
ABCDEFGHIJKLMNOPQRSTUVWXYZ
1234567890

8/10 pt

abcdefghijklmnopqrstuvwxyz
ABCDEFGHIJKLMNOPQRSTUVWXYZ
1234567890

10/12 pt

abcdefghijklmn
opqrstuvwxyz
ABCDEFGHIJKLMN
OPQRSTUVWXYZ
1234567890

18/18 pt

abcdefghijklmn
opqrstuvwxyz
ABCDEFGHIJKLMN
OPQRSTUVWXYZ
1234567890

24/24 pt

The inspiration for this typeface is a children's game called amoeba, created using jellolike shapes. Its soft appearance makes it look a lot like ameba, a single-cell living creature characterized by its changing shape. The font originally formed part of Typos do aCASO, a website put together by a group of Brazilian typographers. It was designed with Fontographer, a program for creating and editing typefaces that softens and merges fonts, creates freehand fonts or converts the sources to editable vectors. The result is a sans serif font with uneven, shapeless characters.

Typographie inspirée d'un jeu d'enfant intitulé amibe qui se compose de formes gélatineuses. Son aspect mou et flasque provoque une sensation semblable aux amibes : des êtres vivants unicellulaires caractérisés par leur allure changeante. Auparavant elles faisaient partie des Tipos do aCASO, un site web créé par un groupe de typographes brésiliens. Cette police a été conçue avec Fontographer, un programme pour la création et l'édition de typographies qui adoucit et fusionne les différentes polices, qui crée des dessins de polices à main levée ou convertit les polices en caractères éditables. Le résultat obtenu est une police sans serif dont les caractères sont irréguliers et sans forme.

Tipografía inspirada en el juego infantil brasileño ameba, el cual se desarrolla a través de formas gelatinosas. Su aspecto blando causa una impresión similar a las amebas, caracterizadas por sus formas cambiantes. Anteriormente formaba parte de Tipos do aCASO, espacio web organizado por un grupo de tipógrafos brasileños. Fue diseñada con Fontographer, un programa para la creación y edición de tipografías que suaviza y fusiona fuentes, crea fuentes a mano alzada o las convierte a vectores editables. El resultado es una tipografía de palo seco cuyos caracteres son irregulares y de construcción amorfa.

Cuneiform

sugargliderz | www.sugargliderz.com

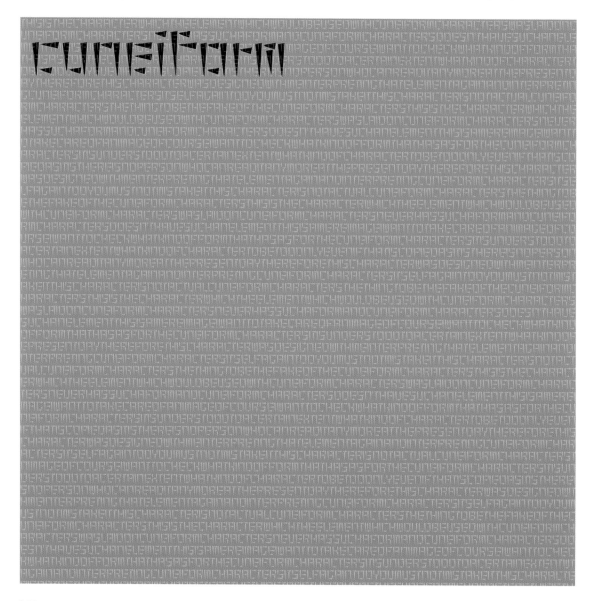

abcdefghijklmnopqrstuvwxyz[àöüßâdæœçñ]
ABCDEFGHIJKLMNOPQRSTUVWXYZ
1234567890(.,:;¡¿€£¥₢-#¾àöüÂ@ßàœçñ)

8/10 pt

abcdefghijklmnopqrstuvwxyz[àöüßâdæœçñ]
ABCDEFGHIJKLMNOPQRSTUVWXYZ
1234567890(.,:;¡¿€£¥₢-#¾àöüÂ@ßàœçñ)

10/12 pt

abcdefghijklmn
opqrstuvwxyz[àöüßâdæœçñ]
ABCDEFGHIJKLMNOPQRSTUVWXYZ
1234567890
(.,:;¡¿€£¥₢-#¾àöüÂ@ßàœçñ)

18/18 pt

abcdefghijklmn
opqrstuvwxyz
[àöüßâdæœçñ]
ABCDEFGHIKLMN
OPQRSTUVWXYZ
1234567890
(.,:;¡¿€£¥₢-#¾àöüÂ@ßàœçñ)

24/24 pt

Generally accepted as being the earliest known form of written expression, the cuneiform script was created by the Sumerians at the end of the fourth millennium BC. Originally, it was a system of pictographs, which was gradually simplified and made more abstract. Cuneiform symbols were written on clay tablets with reeds, producing characters that were shaped like a wedge (cuneiform). This font is an adaptation of cuneiform script, and is composed of loose, discontinuous, individual elements. It is easier to read if the spacing between the characters is increased and more effective in short words.

Connu comme le système d'écriture le plus ancien, le cunéiforme a été créé par les Sumériens à la fin du IVᵉ millénaire avant J.-C. Il est apparu comme un système de pictogrammes qui, avec le temps, s'est simplifié et est devenu plus abstrait. Les signes cunéiformes se réalisaient avec des calames sur une tablette en argile produisant des caractères en forme de coins (cunéiformes). La police de caractères Cuneiform est une adaptation de ce système d'écriture qui se compose d'éléments séparés, de forme non homogène. Il est plus lisible si l'on agrandit l'espace entre chaque caractère et plus efficace si les mots sont courts.

Aceptada comúnmente como la forma más temprana de expresión escrita, la escritura cuneiforme fue creada por los sumerios a finales del siglo IV a.C. Surgió como un sistema de pictogramas que, con el tiempo, se fue simplificando y se volvió más abstracto. Los signos cuneiformes eran escritos mediante cuñas sobre tablillas de arcilla, dando lugar a caracteres en forma de cuña (cuneiformes). Esta fuente es una adaptación de aquella escritura, y como tal se compone de elementos individuales sueltos, de construcción discontinua. Resulta más legible si se amplía el espaciado entre caracteres y funciona mejor en palabras cortas.

Data Trash

Popdog Fonts | popdog_fonts.tripod.com

ABCDEFGHIJKLMNOPQRSTUVWXYZ
1234567890C.,:;?E+—*JΔΦЄЧZHP

8/10 pt

ABCDEFGHIJKLMNOPQRSTUVWXYZ
1234567890C.,:;?E+—*JΔΦЄЧZHP

10/12 pt

ABCDEFGHIJKLMNOPQRSTUVWXYZ
1234567890C.,:;?E+—*JΔΦЄЧZHP

18/18 pt

ABCDEFGHIJKLMN
OPQRSTUVWXYZ
1234567890
C.,:;?E+—*JΔΦЄЧZHP

24/24 pt

ABCDEFGHIJKLMN
OPQRSTUVWXYZ
1234567890
C.,:;?E+—*JΔΦЄЧZHP

32/34 pt

This font represents the merger of retro and futuristic styles of writing. The result is the combination of digital typeface with elements from early videogames and the typeface typical of the Soviet era. The characters are even and follow the same pattern engraved within a rectangle. The letters rest on the baseline and have soft, clean edges. This is an uppercase only, sans serif typeface with Latin and Greek characters, including numbers, punctuation marks and symbols. One of the key characters is the Q with its straight tail, which is projected externally on one side without cutting through the bowl.

Il s'agit d'une fusion entre le style rétro et le style futuriste. Le résultat est un mélange de typographie numérique avec des éléments des premiers jeux vidéo de l'histoire et la typographie de l'ère soviétique. Les caractères sont réguliers et suivent un même modèle tout en étant inscrits dans un rectangle. Les lettres s'appuient sur la ligne de base et les contours sont nets et agréables. Cette typographie sans serif offre des caractères latins et grecs uniquement haut de casse, ainsi que des chiffres, des signes de ponctuation et des symboles. Parmi les caractères emblématiques celui qui se distingue est le Q dont la queue est droite et se prolonge sur le côté sans couper la panse.

Representa la fusión de los estilos retro y futurista. Es resultado de la combinación de la tipografía digital con elementos de los primeros videojuegos de la historia y la tipografía de la era soviética. Los caracteres son regulares y siguen un mismo patrón inscritos en un rectángulo. Las letras se apoyan en la línea base y sus bordes son limpios y suaves. Se trata de una tipografía de palo seco que ofrece caracteres latinos y griegos únicamente de caja alta, junto con números, signos de puntuación y símbolos. Entre los caracteres clave destaca la Q con la cola recta que, sin cortar el anillo, se prolonga externamente por un lado.

Depot Trapharet

Lukyan Turetsky | www.2d.lviv.ua

URBANTYPE
ROCK
INDUSTRIAL

За основу малюнку шрифта Depot Trapharet взято трамвайні щити з описами маршрутів в місті Львові.

ABCDEFGHIJKLMNOPQRSTUVWXYZ[]
1234567890(.,;:?$€&-")[]

8/10 pt

ABCDEFGHIJKLMNOPQRSTUVWXYZ[]
1234567890(.,;:?$€&-")[]

10/12 pt

ABCDEFGHIJKLMNOPQRSTUVWXYZ[]
1234567890(.,;:?$€&-")[]

18/18 pt

ABCDEFGHIJKLMNOPQRSTUVWXYZ[]
1234567890(.,;:?$€&-")[]

24/24 pt

ABCDEFGHIJKLMN
OPQRSTUVWXYZ[]
1234567890
(.,;:?$€&-")[]

32/34 pt

A template-type font with ornamental characters is inspired by the side panels describing the tram routes in Lviv. The tram is the most widely used means of transport in this Ukrainian city. These typefaces, which are also known as Stencil fonts, are characterized by their letters being divided into several parts, making it easier to cut them out whole. Hence, templates can be created so that they can be reproduced on another surface. The result is a sans serif font with parallel edge stems and medium weight and proportions.

Ayant un caractère ornemental, cette police d'écriture s'inspire des panneaux qui indiquent les directions sur le tramway de Lviv. Le tramway est le moyen de transport le plus utilisé dans cette ville ukrainienne. Ces typographies, également connues comme Stencil, se caractérisent par des lettres divisées en plusieurs parties ce qui permet de les découper tout en les conservant dans leur intégralité. Il est donc possible de créer des modèles et de les reproduire sur des superficies différentes. Il en résulte une police sans serif, avec des hampes verticales et des bords parallèles, aux proportions et au poids moyens.

De carácter ornamental tipo plantilla, encuentra su fuente de inspiración en los rótulos que indican las rutas en los tranvías de Lviv, que son el medio de transporte más utilizado en esta ciudad ucraniana. Estas tipografías, también conocidas como stencil, se caracterizan por sus letras divididas en varias partes, facilitando así el poder recortarlas manteniéndolas enteras. De esta manera se pueden crear plantillas para reproducirlas en otras superficie. El resultado es una fuente de palo seco, con astas verticales de bordes paralelos, y de proporciones y peso medios.

Designer Block

K-Type/Keith Bates | www.k-type.com

abcdefghijklmnopqrstuvwxyz[äöüßàèæœçñ]
ABCDEFGHIJKLMNOPQRSTUVWXYZ
1234567890[.,;:?¿$¢£€¥&-*][ÄÖÜÂßÆŒÇÑ]

8/10 pt

abcdefghijklmnopqrstuvwxyz[äöüßàèæœçñ]
ABCDEFGHIJKLMNOPQRSTUVWXYZ
1234567890[.,;:?¿$¢£€¥&-*][ÄÖÜÂßÆŒÇÑ]

10/12 pt

abcdefghijklmn
opqrstuvwxyz[äöüßàèæœçñ]
ABCDEFGHIJKLMNOPQRSTUVWXYZ
1234567890[.,;:?¿$¢£€¥&-*]
[ÄÖÜÂßÆŒÇÑ]

18/18 pt

abcdefghijklmn
opqrstuvwxyz
[äöüßàèæœçñ]
ABCDEFGHIJKLMN
OPQRSTUVWXYZ
1234567890
[.,;:?¿$¢£€¥&-*]
[ÄÖÜÂßÆŒÇÑ]

24/24 pt

A decorative source forming part of the post-modern and futuristic style that draws its inspiration from DesignerShock, Designers Republic and designs from the nineteen nineties. DesignerShock is a group of German-based graphic artists. Basically, they create designer software such as downloadable fonts or screensavers for online distribution. The Designers Republic is a design studio based in the U.K. famous for its unconventional style. The peculiar style of this sans serif font is evident in its continuous construction with rectangular curves and rounded edges.

Police d'écriture décorative dans un style post-moderne et futuriste qui s'inspire de Designer Shock, Designers Republic et du style des années 90. DesignerShock est un collectif d'artistes graphiques dont le siège est en Allemagne. Ils créent principalement des logiciels de design comme des polices à télécharger ou des économiseurs d'écran qu'ils distribuent en ligne. The Designers Republic est un studio de design situé en Angleterre, connu pour son esthétique non-conformiste. Cette police sans serif témoigne d'un style particulier avec une forme homogène, des courbes avec un aspect rectangulaire et des contours arrondis.

Fuente decorativa dentro del estilo post-moderno y futurista que encuentra su inspiración en DesignerShock, The Designers Republic y los diseños de la década de 1990. DesignerShock es un colectivo de artistas gráficos con sede en Alemania, especializados en la creación de software de diseño como fuentes descargables o salvapantallas para distribuirlo en la red; por su parte, The Designers Republic es un estudio de diseño británico conocido por su estética inconformista. Esta fuente de palo seco muestra su peculiar estilo a través de la construcción continua con aspecto de las curvas rectangular y los bordes redondeados.

Discobox

Popdog Fonts | popdog_fonts.tripod.com

ABCDEFGHIJKLMNOPQRSTUVWXYZ
1234567890(.,✳:✳$&–✳)ΔΦΕΥΖΗΡ

8/10 pt

ABCDEFGHIJKLMNOPQRSTUVWXYZ
1234567890(.,✳:✳$&–✳)ΔΦΕΥΖΗΡ

10/12 pt

ABCDEFG HIJKLMN
OPQRSTUVWXYZ
1234567890
(.,✳:✳$&–✳)ΔΦΕΥΖΗΡ

18/18 pt

ABCDEFGHIJKLMN
OPQRSTUVWXYZ
1234567890
(.,✳:✳$&–✳)
ΔΦΕΥΖΗΡ

24/24 pt

This font aims to reproduce the effect of a stamp that has been poorly printed, when the ink runs and creates stains, giving it a distorted look. Its decorative and pictographic characters are very suitable for text headings and small-sized lettering. It is a sans serif font constructed with uneven elements and strokes that generate a shapeless form. Key characters include: the A with a poorly defined apex; the G without a spur; and the Q with a tail cutting through the bowl. This typeface comes in a set of Latin and Greek characters, including numbers, punctuation marks and symbols.

Cette police reproduit la marque d'un tampon mal imprégné, lorsque l'encre coule et fait des taches provoquant un aspect déformé. De caractère décoratif et pictographique, elle convient parfaitement pour des en-têtes et des textes courts. Il s'agit d'une police sans serif composée d'éléments irréguliers dont les traits produisent une construction sans forme. Les caractères clés qui se distinguent sont : le « A » dont la pointe n'est pas définie, le « G » sans empattement et le « Q » dont la queue coupe la panse. Cette typographie existe en caractères latins et grecs. Elle inclut des chiffres, des signes de ponctuation et des symboles.

Busca el efecto de un sello que ha quedo mal estampado, cuando la tinta se corre y genera manchas, provocando un aspecto distorsionado. Esta fuente de carácter decorativo y pictográfico resulta muy apropiada para titulares y textos breves. Se trata de una fuente de palo seco construida a base de elementos irregulares cuyos trazos generan una construcción amorfa. Entre los caracteres clave destacan la A con el vértice indefinido, la G sin espuela y la Q con cola que corta el anillo. Esta tipografía ofrece el set para caracteres latinos y griegos. Incluye números, signos de puntuación y símbolos.

Estuque

Setemeia | www.studiosetemeia.com/blog

ABCDEFGHIJKLMNOPQRSTUVWXYZ

8/10 pt

ABCDEFGHIJKLMNOPQRSTUVWXYZ

10/12 pt

ABCDEFGHIJKLMN
OPQRSTUVWXYZ

18/18 pt

ABCDEFGHIJKLMN
OPQRSTUVWXYZ

24/24 pt

ABCDEFGHI
JKLMNOPQRS
TUVWXYZ

32/34 pt

The term "stucco" (plaster), which translates into Portuguese as *estuque*, comes from the Italian (*stucco*), and is a type of finish or interior or exterior decoration for walls, ceilings and roofs, based on paints and different types of mortar to obtain different textures. This font was created for use on rustic-style walls with an apparent unfinished appearance. It is available in uppercase characters and includes acute, grave and circumflex accents for use with vowels and also the tilde for the Ã. The vigorous strokes are suggestive of a flat brush used as a design tool. This is a decorative sans serif font.

Le mot « stuc », en portugais *estuque*, provient de l'italien *stucco*, une technique de finition ou de décoration pour les plafonds et les murs, aussi bien à l'intérieur qu'à l'extérieur. C'est un mélange de peintures et de différents types de mortiers qui permet d'obtenir diverses textures. Cette police a été créée pour être utilisée sur des murs dont les finitions sont rustiques et semblent inachevées. Elle propose des caractères en haut de casse, et inclut les accents aigus, graves et circonflexes ainsi que le tilde du « Ã ». Les traits énergiques laissent suggérer que l'outil de travail est un pinceau plat. Il s'agit d'une police décorative sans serif.

El término «estuco», o *estuque* en portugués, proviene del italiano *stucco*, una técnica de pintura decorativa para paredes y techos, interiores o exteriores, basada en pinturas y diferentes tipos de morteros, que permite la obtención de diferentes texturas. Esta fuente se creó para ser usada en paredes donde la terminación es más rústica y tiene apariencia de inacabada. Ofrece los caracteres en caja alta e incorpora los acentos agudo, grave y circunflejo para las vocales así como la tilde de la Ã. Los trazos enérgicos hacen referencia al pincel plano como herramienta de diseño. Se trata de una fuente decorativa de palo seco.

12345 YZ $&)

Fine Serif

Galdino Otten | galdinoottenbr.blogspot.com

FINE SERIF

A B C D E F G H I J K L M
N O P Q R S T U V W X Y Z
A B C D E F G H I J K L M N O P Q
R S T U V W X Y Z { $? ! % @ }
1 2 3 4 5 6 7 8 9 0 (& # * :)

GALDINO
OTTEN

ABCDEFGHIJKLMNOPQRSTUVWXYZ[]
ABCDEFGHIJKLMNOPQRSTUVWXYZ
1234567890(-+;:?$&,){ÇÑ}

8/10 pt

ABCDEFGHIJKLMNOPQRSTUVWXYZ[]
ABCDEFGHIJKLMNOPQRSTUVWXYZ
1234567890(-+;:?$&,){ÇÑ}

10/12 pt

ABCDEFGHIJKLMN
OPQRSTUVWXYZ[]
ABCDEFGHIJKLMN
OPQRSTUVWXYZ
1234567890(-+;:?$&,){ÇÑ}

18/18 pt

ABCDEFGHIJKLMN
OPQRSTUVWXYZ[]
ABCDEFGHIJKLMN
OPQRSTUVWXYZ
1234567890(-+;:?$&,){ÇÑ}

24/24 pt

After analyzing the Free Font phenomenon, the designer realized that most designs resort to disparate concepts with impossible shapes. Having reached this conclusion, Galdino Otten decided to spend his time in developing a normal font that would be functional and devoid of any decorative elements or exaggerated thicknesses. The result was a basic serif font, with medium contrast, vertical axis and gradual transition. The set comes in two different-sized groups for uppercase characters. Ideal for applications involving graphic design, using several resources like the printed medium, computer software or television.

Après avoir analysé le phénomène Free Font, le concepteur s'est rendu compte que la plupart des designs utilisaient des concepts extravagants avec des formes impossibles. C'est à ce moment que Galdino Otten a décidé de consacrer son temps à développer une police normale, fonctionnelle, sans éléments décoratifs ni grosseurs exagérées. Le résultat qu'il a obtenu est une police de base avec serif, qui offre un contraste moyen avec un axe vertical et une transition progressive. L'ensemble se compose de deux jeux de taille différente pour des caractères hauts de casse. Il est idéal pour des travaux de design graphique, sur différents supports comme le média imprimé, les supports électroniques ou la télévision.

Tras analizar el fenómeno Free Font, Galdino Otten se dio cuenta de que la mayoría de los diseños recurren a conceptos disparatados con formas imposibles. Por ello, decidió desarrollar una fuente normal, funcional, sin elementos decorativos ni grosores exagerados. El resultado es una fuente básica con serifa, que presenta un contraste medio con eje vertical y transición gradual. El set ofrece dos juegos con tamaños diferentes para caracteres de caja alta. Ideal para aplicar en trabajos de diseño gráfico, tanto para el medio impreso como para soportes digitales.

FlatPack

K-Type/Keith Bates | www.k-type.com

ABCDEFGHIJKLMNOPQRSTUVWXYZ[ÄÖÜßÅØÆŒÇÑ]
ABCDEFGHIJKLMNOPQRSTUVWXYZ
1234567890[.,;:?¿$¢£€¥&-×][ÄÖÜÅØÆŒÇÑ]

8/10 pt

ABCDEFGHIJKLMNOPQRSTUVWXYZ[ÄÖÜßÅØÆŒÇÑ]
ABCDEFGHIJKLMNOPQRSTUVWXYZ
1234567890[.,;:?¿$¢£€¥&-×][ÄÖÜÅØÆŒÇÑ]

10/12 pt

ABCDEFGHIJKLMN
OPQRSTUVWXYZ[ÄÖÜßÅØÆŒÇÑ]
ABCDEFGHIJKLMNOPQRSTUVWXYZ
1234567890
[.,;:?¿$¢£€¥&-×][ÄÖÜÅØÆŒÇÑ]

18/18 pt

ABCDEFGHIJKLMN
OPQRSTUVWXYZ
[ÄÖÜßÅØÆŒÇÑ]
ABCDEFGHIJKLMN
OPQRSTUVWXYZ
1234567890
[.,;:?¿$¢£€¥&-×]
[ÄÖÜÅØÆŒÇÑ]

24/24 pt

Gavin Peacock is an artist living in Brighton, UK, who has taken part in various exhibitions along with several international projects on mail art. His work includes participatory projects, sculpture, installations, photography and video. He is the creator of Flatpack, a game with 1200 plastic modules that can be put together to produce unique structures. This is a work in progress that owes a lot to Lego or Ikea, as well as post-minimal and conceptual art. Each letter in this font has been created from loose individual elements representing the interchangeable parts of a flat-pack carton.

Gavin Peacock est un artiste qui vit à Brighton en Angleterre. Il a participé à de nombreuses expositions et plusieurs projets internationaux sur le Mail art. Son travail comprend des projets participatifs, des sculptures, des installations, des photos et des vidéos. Il est le créateur de Flatpack, un kit de 1 200 modules en plastique qui peuvent être assemblés entre eux pour produire des structures uniques. Il s'agit d'un projet en cours qui doit beaucoup à Lego ou Ikea ainsi qu'à l'art post-minimal et l'art conceptuel. Chaque lettre de cette police est créée à partir d'éléments séparés qui représentent les pièces interchangeables de carton flat-pack.

Gavin Peacock es un artista que reside en Brighton (Reino Unido) y que ha participado en diversas exposiciones, así como en varios proyectos internacionales sobre *mail art* o arte postal. Su trabajo abarca desde proyectos participativos e instalaciones hasta escultura, fotografía y vídeo. Es el creador de Flatpack, un juego de 1.200 módulos de plástico ensamblables entre sí para producir estructuras únicas. Se trata de un proyecto en curso que debe mucho a Lego o Ikea así como al arte *post-minimal* y arte conceptual. Cada letra de esta fuente se ha creado a partir de elementos individuales sueltos que representan las piezas de cartón *flat-pack* intercambiables.

Fresh Bold (Lumio)

Jonathan Sipkema | www.jonathansipkema.com

ABCDEFGHIJKLMNOPQRSTUVWXYZ

8/10 pt

ABCDEFGHIJKLMNOPQRSTUVWXYZ

10/12 pt

ABCDEFGHIJKLMNOPQRSTUVWXYZ

18/18 pt

ABCDEFGHIJKLM
NOPQRSTUVWXYZ

24/24 pt

ABCDEFGHIJKLMN
OPQRSTUVWXYZ

32/34 pt

This font was the idea of Jonathan Sipkema, who wanted to design a typeface that was as thick and basic as possible. Each glyph used the square as the basis for its design, in this way each letter was extracted from the square making as few changes as possible. It is not really suited to running text, but but is ideal to lend a text a bit more oomph. Basically speaking, this font is suitable for logos, posters and experimental work. Sipkema uses the font for his own logo and also for some of his more personal work. Fresh Bold, or Lumio as it is also called, is a modern **Bold** typeface.

Conçue par Jonathan Sipkema dans le but de réaliser une typographie la plus simple et large possible. Chaque glyphe est conçu à partir du carré : forme géométrique qui donne sa forme à chaque lettre réduisant le plus possible les modifications. Elle ne convient pas pour un texte long mais elle est appropriée pour donner à un texte un ton davantage exclamatif. Cette police s'utilise principalement pour des logotypes, des posters ou des travaux expérimentaux. Sipkema utilise cette police pour son propre logotype et pour certains travaux personnels. Fresh Bold, également appelée Lumio, est une typographie Bold moderne.

Jonathan Sipkema ideó esta tipografía con la intención de que fuera lo más básica y gruesa posible. Cada glifo se ha diseñado a partir del cuadrado: de esta forma se ha extraído cada letra procurando el mínimo de modificaciones posibles. No resulta muy adecuada para texto corrido, pero sí lo es para proporcionar a cierto texto un tono extra de exclamación. Esta fuente está básicamente indicada para logotipos, pósters y obras experimentales. Sipkema utiliza la fuente para su propio logotipo así como para algunos trabajos personales. Fresh Bold, también llamada Lumio, es una tipografía Bold moderna.

Glasnost

Popdog Fonts | popdog_fonts.tripod.com

abcdefghijklmnopqrstuvwxyz[ξφςίεψznρ]
ABCDEFGHIJKLMNCPQRSTUVWXYZ
1234567890(.,;:?!0$A&-*){ΔΦ&FΨZHP}

8/10 pt

abcdefghijklmnopqrstuvwxyz[ξφςίεψznρ]
ABCDEFGHIJKLMNCPQRSTUVWXYZ
1234567890(.,;:?!0$A&-*){ΔΦ&FΨZHP}

10/12 pt

abcdefghijklmnopqrstuvwxyz[ξφςίεψznρ]
ABCDEFGHIJKLMNCPQRSTUVWXYZ
1234567890(.,;:?!0$A&-*){ΔΦ&FΨZHP}

18/18 pt

abcdefghijklmn
opqrstuvwxyz[ξφςίεψznρ]
ABCDEFGHIJKLMNCPQRSTUVWXYZ
1234567890
(.,;:?!0$A&-*){ΔΦ&FΨZHP}

24/24 pt

This font appears to be heavily eroded to the extent that some of the constructive elements of the letters have been lost. The discontinuous outline of this decorative font casts a shadow on the background, which remains behind the letter. It is excellent for headings or large typeface. This sans serif font includes a set of Latin and Greek characters. Despite the amputation of certain elements, it is possible to imagine some of the key features such as: a double-story lowercase a; a lowercase e with a cross stroke; a lowercase f resting on the base line; and an uppercase A with a straight apex.

Cette police est extrêmement érodée, au point d'en perdre certains éléments des lettres. Le contour discontinu de cette police d'écriture décorative projette une ombre que l'on aperçoit au second plan. Elle est appropriée pour les en-têtes ou la typographie de grande taille. Il s'agit d'une police sans serif qui comprend les caractères latins et grecs. Malgré l'amputation de certains éléments, il est possible de deviner les caractéristiques de quelques éléments clés comme : un « a » bas de casse en script, un « e » bas de casse avec une barre horizontale, un « f » bas de casse qui s'appuie sur la ligne de base, un « A » haut de casse dont la pointe est droite.

Resulta fuertemente erosionada, hasta perder parte de los elementos constructivos de las letras. El contorno discontinuo de esta fuente decorativa proyecta una sombra en el fondo que queda en segundo plano. Resulta muy adecuada para encabezamientos o tipografía a gran tamaño. Esta fuente de palo seco incluye el set de caracteres latinos y griegos. A pesar de las amputaciones de ciertos elementos, se intuyen las características de algunos caracteres: a de caja baja de dos pisos, e de caja baja con barra horizontal, f de caja baja que se apoya en la línea base y A de caja alta con vértice recto.

Goca Logotype Beta

Jonas Borneland Hansen | www.borneland.com

GOCA
LOGOTYPE
"BETA"

ABCDEFGHIJKL
MNOPQRSTUV
WXYZÆØÅ

ABCDEFGHIJKLMNOPQRSTUVWXYZ[ÅØÆ]
1234567890(.,;:?-*)

8/10 pt

ABCDEFGHIJKLMNOPQRSTUVWXYZ[ÅØÆ]
1234567890(.,;:?-*)

10/12 pt

ABCDEFGHIJKLMN
OPQRSTUVWXYZ[ÅØÆ]
1234567890(.,;:?-*)

18/18 pt

ABCDEFGHIJKLMN
OPQRSTUVWXYZ[ÅØÆ]
1234567890(.,;:?-*)

24/24 pt

ABCDEFGHI
JKLMNOPQR
STUVWXYZ[ÅØÆ]
1234567890(.,;:?-*)

32/34 pt

This font is perfect for logo designs. However, the typographer suggests that it should be used freely. The font only offers uppercase letters and numbers, apart from a complete set of symbols and punctuation marks. The characters are clearly of continuous construction, with a curved, circular appearance. The lines that are normally straight are also curved. The stems have parallel edges and the bars occupy a central position. In some cases, the stems and bowls are not joined together. This is a sans serif font of ample proportions and no modulation.

Elle convient parfaitement au design de logotypes. Cependant, le typographe propose de l'utiliser librement. Cette police offre uniquement des lettres haut de casse ainsi que toute une série de symboles et de signes de ponctuation. Les caractères présentent une forme homogène avec des courbes circulaires et les lignes qui en principe sont droites, sont ici arrondies. Les hampes verticales ont des bords parallèles et les traverses sont placées au milieu de la lettre. Dans certains cas, les hampes et les panses ne se touchent pas. Cette police sans serif possède de grandes proportions et n'a pas de modulation.

Resulta muy adecuada para el diseño de logotipos. Sin embargo, el tipógrafo propone utilizarla libremente. La fuente ofrece caracteres únicamente de caja alta y números, además de un set completo de símbolos y signos de puntuación. Los caracteres muestran una construcción continua con aspecto de las curvas circular, y las líneas que normalmente son rectas se vuelven curvadas. Las astas verticales son de bordes paralelos y las astas transversales se sitúan en posición central. En algunos casos, las astas y anillos no llegan a tocarse. Esta fuente de palo seco es de proporciones anchas y no tiene modulación.

Grixel Acme

Nikos Giannakopoulos | www.grixel.gr

abcdefghijklmnopqrstuvwxyz[ööÜßåœœœœçÑ]
ABCDEFGHIJKLMNOPQRSTUVWXYZ
1234567890(.,:?¿$¢£₤¥&-*){ÄÖÜÅØÆŒÇÑ}

8/10 pt

abcdefghijklmn
opqrstuvwxyz[ööÜßåœœœœçÑ]
ABCDEFGHIJKLMNOPQRSTUVWXYZ
1234567890
(.,:?¿$¢£₤¥&-*){ÄÖÜÅØÆŒÇÑ}

8/10 pt

ABCDEFGHIJKLMNOPQRSTUVWXYZ
1234567890(.,:?¿$¢£₤¥&-*){ÄÖÜÅØÆŒÇÑ}

8/10 pt

abcdefghijklmnopqrstuvwxyz
[ööÜßåœœœœçÑ]
ABCDEFGHIJKLMNOPQRSTUVWXYZ
1234567890
[.,:?¿$¢£₤¥&-*){ÄÖÜÅØÆŒÇÑ}

10/12 pt

abcdefghijklmn
opqrstuvwxyz[ööÜßåœœœœçÑ]
ABCDEFGHIJKLMN
OPQRSTUVWXYZ
1234567890
[.,:?¿$¢£₤¥&-*){ÄÖÜÅØÆŒÇÑ}

10/12 pt

ABCDEFGHIJKLMNOPQRSTUVWXYZ
1234567890
[.,;:?¿$¢£₤¥&-*){ÄÖÜÅØÆŒÇÑ}

10/12 pt

The Grixel fonts are vector-based Greek pixel typefaces that can be used at 8 px in Flash and Photoshop with the text still remaining clean and crisp on the screen. Grixel Acme is a linear, linear, sans serif font family that includes the characters used by Turkish and Greek, and the languages of Central and Western Europe. Fonts of this nature are essentially geometric, and are formed by typeface with an even thickness of stroke, and without any contrast or modulation. They are characterized by the fact that they can generate huge families, with a great many variations, even though they are not very legible in running text.

Grixel est une police vectorielle et pixélisée grecque qui peut être utilisée en taille de 8 px dans Flash et Photoshop en gardant la clarté du texte à l'écran. Grixel Acme est une typographie sans serif, de type linéaire qui inclut des caractères de plusieurs régions : Europe centrale, Europe occidentale, Turquie et Grèce. Les polices de ce type sont principalement géométriques, avec un trait d'une grosseur uniforme, sans contraste ni modulation. Ce qui les caractérise est le fait de pouvoir créer de nombreuses familles, avec plusieurs variantes, bien que la lisibilité ne soit pas très bonne pour des textes longs.

Las fuentes Grixel son fuentes griegas vectoriales y pixeladas que se pueden utilizar a un tamaño de 8 px en Flash y Photoshop, al tiempo que el texto se conserva limpio en pantalla. Grixel Acme es familia tipográfica de palo seco, de tipo lineal que incluye caracteres centroeuropeos, de Europa Occidental, turcos y griegos. Estas fuentes están formadas por tipos de un grosor de trazo uniforme, sin contraste ni modulación, y son esencialmente geométricas. Se caracterizan porque admiten familias larguísimas, con numerosas variantes, a pesar de que su legibilidad suele ser mala para texto corrido.

abcdefghijklmnopqrstuvwxyz[äöüßåøæœçñ]
ABCDEFGHIJKLMNOPQRSTUVWXYZ
1234567890(.,:?¿$¢£€¥&-*){ÄÖÜÅØÆŒÇÑ}

8/10 pt

abcdefghijklmnopqrstuvwxyz[äöüßåøæœçñ]
ABCDEFGHIJKLMNOPQRSTUVWXYZ
1234567890(.,:?¿$¢£€¥&-*){ÄÖÜÅØÆŒÇÑ}

8/10 pt

abcdefghijklmnopqrstuvwxyz[äöüßåøæœçñ]
ABCDEFGHIJKLMNOPQRSTUVWXYZ
1234567890(.,:?¿$¢£€¥&-*){ÄÖÜÅØÆŒÇÑ}

8/10 pt

abcdefghijklmnopqrstuvwxyz[äöüßåøæœçñ]
ABCDEFGHIJKLMNOPQRSTUVWXYZ
1234567890(.,:?¿$¢£€¥&-*){ÄÖÜÅØÆŒÇÑ}

10/12 pt

abcdefghijklmnopqrstuvwxyz[äöüßåøæœçñ]
ABCDEFGHIJKLMNOPQRSTUVWXYZ
1234567890(.,:?¿$¢£€¥&-*){ÄÖÜÅØÆŒÇÑ}

10/12 pt

abcdefghijklmnopqrstuvwxyz[äöüßåøæœçñ]
ABCDEFGHIJKLMNOPQRSTUVWXYZ
1234567890(.,:?¿$¢£€¥&-*){ÄÖÜÅØÆŒÇÑ}

10/12 pt

abcdefghijklmnopqrstuvwxyz[äöüßåøæœçñ]
ABCDEFGHIJKLMNOPQRSTUVWXYZ
1234567890[.,:;?¿$¢£€¥&-*]{ÅÖÜÄØÆŒÇÑ}

8/10 pt

abcdefghijklmnopqrstuvwxyz[äöüßåøæœçñ]
ABCDEFGHIJKLMNOPQRSTUVWXYZ
1234567890[.,:;?¿$¢£€¥&-*]{ÅÖÜÄØÆŒÇÑ}

8/10 pt

abcdefghijklmnopqrstuvwxyz[äöüßåøæœçñ]
ABCDEFGHIJKLMNOPQRSTUVWXYZ
1234567890[.,:;?¿$¢£€¥&-*]{ÅÖÜÄØÆŒÇÑ}

8/10 pt

abcdefghijklmnopqrstuvwxyz[äöüßåøæœçñ]
ABCDEFGHIJKLMNOPQRSTUVWXYZ
1234567890[.,:;?¿$¢£€¥&-*]{ÅÖÜÄØÆŒÇÑ}

10/12 pt

abcdefghijklmnopqrstuvwxyz[äöüßåøæœçñ]
ABCDEFGHIJKLMNOPQRSTUVWXYZ
1234567890[.,:;?¿$¢£€¥&-*]{ÅÖÜÄØÆŒÇÑ}

10/12 pt

abcdefghijklmnopqrstuvwxyz[äöüßåøæœçñ]
ABCDEFGHIJKLMNOPQRSTUVWXYZ
1234567890[.,:;?¿$¢£€¥&-*]{ÅÖÜÄØÆŒÇÑ}

10/12 pt

Hammerhead Regular/Bold/Black

Felix Braden | www.floodfonts.com

ergang der feudalen Gesellschaft hervorgegangene mod-
Gesellschaft hat die Klassengegensätze nicht aufgehoben.
Klassen, neue Bedingungen der Unterdrückung, neue Gestal-
es an die Stelle der alten gesetzt. Unsere Epoche, die Epoche
zeichnet sich jedoch dadurch aus, daß sie die Klassengegen-
hat. Die ganze Gesellschaft spaltet sich mehr und mehr in
che Lager, in zwei große, einander direkt gegenüberstehende
isie und Proletariat. Aus den Leibeigenen des Mittelalters
irger der ersten Städte hervor; aus dieser Pfahlbürgerschaft
die ersten Elemente der Bourgeoisie.

sellschaft spaltet sich mehr und mehr in zwei
iche Lager, in zwei große, einander direkt
ehende Klassen: Bourgeoisie und Proletariat.

black
bold

zünftige Betriebsweise der Industrie reichte nicht
n Märkten anwachsenden Bedarf. Die Manufaktur
meister wurden verdrängt durch den industriel-
g der Arbeit zwischen den verschiedenen Korpo-
er Teilung der Arbeit in der einzelnen Werkstatt
en die Märkte, immer stieg der Bedarf. Auch die
mehr aus. Da revolutionierte der Dampf und die
le Produktion. An die Stelle der Manufaktur trat
rie, an die Stelle des industriellen Mittelstandes
llionäre, die Chefs ganzer industrieller Armeen.
iese hat wieder auf die Ausdehnung der Industrie
selben Maße, worin Industrie, Handel, Schiffahrt,
nten, in demselben Maße entwickelte sich die
e ihre Kapitalien, drängte sie alle vom Mittelalter
in den Hintergrund.

Die Entdeckung Amerikas, die Um-
schiffung Afrikas schufen der auf-
kommenden Bourgeoisie ein neues
Terrain. Der ostindische und chine-
sische Markt, die Kolonisierung von
Amerika, der Austausch mit den
Kolonien, die Vermehrung der
Tauschmittel und der Waren
überhaupt gaben dem Handel, der
Schiffahrt, der Industrie einen nie
gekannten Aufschwung und damit
dem revolutionären Element in der
zerfallenden feudalen Gesellschaft
eine rasche Entwicklung.

Freier und Sklave, Patrizier und Plebejer, Baron und Leib-
eigener, Zunftbürger und Gesell, kurz, Unterdrücker und
Unterdrückte standen in stetem Gegensatz zueinander,
führten einen ununterbrochenen, bald versteckten, bald
offenen Kampf, einen Kampf, der jedesmal mit einer revolutionären Umgestaltung der ganzen Gesellschaft endete oder
mit dem gemeinsamen Untergang der kämpfenden Klassen.

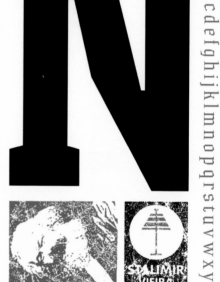

abcdefghijklmnopqrstuvwxyz

ABCDEFGHIJKLMNOPQRSTUVWXZ 1234567890 ★

Hammerhead

abcdefghijklmnopqrstuvwxyz[äöüʁåøæœçñ]
ABCDEFGHIJKLMNOPQRSTUVWXYZ
1234567890(.,;:?¿$¢£¥ʚ-*){ÄÖÜÅØÆŒÇÑ}

8/10 pt

abcdefghijklmnopqrstuvwxyz[äöüʁåøæœçñ]
ABCDEFGHIJKLMNOPQRSTUVWXYZ
1234567890(.,;:?¿$¢£¥ʚ-*){ÄÖÜÅØÆŒÇÑ}

8/10 pt

abcdefghijklmnopqrstuvwxyz[äöüʁåøæœçñ]
ABCDEFGHIJKLMNOPQRSTUVWXYZ
1234567890(.,;:?¿$¢£¥ʚ-*){ÄÖÜÅØÆŒÇÑ}

8/10 pt

abcdefghijklmn
opqrstuvwxyz[äöüʁåøæœçñ]
ABCDEFGHIJKLMNOPQRSTUVWXYZ
1234567890(.,;:?¿$¢£¥ʚ-*){ÄÖÜÅØÆŒÇÑ}

18/18 pt

abcdefghijklmn
opqrstuvwxyz[äöüʁåøæœçñ]
ABCDEFGHIJKLMNOPQRSTUVWXYZ
1234567890(.,;:?¿$¢£¥ʚ-*){ÄÖÜÅØÆŒÇÑ}

18/18 pt

abcdefghijklmn
opqrstuvwxyz[äöüʁåøæœçñ]
ABCDEFGHIJKLMNOPQRSTUVWXYZ
1234567890(.,;:?¿$¢£¥ʚ-*){ÄÖÜÅØÆŒÇÑ}

18/18 pt

Hammerhead is the modern interpretation of the Renaissance Antiqua typeface. It has been constructed without any curves, by using straight lines, which generate angles along the outline of the glyphs. There is marked contrast and the font takes on the aspect of Blackletter or Gothic script. The flourishes are cut at right angles and the serifs increase in proportion to the weight of the font. The thick letters have a peculiar shape reminiscent of sturdy iron girders. Despite the font's extraordinary details, Hammerhead is clearly legible even in small font sizes.

Hammerhead est l'interprétation moderne de la typographie Rennaissance Antiqua. Elle a été conçue en évitant les courbes, utilisant les lignes droites pour créer des angles au niveau du contour des glyphes. Cela provoque un contraste et donne à cette police l'aspect de lettre gothique. Les contours semblent coupés à angle droit et les empattements s'agrandissent en fonction de la taille de la police. Les lettres grasses ont une forme singulière qui fait penser à des poutres en fer robustes. Malgré tous les détails étranges, Hammerhead est une police parfaitement lisible même pour des textes avec des petites tailles de caractères.

Hammerhead es la interpretación moderna de la tipografía Rennaissance Antiqua. Se ha construido evitando las curvas, sirviéndose de líneas rectas que generan ángulos en el contorno de los glifos. El contraste queda remarcado y la fuente adopta un aspecto de letra gótica. Los remates aparecen cortados en ángulo recto y las serifas se van agrandando proporcionalmente con el peso de la fuente. Las letras gruesas adoptan una forma singular que recuerda a recias vigas de hierro. A pesar de los extraordinarios detalles de la Hammerhead, esta fuente resulta claramente legible incluso en tamaños de fuente pequeños.

Hausbau

Anton Studer | www.bubentraum.com

ABCDEFGHIJKLMNOPQRSTUVWXYZ
ABCDEFGHIJKLMNOPQRSTUVWXYZ
. , ÀÖÜ

8/10 pt

ABCDEFGHIJKLMNOPQRSTUVWXYZ
ABCDEFGHIJKLMNOPQRSTUVWXYZ
. , ÀÖÜ

10/12 pt

ABCDEFGHIJKLMN
OPQRSTUVWXYZ
ABCDEFGHIJKLMN
OPQRSTUVWXYZ
. , ÀÖÜ

18/18 pt

ABCDEFGHIJKLMN
OPQRSTUVWXYZ
ABCDEFGHIJKLMN
OPQRSTUVWXYZ
. , ÀÖÜ

24/24 pt

This font has both upper and lowercase characters, with basic punctuation marks such as the period and comma. It is obviously a pictogram type of decorative font. The letters, engraved on a square block with fixed dimensions, are formed using architectural motifs alluding to elements like windows, roofs and chimney stacks. The spacing between the words is very unusual and is obtained by means of a grid with a positive value, which makes the space invisible. As the text is written, the font erects a building all by itself.

Cette police propose la représentation graphique des caractères aussi bien haut que bas de casse, avec des signes de ponctuation simples comme le point et la virgule. Il s'agit manifestement d'une police décorative composée de pictogrammes. Les lettres, inscrites dans un carré aux dimensions fixes, sont formées par des motifs architecturaux qui font référence à des éléments comme les fenêtres, les toitures ou les cheminées. D'une forme plutôt étrange, l'espace entre les mots est représenté par un carré noir ce qui le rend davantage visible. Ainsi, au fur et à mesure que le texte est écrit, cette police de caractères construit un bâtiment à travers les mots.

Ofrece la representación gráfica correspondiente a los caracteres de caja alta y baja, con signos de puntuación básicos como el punto y la coma. Se trata de una fuente claramente decorativa de tipo pictográfico. Las letras, inscritas en bloques cuadrados de dimensiones fijas, se forman a través de motivos arquitectónicos, que hacen referencia a elementos como ventanas, tejados o chimeneas. De forma peculiar, el espaciado entre palabras se representa a través de un cuadrado con el cuerpo relleno, por lo que el espacio se vuelve visible. De esta manera, a medida que se escribe el texto, la fuente va construyendo un edificio por sí misma.

Hip Priest

Popdog Fonts | popdog_fonts.tripod.com

ABCDEFGHIJKLMNOPQRSTUVWXYZ
1234567890(.,;:?✳8-*)ΔΦEΨZHP

8/10 pt

ABCDEFGHIJKLMNOPQRSTUVWXYZ
1234567890(.,;:?✳8-*)ΔΦEΨZHP

10/12 pt

ABCDEFGHIJKLMNOPQRSTUVWXYZ
1234567890(.,;:?✳8-*)ΔΦEΨZHP

18/18 pt

ABCDEFGHIJKLMNOPQRSTUVWXYZ
1234567890(.,;:?✳8-*)ΔΦEΨZHP

24/24 pt

ABCDEFGHIJKLMN
OPQRSTUVWXYZ
1234567890
(.,;:?✳8-*)ΔΦEΨZHP

24/24 pt

This font is only available in uppercase and offers the set of characters for the Latin and Greek alphabets. It is an informal script seemingly constructed using a narrow brush as the design tool, resulting in very fine, rough strokes producing a loose or discontinuous construction. The aspect of the curves is deformed and devoid of modulation. The font is sans serif, of medium weight, with bowls and stems that do not quite join together. Key uppercase characters include: the G with a vertical spur; the Q with a tail that cuts through the bowl; and the R with a straight tail.

Uniquement disponible en haut de casse, cette police existe en caractères grecs et latins. Il s'agit d'une écriture informelle dont la conception semble avoir été réalisée à partir d'une brosse étroite. Il en résulte des traits fins peints subitement qui produisent une construction détachée ou discontinue. Les courbes semblent déformées et ne présentent aucune modulation. Cette police est sans serif, de poids moyen, dont les panses ne rejoignent pas les hampes. Parmi les caractères emblématiques il convient de citer : le « G » avec un empattement vertical, le « Q » dont la queue coupe la panse et le « R » avec une queue droite.

Únicamente disponible en caja alta, ofrece el set de caracteres para los alfabetos griego y latino. Se trata de una escritura informal cuya construcción hace referencia a una brocha estrecha como herramienta de diseño. El resultado son unos trazos finos bruscamente pintados que generan una construcción suelta o discontinua. El aspecto de las curvas es deforme y no muestra modulación. Se trata de una fuente de palo seco, de peso medio, con anillos y astas que no llegan a tocarse. Entre los caracteres clave de caja alta destacan: la G con espuela vertical, la Q con cola que corta el anillo y la R con cola recta.

HOCUS FOCUS

BLAAS CHEWING GUM

In elk pakje **HOCUS FOCUS** bevindt zich een blanco-toverkaart welke U zonder moeite in een mooie foto kunt omtoveren. Dompel dit kaartje even in zuiver water - druk het gedurende 10 seconden op de witte binnenzijde van de bedrukte omslag der tablet - en ogenblikkelijk komt het beeld te voorschijn.

OPGELET: geldig tot en met 25 mei 1949

abcdefghijklmnopqrstuvwxyz
ABCDEFGHIJKLMNOPQRSTUVWXYZ
1234567890.:-

8/10 pt

abcdefghijklmnopqrstuvwxyz
ABCDEFGHIJKLMNOPQRSTUVWXYZ
1234567890.:-

10/12 pt

abcdefghijklmnopqrstuvwxyz
ABCDEFGHIJKLMNOPQRSTUVWXYZ
1234567890.:-

18/18 pt

abcdefghijklmn
opqrstuvwxyz
ABCDEFGHIJKLMN
OPQRSTUVWXYZ
1234567890.:-

24/24 pt

Hocus Focus is based on the typeface used in the signs for old chewing gum adverts. The typographer redrew the design of each letter by hand and then made the necessary adjustments to capture the essence of his idea. The result is a sans serif font with a rough outline. It displays a very black outline flecked with irregular white incrustations, to achieve a more worn, distressed look. The stems are wide and have parallel edges. The font is constructed in a continuous fashion with circular curves, devoid of any modulation. The set offers upper and lowercase characters and numbers.

Cette police s'inspire de la typographie utilisée sur les enseignes des anciennes publicités de chewing-gum. Le typographe a redessiné à la main chaque lettre puis il a peaufiné les détails afin de refléter son idée. Le résultat est une police de caractères sans serif aux contours rugueux. Elle présente des traits très noirs avec des taches blanches incrustées de manière irrégulière afin d'obtenir un aspect vieilli. Les hampes sont larges et les bords sont parallèles. Il s'agit d'une police de forme continue, avec un aspect arrondi de la courbe, sans modulation. La police propose des caractères haut et bas de casse ainsi que des chiffres.

La fuente se basa en la tipografía utilizada en los anuncios antiguos de chicle. El tipógrafo redibujó a mano el diseño de cada letra y posteriormente realizaría los ajustes necesarios con el fin de plasmar su idea. El resultado es una fuente de palo seco de contorno rugoso. Presenta un trazo muy negro con motas blancas incrustadas de forma irregular, para lograr un aspecto más envejecido. Las astas son anchas y de bordes paralelos. Se trata de una fuente de construcción continua, con aspecto de las curvas circular, sin modulación. El set ofrece caracteres de caja alta y de caja baja junto con números.

Hut Sut Ralston NF

Nick's Fonts | www.nicksfonts.com

ÅÖÜ

abcdefghijklmnopqrstuvwxyz[äöüßåøæœçñ]
ABCDEFGHIJKLMNOPQRSTUVWXYZ
1234567890(.,:;?¿$¢£€¥&-*){ÅÖÜÅØÆŒÇÑ}

8/10 pt

abcdefghijklmnopqrstuvwxyz[äöüßåøæœçñ]
ABCDEFGHIJKLMNOPQRSTUVWXYZ
1234567890(.,:;?¿$¢£€¥&-*){ÅÖÜÅØÆŒÇÑ}

10/12 pt

abcdefghijklmn
opqrstuvwxyz[äöüßåøæœçñ]
ABCDEFGHIJKLMNOPQRSTUVWXYZ
1234567890
(.,:;?¿$¢£€¥&-*){ÅÖÜÅØÆŒÇÑ}

18/18 pt

abcdefghijklmn
opqrstuvwxyz[äöüßåøæœçñ]
ABCDEFGHIJKLMN
OPQRSTUVWXYZ
1234567890
(.,:;?¿$¢£€¥&-*){ÅÖÜÅØÆŒÇÑ}

24/24 pt

This font represents a style reminiscent of ArtDeco with serifs. The flourishes are all even with soft, clean edges. The font has an all but imperceptible modulation and the characters are aligned with the baseline. Key characters include: the double-storied lowercase a; the lowercase g with its loop not joined by a link, and with an ear that has been prolonged upwards. Then there is the uppercase A with its apex and prolongation; and the uppercase R with a prolonged curving tail. This font is particularly suitable for advertising, packaging and headlines.

Cette police avec empattement fait penser au style Art déco. Les empattements sont uniformes avec des contours doux et nets. Les modulations de cette police ne sont presque pas visibles, les caractères sont alignés sur la ligne de base. Les caractères clés sont d'une part : le « a » bas de casse en script, le « g » bas de casse dont la boucle est reliée à la panse sans délié de jonction et dont l'oreille se prolonge vers le haut. D'autre part : le « A » haut de casse avec une pointe et un prolongement puis le « R » haut de casse avec une queue courbée prolongée. Cette police convient parfaitement aux publicités, au packaging ou aux gros titres.

Es una fuente de estilo Art decó con serifa. Los remates son uniformes con los bordes suaves y limpios. Presenta una modulación casi imperceptible y los caracteres están alineadas con la línea base. Entre los caracteres clave se encuentran: la a de caja baja de dos pisos, la g de caja baja con ojal sin cuello y con oreja prolongada hacia arriba. Por otra parte están la A de caja alta con vértice y prolongación y la R de caja alta con cola curva prolongada. Esta fuente resulta muy apropiada para publicidad, *packaging* y titulares.

Gummimauer

Through the eyes

of an eleven year old child

The World

looks different.

Zirkuspferd

abcdefghijklmnopqrstuvwxyz[äöüßåçñ]
ABCDEFGHIJKLMNOPQRSTUVWXYZ
1234567890(.,;:?¿$¢£€&-*){ÄÖÜÅÇÑ}

8/10 pt

abcdefghijklmnopqrstuvwxyz[äöüßåçñ]
ABCDEFGHIJKLMNOPQRSTUVWXYZ
1234567890(.,;:?¿$¢£€&-*){ÄÖÜÅÇÑ}

10/12 pt

abcdefghijklmn
opqrstuvwxyz[äöüßåçñ]
ABCDEFGHIJKLMNOPQRSTUVWXYZ
1234567890(.,;:?¿$¢£€&-*){ÄÖÜÅÇÑ}

18/18 pt

abcdefghijklmn
opqrstuvwxyz[äöüßåçñ]
ABCDEFGHIJKLMNOPQRSTUVWXYZ
1234567890
(.,;:?¿$¢£€&-*){ÄÖÜÅÇÑ}

24/24 pt

This is one of the earliest fonts designed by Hannes von Döhren and looks very much like handwriting, with some unusually shaped letters. This is a type of calligraphy that uses a fine brush as the design tool. The spontaneous strokes create a natural appearance. The edges of the type are uneven, as if drawn by hand. There is no modulation and the characters, which are not joined up, do not rest on the baseline. This font is a good choice for headings or shorto to medium length blocks of text. The designer uses it to advertise and decorate a big birthday party.

Conçue par Hannes von Döhren, HVD Age11 est une des premières polices du designer graphique qui ressemble à une écriture manuscrite, avec des formes inhabituelles. Il s'agit d'une typographie qui relève de la calligraphie et dont l'outil de conception semble être un pinceau fin. Les traits spontanés lui donnent un aspect naturel. Les bords des lettres semblent irréguliers, comme si les caractères étaient dessinés à la main. Il n'existe aucune modulation et les caractères, sans être reliés, ne reposent pas sur la ligne de base. Cette police convient pour les titres ou les textes courts ou d'une longueur moyenne. Le designer propose de l'utiliser pour annoncer et décorer une grande fête d'anniversaire.

Es una de las primeras fuentes diseñadas por Hannes von Döhren (HVD Fonts), que ofrece un aspecto de escritura a mano, con formas inusuales. Se trata de una tipografía caligráfica que hace referencia al pincel fino como herramienta de diseño. Los trazos espontáneos generan un aspecto natural. Los bordes de la tipografía son irregulares, como dibujados a mano. No presenta modulación y los caracteres sin unión no se apoyan en la línea base. Una buena opción para títulos o bloques de texto cortos o de longitud media. El diseñador propone usarla para anunciar y decorar una gran fiesta de cumpleaños.

PÜREE

437 Kartoffelpuffer

Pommes Frites

Die dümmsten Bauern

Die klassischen French Fries

Aber mit einer Portion Ketchup & Mayo!

ERDAPFEL

abcdefghijklmnopqrstuvwxyz[äöüßåøæœçñ]
ABCDEFGHIJKLMNOPQRSTUVWXYZ
1234567890(.,;:?¿$¢£€¥&-*){ÄÖÜÅØÆŒÇÑ}

8/10 pt

abcdefghijklmnopqrstuvwxyz[äöüßåøæœçñ]
ABCDEFGHIJKLMNOPQRSTUVWXYZ
1234567890(.,;:?¿$¢£€¥&-*){ÄÖÜÅØÆŒÇÑ}

10/12 pt

abcdefghijklmn
opqrstuvwxyz[äöüßåøæœçñ]
ABCDEFGHIJKLMN
OPQRSTUVWXYZ
1234567890
(.,;:?¿$¢£€¥&-*){ÄÖÜÅØÆŒÇÑ}

18/18 pt

abcdefghijklmn
opqrstuvwxyz[äöüßåøæœçñ]
ABCDEFGHIJKLMN
OPQRSTUVWXYZ
1234567890
(.,;:?¿$¢£€¥&-*)
{ÄÖÜÅØÆŒÇÑ}

24/24 pt

The initial question challenged the idea of creating a typeface from such an ill-defined material as the potato. Therefore four friends spent all night cutting up 8 kg of potatoes in the kitchen. Next they printed them on paper and then scanned the printouts so that they could work on the design digitally. The font has the same serifs and a black roughly drawn stroke. The contrast is exaggerated, with a vertical axis and instant transition. The result is a dirty font but one that is "as noble as a classical music concert" – to put it in the words of the typographer, who at the same time would also like to thank Felix, Robin and Carro for their help.

L'idée première était de créer une typographie à partir d'un élément aussi imprécis que la pomme de terre. Ainsi, quatre amis se sont mis à couper huit kilos de pommes de terres pendant toute une nuit dans la cuisine. Puis ils les ont imprimées sur une feuille et ils ont scanné les photocopies pour les retravailler numériquement. La police présente des empattements uniformes et un trait noir avec des imperfections. Cela met en avant un contraste exagéré avec un axe vertical et une transition instantanée. Le résultat est une police sale mais « noble comme un concert de musique classique », selon les dires du typographe qui remercie également la collaboration de : Felix, Robin et Carro.

¿Qué aspecto tendría una tipografía clásica realizada con un material tan indefinido como la patata? Movidos por esta curiosidad, cuatro amigos se pasaron toda una noche en la cocina recortando caracteres en ocho kilos de patatas; luego imprimieron en papel las letras y las escanearon para trabajar el diseño digitalmente. La fuente presenta remates uniformes y un trazo negro con imperfecciones. Existe un contraste exagerado con eje vertical y transición instantánea. El resultado es una fuente sucia pero «noble como un concierto de música clásica», según el propio tipógrafo, que agradece la colaboración de Felix, Robin y Carro.

abcdefghijklmnopqrstuvwxyz[äöüßåøæœçñ]
ABCDEFGHIJKLMNOPQRSTUVWXYZ
1234567890(.,;:?¿$¢£€¥&-*){ÄÖÜÅØÆŒÇÑ}

8/10 pt

abcdefghijklmnopqrstuvwxyz[äöüßåøæœçñ]
ABCDEFGHIJKLMNOPQRSTUVWXYZ
1234567890(.,;:?¿$¢£€¥&-*){ÄÖÜÅØÆŒÇÑ}

10/12 pt

abcdefghijklmn opqrstuvwxyz[äöüßåøæœçñ] ABCDEFGHIJKLMN OPQRSTUVWXYZ 1234567890 (.,;:?¿$¢£€¥&-*){ÄÖÜÅØÆŒÇÑ}

18/18 pt

abcdefghijklmn opqrstuvwxyz [äöüßåøæœçñ] ABCDEFGHIJKLMN OPQRSTUVWXYZ 1234567890 (.,;:?¿$¢£€¥&-*) {ÄÖÜÅØÆŒÇÑ}

24/24 pt

The name refers to the font's two main characteristics: the comic style of lettering and serif. The aim was to design the letters imitating the typeface found in a comic. The font is mainly distinguished by the design of its serifs, which are dense and rectangular in shape, establishing an angular relationship with the strokes. Its robust, geometric design is striking for its contemporary, modern, stable appearance. Originally created for applications in informal situations, headlines, posters and exhibitions, it is too heavy for small size lettering and is therefore not recommended for blocks of text.

Le nom fait référence aux deux caractéristiques principales de cette police : un style de bande dessinée (comic) et des lettres avec empattement (serif). Elle a été conçue avec l'intention d'imiter les lettres d'une bande dessinée. La police se distingue principalement par la forme des empattements, denses et rectangulaires, qui établissent une relation angulaire avec les traits. La forme géométrique et robuste attire l'attention par son aspect contemporain, moderne et stable. Elle a été créée dans le but d'être utilisée pour des situations informelles, des gros titres, des affiches et des expositions. Les caractères sont trop gras pour des petites tailles de police, pour cela HVD Comic Serif Pro n'est pas recommandée pour des textes longs.

El nombre hace referencia a sus dos características principales: el estilo cómic y la serifa. Se ha diseñado con la intención de imitar las letras de un *comic book*. La fuente se distingue por sus remates, que son densos y rectangulares, y establecen una relación angular con los trazos. Su diseño geométrico y robusto llama la atención por su apariencia contemporánea, moderna y estable. Se creó originalmente para contextos informales, titulares, carteles y material para exposiciones. No se recomienda para bloques de texto, porque con tamaños pequeños queda demasiado gruesa.

HVD Edding 780

HVD Fonts | www.hvdfonts.com

Just Writing

some cool letters

Stift & Schreibunterlage

Better Move Quick

This wall should stay clean!

Paper is boring

abcdefghijklmnopqrstuvwxyz[äöüßåøæœçñ]
ABCDEFGHIJKLMNOPQRSTUVWXYZ
1234567890(.,;:?¿$¢£€¥£-*}{ÄÖÜÅØÆŒÇÑ}

8/10 pt

abcdefghijklmnopqrstuvwxyz[äöüßåøæœçñ]
ABCDEFGHIJKLMNOPQRSTUVWXYZ
1234567890(.,;:?¿$¢£€¥£-*}{ÄÖÜÅØÆŒÇÑ}

10/12 pt

abcdefghijklmnopqrstuvwxyz[äöüßåøæœçñ]
ABCDEFGHIJKLMNOPQRSTUVWXYZ
1234567890
(.,;:?¿$¢£€¥£-*}{ÄÖÜÅØÆŒÇÑ}

18/18 pt

abcdefghijklmn
opqrstuvwxyz[äöüßåøæœçñ]
ABCDEFGHIJKLMN
OPQRSTUVWXYZ
1234567890
(.,;:?¿$¢£€¥£-*}{ÄÖÜÅØÆŒÇÑ}

24/24 pt

The letters of this font were drawn with an Edding 780 paint marker before being scanned and perfected on the computer. The result is a font that is fun and entertaining, appropriate for publicity designs – as it has a certain childlike quality. Fonts of this nature are characterized by their uneven, informal appearance. There are no common features or ligatures between different characters: they emulate handwriting. This particular font is an informal serifless typeface, with aliased edges and uneven strokes, with no modulation whatsoever.

Les caractères de cette police ont été dessinés avec un marqueur Edding 780 puis scannés et peaufinés à l'ordinateur. Le résultat est une lettre gaie et amusante, appropriée pour le graphisme publicitaire, en particulier pour les publicités à caractère enfantin. L'apparence irrégulière et désinvolte caractérise ce genre de polices. Les différents caractères n'ont pas de traits communs ni de ligatures, ils imitent une écriture à main levée. Il s'agit d'une police informelle sans serif qui relève de la calligraphie, avec des contours irréguliers et des traits non uniformes, sans aucun type de modulation.

Las letras de esta fuente han sido dibujadas con un rotulador Edding 780 para ser posteriormente escaneadas y afinadas en el ordenador. El resultado es una letra alegre y divertida, apropiada para diseños publicitarios, sobre todo con un cierto carácter infantil. Este tipo de fuentes se caracterizan por tener una apariencia irregular y desenfadada. No existen rasgos comunes ni ligadura entre distintos caracteres sino que emulan la escritura a mano alzada. Se trata de una fuente caligráfica informal de palo seco, de bordes irregulares y trazos no uniformes donde no se crea ningún tipo de modulación.

ABCDEFGHIJKLMNOPQRSTUVWXYZ[ÄÖÜßÅÆŒÇÑ]
ABCDEFGHIJKLMNOPQRSTUVWXYZ
1234567890(.,;:?¿$£€¥&-*) (ÄÖÜÅÆŒÇÑ)

8/10 pt

ABCDEFGHIJKLMNOPQRSTUVWXYZ[ÄÖÜßÅÆŒÇÑ]
ABCDEFGHIJKLMNOPQRSTUVWXYZ
1234567890(.,;:?¿$£€¥&-*) (ÄÖÜÅÆŒÇÑ)

10/12 pt

ABCDEFGHIJKLMN
OPQRSTUVWXYZ[ÄÖÜßÅÆŒÇÑ]
ABCDEFGHIJKLMN
OPQRSTUVWXYZ
1234567890
(.,;:?¿$£€¥&-*) (ÄÖÜÅÆŒÇÑ)

18/18 pt

ABCDEFGHIJKLMN
OPQRSTUVWXYZ
[ÄÖÜßÅÆŒÇÑ]
ABCDEFGHIJKLMN
OPQRSTUVWXYZ
1234567890
(.,;:?¿$£€¥&-*)
(ÄÖÜÅÆŒÇÑ)

24/24 pt

This font can be classified as belonging to the group of stencil typefaces. In this case, however, it is not a font that is made up of separate template lettering, but one that simulates the effect of spray-painting the letters that have been created using a stencil. It is also characterized by its grunge and graffiti effect, with jagged edges and its seemingly worn or eroded appearance. It is constructed from a mass of vector-based dots so as to better simulate the effect of spray-painting and possible splashing as a result of using this technique. The font includes a large range of accents and symbols such as the euro sign.

On peut classer cette police dans le groupe de typographie Stencil. Il ne s'agit pas ici d'une police réalisée à partir d'un modèle de lettres discontinues mais de la simulation de l'effet de la peinture en aérosol à travers un pochoir. Elle se caractérise par un style grunge et ressemble à des graffitis, avec les bords rugueux et un effet final usé, érodé. Elle est réalisée à partir de nombreux points vectoriels pour mieux imiter l'effet de la peinture en bombe et les éventuelles éclaboussures que cette technique peut provoquer. Cette police comporte une grande variété d'accents et de symboles tels que l'euro.

Se puede clasificar dentro del grupo de tipografías stencil. En este caso, no se trata de una fuente con letras de plantilla de construcción discontinua, sino de la simulación del efecto de pintura con *spray* generado en las letras creadas a través de una plantilla. También se caracteriza por un estilo *grunge* y grafiti, con los bordes rugosos y un efecto final gastado, como erosionado. Está construida a base de muchos puntos vectoriales para imitar mejor el efecto de pintura con *spray* y las posibles salpicaduras provocadas por esta técnica. Incluye una gran variedad de acentos y símbolos como el del euro.

HVD Poster

HVD Fonts | www.hvdfonts.com

700 PT

ABCDEFGHIJKLMNOPQRSTUVWXYZ
1234567890(.,;:?¿$₡£€¥&-×){ÄÖÜÅØÆŒÇÑ}

8/10 pt

ABCDEFGHIJKLMNOPQRSTUVWXYZ
1234567890(.,;:?¿$₡£€¥&-×){ÄÖÜÅØÆŒÇÑ}

10/12 pt

ABCDEFGHIJKLMNOPQRSTUVWXYZ
1234567890
(.,;:?¿$₡£€¥&-×){ÄÖÜÅØÆŒÇÑ}

18/18 pt

ABCDEFGHIJKLMN
OPQRSTUVWXYZ
1234567890
(.,;:?¿$₡£€¥&-×){ÄÖÜÅØÆŒÇÑ}

24/24 pt

ABCDEFGHIJKLMN
OPQRSTUVWXYZ
1234567890
(.,;:?¿$₡£€¥&-×)
{ÄÖÜÅØÆŒÇÑ}

32/34 pt

This large format font has a very elegant appearance. The two uppercase variants offer a very detailed design, built up from a mass of vector-based dots. The result is a sans serif font, constructed in a continuous fashion. The curves are given a slightly angular appearance. It displays exaggerated contrast modulation, with bowls and stems that come together and virtually closed arcs. The characters are jagged, as if drawn by hand, and do not rest on the baseline. The font includes the grave and acute accents, circumflex, dieresis and main punctuation marks, together with a large variety of symbols.

Cette police de caractères a un aspect très élégant pour les grands formats. Avec deux variantes haut de casse, elle offre un design très détaillé avec une série de points vectoriels. Il en résulte une police sans serif, avec des formes homogènes et un traitement des courbes qui les rend légèrement carrées. Elle présente une modulation de contraste exagéré, avec des panses et des hampes qui se rejoignent et des arches presque fermées. Les caractères sont irréguliers, comme s'ils étaient dessinés à la main et ne reposaient pas sur la ligne de base. Elle comporte : les accents graves, aigus, circonflexes, les trémas et les principaux signes de ponctuation ainsi qu'une grande variété de symboles.

En tamaños grandes esta fuente resulta muy elegante. Con dos variantes de caja alta, ofrece un diseño muy detallado con muchos puntos vectoriales. Es una fuente de palo seco, de construcción continua y con un tratamiento de las curvas que las hace ligeramente cuadradas. Muestra una modulación de contraste exagerado, con anillos y astas que se tocan y los arcos casi cerrados. Los caracteres son irregulares, como dibujados a mano, y no se apoyan en la línea base. Incluye los acentos grave, agudo y circunflejo, la diéresis y los signos de puntuación principales, junto con una gran variedad de símbolos.

HVD Fonts | www.hvdfonts.com

ABCDEFGHIJKLMNOPQRSTUVWXYZ[ÄÖÜSSÅØÆŒÇÑ]
ABCDEFGHIJKLMNOPQRSTUVWXYZ
1231C4890C.,;:?2$f£€¥&-*)(ÄÖÜÀØ ÆŒÇÑ)

8/10 pt

ABCDEFGHIJKLMNOPQRSTUVWXYZ[ÄÖÜSSÅØÆŒÇÑ]
ABCDEFGHIJKLMNOPQRSTUVWXYZ
1231C4890C.,;:?2$f£€¥&-*)(ÄÖÜÀØ ÆŒÇÑ)

10/12 pt

ABCDEFGHIJKLMN
OPQRSTUVWXYZ[ÄÖÜSSÅØÆŒÇÑ]
ABCDEFGHIJKLMNOPQRSTUVWXYZ
1231C4890
C.,;:?2$f£€¥&-*)(ÄÖÜÀØ ÆŒÇÑ)

18/18 pt

ABCDEFGHIJKLMN
OPQRSTUVWXYZ
[ÄÖÜSSÅØÆŒÇÑ]
ABCDEFGHIJKLMN
OPQRSTUVWXYZ
1231C4890
C.,;:?2$f£€¥&-*)
(ÄÖÜÀØ ÆŒÇÑ)

24/24 pt

The HVD letters verge on the unpleasant to the point of actually becoming interesting. They were cut out from a screwed up tatty piece of paper and then scanned to enable their outlines to be digitally modified. The result is a broad, black typeface with the characters not resting on the baseline. The design of this shapeless font, which is of continuous construction, suggests that a pair of scissors were used to create the letters. The set includes two different groups of uppercase letters. The unusual appearance of the design is due to the positive counter of the A, B, D, O and U.

Les lettres HVD frôlent une sensation désagréable au point de devenir intéressantes. Elles ont été découpées dans une feuille froissée, plutôt sale puis elles ont été scannées afin de modifier les contours de façon numérique. Le résultat est une typographie de chasse large, noire dont les caractères ne reposent pas sur la ligne de base. Avec une construction continue, le design de cette police d'écriture amorphe fait référence aux ciseaux comme élément de création. Elle propose deux variantes haut de casse avec touche singulière au niveau du design des caractères « A », « B », « D », « O », « U » dont le contrepoinçon est entièrement colorié.

Las letras HVD Rowdy rozan el límite de lo desagradable, hasta el punto de convertirse en interesantes. Se han recortado a partir de una hoja de papel arrugado, medio sucio, y luego se han escaneado para poder modificar los contornos digitalmente. El resultado es una tipografía ancha, de espesor negro, cuyos caracteres no se apoyan en la línea base. De construcción continua, el diseño de esta fuente amorfa hace referencia a las tijeras como herramienta de creación. El set incluye dos juegos distintos de caja alta. El toque singular del diseño se encuentra en los caracteres A, B, D, O y U, que presentan la contraforma rellena.

Schablone

I need a plotter

spraypaint and a sharp knife

Dark Night

Mathematisch Modularen System

3 Dimensional

abcdefghijklmnopqrstuvwxyz[äöüßç]
ABCDEFGHIJKLMNOPQRSTUVWXYZ
1234567890(.,;:?$&8-*){ÄÖÜÇ}

8/10 pt

abcdefghijklmnopqrstuvwxyz[äöüßç]
ABCDEFGHIJKLMNOPQRSTUVWXYZ
1234567890(.,;:?$&8-*){ÄÖÜÇ}

8/10 pt

abcdefghijklmnopqrstuvwxyz[äöüßç]
ABCDEFGHIJKLMNOPQRSTUVWXYZ
1234567890(.,;:?$&8-*){ÄÖÜÇ}

10/12 pt

abcdefghijklmnopqrstuvwxyz[äöüßç]
ABCDEFGHIJKLMNOPQRSTUVWXYZ
1234567890(.,;:?$&8-*){ÄÖÜÇ}

10/12 pt

abcdefghijklmn
opqrstuvwxyz[äöüßç]
ABCDEFGHIJKLMNOPQRSTUVWXYZ
1234567890(.,;:?$&8-*){ÄÖÜÇ}

18/18 pt

abcdefghijklmn
opqrstuvwxyz[äöüßç]
ABCDEFGHIJKLMNOPQRSTUVWXYZ
1234567890(.,;:?$&8-*){ÄÖÜÇ}

18/18 pt

This font belongs to the group of stencil-type decorative typefaces. These typically have their letters divided into several parts so that they can be cut out in one piece and reproduced on other surfaces using templates. The font has a discontinuous construction since each letter is formed from a limited set of loose elements. The characters follow the same pattern, with single space widths for the capitals. The set offers the variants Regular and Block in both upper and lowercase letters and also includes the acute and grave accents, circumflex and dieresis for the vowels and a large variety of punctuation marks and symbols.

Elle appartient au groupe de typographie décorative du genre Stencil. Ce type de polices se caractérise par des lettres divisées en plusieurs parties ce qui permet de les découper tout en gardant la forme de chacune et de les reproduire sur d'autres superficies à l'aide de pochoirs. La construction de cette police est discontinue étant donné que chaque lettre est composée d'un ensemble limité d'éléments séparés. Les caractères suivent un même modèle, avec des capitales à chasse fixe. Il existe deux variantes, Regular et Block, haut et bas de casse. Elle inclut : les accents graves, aigus et circonflexes, les trémas ainsi qu'une grande variété de signes de ponctuation et de symboles.

Pertenece al grupo de tipografías decorativas tipo stencil. Estas se caracterizan por sus letras divididas en varias partes para poder recortarlas y reproducirlas en otras superficies mediante plantillas. Esta fuente muestra una construcción discontinua, ya que cada letra se ha formado a partir de un conjunto limitado de elementos sueltos. Los caracteres siguen un mismo patrón, con anchuras de capitales monoespaciadas. El set ofrece las variantes Regular y Block de caja alta y baja. También incluye los acentos agudo, grave y circunflejo, la diéresis para las vocales y una gran variedad de signos de puntuación y símbolos.

HVD Fonts | www.hvdfonts.com

abcdefghijklmnopqrstuvwxyz[äöüñ...]
ABCDEFGHIJKLMNOPQRSTUVWXYZ
1234567890(.,;:?¿$¢£¥&-*)

8/10 pt

abcdefghijklmnopqrstuvwxyz[...]
ABCDEFGHIJKLMNOPQRSTUVWXYZ
1234567890(.,;:?¿$¢£¥&-*)

8/10 pt

abcdefghijklmnopqrstuvwxyz[...]
ABCDEFGHIJKLMNOPQRSTUVWXYZ
1234567890(.,;:?¿$¢£¥&-*)

10/12 pt

abcdefghijklmnopqrstuvwxyz[...]
ABCDEFGHIJKLMNOPQRSTUVWXYZ
1234567890(.,;:?¿$¢£¥&-*)

10/12 pt

abcdefghijklmnopqrstuvwxyz[...]
ABCDEFGHIJKLMNOPQRSTUVWXYZ
1234567890 (.,;:?¿$¢£¥&-*)

18/18 pt

abcdefghijklmnopqrstuvwxyz[...]
ABCDEFGHIJKLMNOPQRSTUVWXYZ
1234567890(.,;:?¿$¢£¥&-*)

18/18 pt

This three-dimensional typeface is very much in keeping with the style used in illustrations. It comes in two variants: one regular and the other, which has the same construction and shape, but with the area contained inside the outline having a positive value. This is an informal sans serif font, with the characters not resting on the baseline to create a sense of movement. The letters are uneven, as if they had been drawn by hand, and not joined up in any way. It is appropriate for projects that are not very formal, for titles or billboards but not really recommended for running text.

Dessinée en trois dimensions, cette typographie a un aspect qui fait penser à une illustration. Il existe deux variantes : une normale et l'autre avec la même forme mais l'intérieur des caractères est plein. Il s'agit d'une police informelle sans serif, dont les caractères ne reposent pas sur la ligne de base afin de donner une sensation de mouvement. Les lettres sont irrégulières, comme si elles étaient dessinées à la main, et ne sont pas reliées entre elles. Elle convient pour des projets qui ne sont pas formels, pour des titres ou des affiches publicitaires. Elle n'est pas recommandée pour un texte long.

Dibujada en tres dimensiones, esta tipografía tiene un aspecto que recuerda en todo momento a una ilustración. Ofrece dos variantes: una Regular y otra que resulta igual en construcción y forma pero con el interior del trazo relleno. Se trata de una fuente de palo seco de carácter informal, cuyos caracteres no se apoyan en la línea base para generar una sensación de movimiento. Las letras son irregulares, como dibujadas a mano, y no existe unión entre ellas. Resulta apropiada para proyectos poco formales, para títulos o diseño de carteles publicitarios pero muy poco recomendada para texto corrido.

Ibiscus

Ewen Prigent | www.laboitegraphique.fr

ABCDEFGHIJKLMNOPQRSTUUWXYZ
1234567890[.,;:?-)ÄÖÜ

8/10 pt

ABCDEFGHIJKLMNOPQRSTUUWXYZ
1234567890[.,;:?-)ÄÖÜ

10/12 pt

ABCDEFGHIJKLMNOPQRSTUUWXYZ
1234567890[.,;:?-)ÄÖÜ

18/18 pt

ABCDEFGHIJKLMN
OPQRSTUUWXYZ
1234567890[.,;:?-)ÄÖÜ

24/24 pt

ABCDEFGHIJKLMN
OPQRSTUUWXYZ
1234567890
[.,;:?-)ÄÖÜ

32/34 pt

The aim of this typeface is to create a set of modern and robust organic characters through the meticulous treatment of form. The letters are built up through a combination of quarter and semi-circles forming curves and countercurves reminiscent of plant forms. This results in a continuous stroke giving the curves in the letters a somewhat square appearance. The stem terminals in this font, which is sans serif, taper into a point. The key characters are described below: the A has a rounded apex; the G has no spur; the Q has a short tail; and the J rests on the baseline.

Cette typographie a pour objectif de créer un ensemble de caractères organique, moderne et robuste à l'aide d'un traitement épuré de la forme. Les lettres sont formées par une combinaison de quart et de demi-cercles qui produisent des courbes et des contre-courbes faisant penser à des plantes. Il en résulte un tracé de forme continue, avec un aspect carré de la courbe. Les extrémités des hampes de cette police sans serif sont pointues. Voici les principaux caractères qui se distinguent : le « A » avec une pointe arrondie, le « G » sans empattement, le « Q » avec une queue toute petite et le « J » qui repose sur la ligne de base.

La intención de esta tipografía es crear un juego de caracteres orgánico, moderno y robusto a través de un tratamiento depurado de la forma. Las letras se constituyen a través de una combinación de cuartos y medios círculos que provocan curvas y contracurvas que apelan a formas vegetales. El resultado es un trazo de construcción continua, con un aspecto de la curva cuadrado. Esta fuente de palo seco muestra los extremos de las astas en forma de pico. Los caracteres clave destacados se describen a continuación: la A con el ápice redondeado, la G sin espuela, la Q con cola corta y la J que se apoya en la línea base.

THE ROMAN
ITALIC &
BLACK LETTER
bequeathed to the
University of Oxford by
Dr. JOHN FELL

OXFORD
PRINTED FOR THE TYPOPHILES
AT THE UNIVERSITY PRESS
1951

abcdefghijklmnopqrstuvwxyz[äöüßåøæœçñ]
ABCDEFGHIJKLMNOPQRSTUVWXYZ
1234567890(.,;:?¡$¢£€¥&-*){ÄÖÜÅØÆŒÇÑ}

8/10 pt

abcdefghijklmnopqrstuvwxyz[äöüßåøæœçñ]
ABCDEFGHIJKLMNOPQRSTUVWXYZ
1234567890(.,;:?¡$¢£€¥&-){ÄÖÜÅØÆŒÇÑ}*

8/10 pt

ABCDEFGHIJKLMNOPQRSTUVWXYZ[ÄÖÜSSÅØÆŒÇÑ]
ABCDEFGHIJKLMNOPQRSTUVWXYZ
1234567890(.,;:?¡$¢£€¥&-*){ÄÖÜÅØÆŒÇÑ}

8/10 pt

abcdefghijklmnopqrstuvwxyz[äöüßåøæœçñ]
ABCDEFGHIJKLMNOPQRSTUVWXYZ
1234567890(.,;:?¡$¢£€¥&-*){ÄÖÜÅØÆŒÇÑ}

10/12 pt

abcdefghijklmnopqrstuvwxyz[äöüßåøæœçñ]
ABCDEFGHIJKLMNOPQRSTUVWXYZ
1234567890(.,;:?¡$¢£€¥&-){ÄÖÜÅØÆŒÇÑ}*

10/12 pt

ABCDEFGHIJKLMNOPQRSTUVWXYZ[ÄÖÜSSÅØÆŒÇÑ]
ABCDEFGHIJKLMNOPQRSTUVWXYZ
1234567890(.,;:?¡$¢£€¥&-*){ÄÖÜÅØÆŒÇÑ}

10/12 pt

This typeface, a reproduction of some of the versions belonging to the well-known Fell Types font family, takes its name from its creator John Fell, bishop of Oxford in the 17th century. This project does not pursue any philological purpose, just the desire to offer fonts that are unique in the history of typography. The glyphs not included in the font itself were created and added to the set, which is suitable for Turkish, and Western, Central European and Baltic languages. The kerning has been carried out with great care so as to obtain the highest quality typeface. This has been done by using the autospacing and autokerning tool in the iKem software developed by the author himself.

Cette police est une reproduction de certaines versions de la célèbre famille Fell Types, dont le nom provient de son créateur John Fell, évêque d'Oxford au XVIIe siècle. Les glyphes qui ne font pas partie du matériel d'origine ont été créés et ajoutés. La police convient aux langues occidentales, baltiques, turques et d'Europe centrale. L'interlettrage a été effectué méticuleusement afin d'obtenir une meilleure qualité. Pour cela les programmes autospacing et autokerning du logiciel iKern, conçu par l'auteur même, ont été utilisés.

Reproducción de algunas de las versiones de la conocida familia Fell Types, esta tipografía toma el nombre de su creador, John Fell, obispo de Oxford en siglo XVII. Este proyecto no obedece a ningún intento filológico sino al deseo de facilitar fuentes únicas en la historia de la tipografía. Los glifos no incluidos la fuente fueron creados y añadidos al set, apto para lenguas occidentales, centroeuropeas, bálticas y turcas. El interletraje se ha realizado meticulosamente con la intención de obtener la mejor calidad. Para ello se han utilizando las herramientas *autospacing* y *autokerning* del software iKern desarrollado por el mismo autor.

abcdefghijklmnopqrstuvwxyz[äöüßåøæœçñ]
ABCDEFGHIJKLMNOPQRSTUVWXYZ
1234567890(.,;:?¿$¢£€¥&-*){ÄÖÜÅØÆŒÇÑ}

8/10 pt

abcdefghijklmnopqrstuvwxyz[äöüßåøæœçñ]
ABCDEFGHIJKLMNOPQRSTUVWXYZ
1234567890(.,;:?¿$¢£€¥&-){ÄÖÜÅØÆŒÇÑ}*

8/10 pt

ABCDEFGHIJKLMNOPQRSTUVWXYZ[ÄÖÜSSÅØÆŒÇÑ]
ABCDEFGHIJKLMNOPQRSTUVWXYZ
1234567890(.,;:?¿$¢£€¥&-*){ÄÖÜÅØÆŒÇÑ}

8/10 pt

abcdefghijklmnopqrstuvwxyz[äöüßåøæœçñ]
ABCDEFGHIJKLMNOPQRSTUVWXYZ
1234567890(.,;:?¿$¢£€¥&-*){ÄÖÜÅØÆŒÇÑ}

18/18 pt

abcdefghijklmnopqrstuvwxyz[äöüßåøæœçñ]
ABCDEFGHIJKLMNOPQRSTUVWXYZ
1234567890(.,;:?¿$¢£€¥&-){ÄÖÜÅØÆŒÇÑ}*

18/18 pt

ABCDEFGHIJKLMNOPQRSTUVWXYZ[ÄÖÜSSÅØÆŒÇÑ]
ABCDEFGHIJKLMNOPQRSTUVWXYZ
1234567890(.,;:?¿$¢£€¥&-*){ÄÖÜÅØÆŒÇÑ}

18/18 pt

abcdefghijklmnopqrstuvwxyz[äöüßåøæœçñ]
ABCDEFGHIJKLMNOPQRSTUVWXYZ
1234567890(.,;:?¿$¢£€¥&-*){ÄÖÜÅØÆŒÇÑ}

8/10 pt

abcdefghijklmnopqrstuvwxyz[äöüßåøæœçñ]
ABCDEFGHIJKLMNOPQRSTUVWXYZ
1234567890(.,;:?¿$¢£€¥&-){ÄÖÜÅØÆŒÇÑ}*

8/10 pt

ABCDEFGHIJKLMNOPQRSTUVWXYZ[ÄÖÜSSÅØÆŒÇÑ]
ABCDEFGHIJKLMNOPQRSTUVWXYZ
1234567890(.,;:?¿$¢£€¥&-*){ÄÖÜÅØÆŒÇÑ}

8/10 pt

abcdefghijklmnopqrstuvwxyz[äöüßåøæœçñ]
ABCDEFGHIJKLMNOPQRSTUVWXYZ
1234567890(.,;:?¿$¢£€¥&-*){ÄÖÜÅØÆŒÇÑ}

18/18 pt

abcdefghijklmnopqrstuvwxyz[äöüßåøæœçñ]
ABCDEFGHIJKLMNOPQRSTUVWXYZ
1234567890(.,;:?¿$¢£€¥&-){ÄÖÜÅØÆŒÇÑ}*

18/18 pt

ABCDEFGHIJKLMNOPQRSTUVWXYZ[ÄÖÜSSÅØÆŒÇÑ]
ABCDEFGHIJKLMNOPQRSTUVWXYZ
1234567890(.,;:?¿$¢£€¥&-*){ÄÖÜÅØÆŒÇÑ}

18/18 pt

Insecurity

K-Type/Keith Bates | www.k-type.com

CRITIQUE OF SECURITY
MARK NEOCLEOUS

8/10 pt

10/12 pt

18/18 pt

24/24 pt

Somewhere between a dingbat, pictogram and legible type, this font received a commendation in the FUSE Typeface Competition. The idea was to convey the theme of security and an intuitive and eclectic set of images was compiled for the font by searching Google on the subject of Pop Art. The characters in this decorative pictographic font are built up from: characters like the thief, objects like surveillance cameras, keys, pistols, locks, telephones and an assortment of signs. It is available in both upper and lowercase characters and numbers. It is not designed for use in running text, but rather for sporadic, isolated use.

À mi-chemin entre le dingbat, le pictogramme et la police lisible, cette typographie a reçu une mention au concours de typographie FUSE. Ayant comme objectif de refléter le thème de la sécurité cette police rassemble des images de manière intuitive et éclectique, à partir d'une recherche sur Google du thème Pop Art. Les caractères de cette police décorative et pictographique se composent de : personnages comme le voleur, d'objets comme les caméras de sécurité, les clés, les pistolets, les cadenas, les téléphones et divers panneaux. Elle propose des caractères haut et bas de casse ainsi que des chiffres. Elle n'est pas conçue pour rédiger des textes mais pour un usage sporadique et isolé.

A caballo entre el dingbat, el pictograma y la fuente legible, esta tipografía recibió una mención en el concurso de tipografía FUSE. Con el propósito de reflejar el tema de la seguridad, la fuente recopila imágenes Pop Art de un modo intuitivo y ecléctico, a partir de la búsqueda de este concepto en Google. Los caracteres de esta fuente decorativa y pictográfica se construyen a base de personajes como el ladrón y objetos como cámaras de seguridad, llaves, pistolas, candados, teléfonos y señales varias. Ofrece caracteres de caja alta y baja y números. No está pensada para texto corrido, sino para un uso esporádico y aislado.

Insight Issue

Galdino Otten | galdinoottenbr.blogspot.com

Insight Issue

November. 2009

this font was conceived with the intention to make possible to creative of advertising and design the freedom to create title of texts, short texts, logotypes, marks, and any another artistic work being able to modify each letter with the purpose to personalize its work in accordance with its infinite creativity.

A B C
x y z

ABCDEFGHIJKLM
NOPQRSTUVWXYZ
abcdefghijklmnop
rstuvwxyz{$?!%@}
1234567890(&#+:)

abcdefghijKlmnopqrstuvwxyz[äöüßåøæœçñ]
ABCDEFGHIJKLMNOPQRSTUVWXYZ
1234567890(..::?;$¢£€¥&-*){ÄÖÜÅØÆŒÇÑ}

8/10 pt

abcdefghijKlmnopqrstuvwxyz[äöüßåøæœçñ]
ABCDEFGHIJKLMNOPQRSTUVWXYZ
1234567890(..::?;$¢£€¥&-*){ÄÖÜÅØÆŒÇÑ}

10/12 pt

abcdefghijKlmn
opqrstuvwxyz[äöüßåøæœçñ]
ABCDEFGHIJKLM
NOPQRSTUVWXYZ
1234567890
(..::?;$¢£€¥&-*){ÄÖÜÅØÆŒÇÑ}

18/18 pt

abcdefghijKlmn
opqrstuvwxyz
[äöüßåøæœçñ]
ABCDEFGHIJKLMN
OPQRSTUVWXYZ
1234567890
(..::?;$¢£€¥&-*)
{ÄÖÜÅØÆŒÇÑ}

24/24 pt

The soft, clean edges make this decorative font ideal for creating headings and titles, short texts or logos. It belongs to the group of fonts with the old style of serif, with uneven spacing and medium weight. The separate characters are aligned with the baseline and the stems have parallel edges with very heavy Roman flourishes. The set offers upper and lowercase characters along with all types of accents, punctuation marks and a large variety of symbols plus the numbers. This typeface offers complete freedom to make changes in each letter in keeping with the artistic requirements of each piece of work.

Avec des contours doux et nets, cette police d'écriture décorative convient parfaitement pour rédiger des titres, des textes courts ou des logotypes. Elle appartient au groupe de polices avec un empattement d'un style ancien, un espacement irrégulier et un poids moyen. Les caractères non reliés sont alignés sur la ligne de base et les hampes verticales ont les bords parallèles, avec un empattement romain très épais. La police propose des caractères haut et bas de casse avec tout type d'accents, de signes de ponctuation et une grande série de symboles ainsi que les chiffres. Cette typographie offre une liberté absolue pour modifier les lettres en fonction des besoins artistiques de chaque travail.

De bordes suaves y limpios, esta fuente decorativa resulta ideal para crear títulos, textos cortos o logotipos. Pertenece al grupo de las fuentes con serifa de viejo estilo, con espaciado irregular y peso medio. Los caracteres sin unión están alineados con la línea base y las astas verticales son de bordes paralelos, con remates romanos muy gruesos. El set ofrece caracteres de caja alta y baja junto con todo tipo de acentos, signos de puntuación y una gran variedad de símbolos, así como la serie de números. Esta tipografía ofrece total libertad para modificar cada letra de acuerdo a las necesidades artísticas de cada trabajo.

Kato

K-Type/Keith Bates | www.k-type.com

abcdefghijklmnopqrstuvwxyz[äöüßåœçñ]
ABCDEFGHIJKLMNOPQRSTUVWXYZ
1234567890(.,;:?¿$¢€£¥Ω-*)[äöüåœ æœçñ]

8/10 pt

abcdefghijklmnopqrstuvwxyz[äöüßåœçñ]
ABCDEFGHIJKLMNOPQRSTUVWXYZ
1234567890(.,;:?¿$¢€£¥Ω-*)[äöüåœ æœçñ]

10/12 pt

abcdefghijklmn
opqrstuvwxyz[äöüßåœçñ]
ABCDEFGHIJKLMNOPQRSTUVWXYZ
1234567890
(.,;:?¿$¢€£¥Ω-*)[äöüåœ æœçñ]

18/18 pt

abcdefghijklmn
opqrstuvwxyz[äöüßåœçñ]
ABCDEFGHIJKLMN
OPQRSTUVWXYZ
1234567890
(.,;:?¿$¢€£¥Ω-*)
[äöüåœ æœçñ]

24/24 pt

Japanese writing is composed of two syllabaries: *hiragana* and *katakana*, with kana being the term used to refer to both of these writing systems together. These characters, unlike their *kanji* counterparts (used in the Japanese language solely to express concepts), do not have any conceptual value, they are merely phonetic symbols. The font, which strangely enough owes its name to the servant working for Inspector Clouseau in the Pink Panther movies, draws on *kana* characters for its adaptation to the Latin alphabet. The upper and lowercase characters are designed to be used separately, although they can always be combined to achieve a more cryptographic effect.

L'écriture japonaise se compose de deux syllabaires : le *hiragana* et le *katakana*, qui composent le *kana*. Ces caractères, contrairement au *kanji* (utilisé dans la langue japonaise afin d'exprimer uniquement des concepts), n'ont aucune valeur conceptuelle, uniquement phonétique. Cette police, qui curieusement doit son nom au valet de l'inspecteur Clouseau dans les films de la Panthère Rose, s'inspire des caractères *kana* pour être adaptée à l'alphabet latin. Les caractères haut et bas de casse ont été conçus pour être utilisés séparément, bien qu'ils puissent être mélangés pour un effet plus cryptographique.

La escritura japonesa se compone de dos silabarios: el *hiragana* y el *katakana*, y el conjunto de los dos se conoce como *kana*. Estos caracteres, al contrario que los *kanji* (utilizados en la lengua japonesa para expresar sólo conceptos), no tienen ningún valor conceptual, sino únicamente fonético. Esta fuente, que peculiarmente debe su nombre al sirviente del Inspector Clouseau en las películas de la Pantera Rosa, se inspira en los caracteres *kana* para su adaptación al alfabeto latino. Los caracteres de caja alta y baja se han diseñado para usarlas separadamente, aunque siempre se pueden combinar para un efecto más criptográfico.

KleeCapscript

K-Type/Keith Bates | www.k-type.com

pushing the envelope

abcdefghijklmnopqrstuvuuxyz(äöüßåøæœçñ)
ABCDEFGHIJKLMNOPQRSTUVWXYZ
1234567890(.,;:?¿\$¢£€¥&-*)(ÄÖÜÅØÆŒÇÑ)

8/10 pt

abcdefghijklmnopqrstuvuuxyz(äöüßåøæœçñ)
ABCDEFGHIJKLMNOPQRSTUVWXYZ
1234567890(.,;:?¿\$¢£€¥&-*)(ÄÖÜÅØÆŒÇÑ)

10/12 pt

abcdefghijklmn
opqrstuvuuxyz(äöüßåøæœçñ)
ABCDEFGHIJKLMNOPQRSTUVWXYZ
1234567890
(.,;:?¿\$¢£€¥&-*){ÄÖÜÅØÆŒÇÑ}

18/18 pt

abcdefghijklmn
opqrstuvuuxyz
(äöüßåøæœçñ)
ABCDEFGHIJKLMN
OPQRSTUVWXYZ
1234567890
(.,;:?¿\$¢£€¥&-*)
{ÄÖÜÅØÆŒÇÑ}

24/24 pt

KleeCapScript is based on the lovely diminutive handwritten lettering of US artist Emma Klee in her mail art invitation for the Color Museum project. The designer has consistently endeavored to remain faithful to the style of the original invitation. The uppercase characters are based on the caps used by Emma and the lowercase letters have been freely adapted from her own calligraphic style of writing. The font is designed either for use in words only containing capital letters or else for calligraphic purposes, but without any alternation. The result is a sans serif font with uneven edges.

KleeCapScript s'inspire de la belle et toute petite écriture à la main qui figure sur l'invitation art postal de l'artiste américaine Emma Klee pour le projet Color Museum. La graphiste a essayé de rester fidèle au style originel de l'invitation. Les caractères haut de casse se fondent sur les majuscules qu'utilisait Emma et ceux bas de casse s'adaptent librement à son écriture de style calligraphique. Cette police a été conçue afin d'être utilisée soit pour des mots formés uniquement par des majuscules soit sous forme de calligraphie, mais sans alterner. Le résultat est une police de caractères sans serif avec des bords irréguliers.

KleeCapScript hace referencia a la bonita y diminuta escritura realizada a mano en la invitación de arte postal de la artista estadounidense Emma Klee para el proyecto Color Museum. La diseñadora ha buscado en todo momento la fidelidad al estilo de la invitación original. Los caracteres en caja alta se basan en las letras mayúsculas empleadas por Emma y los de caja baja se adaptan libremente partiendo de su escritura de estilo caligráfico. La fuente ha sido diseñada o bien para ser utilizada en palabras en caja alta, o bien en forma de caligrafía, pero sin alternar. El resultado es una fuente de palo seco de bordes irregulares.

Komodore Normal/Destroy

Font-o-Rama | www.font-o-rama.com

ABCDEFGHIJKLMNOPQRSTUVWXYZ
1234567890(.,;:?$-×){äöüàêçñ}

8/10 pt

ABCDEFGHIJKLMNOPQRSTUVWXYZ
1234567890(.,;:?$-×){äöüàêçñ}

8/10 pt

ABCDEFGHIJKLMNOPQRSTUVWXYZ
1234567890(.,;:?$-×){äöüàêçñ}

10/12 pt

ABCDEFGHIJKLMNOPQRSTUVWXYZ
1234567890(.,;:?$-×){äöüàêçñ}

10/12 pt

ABCDEFGHIJKLMN
OPQRSTUVWXYZ
1234567890
(.,;:?$-×){äöüàêçñ}

18/18 pt

ABCDEFGHIJKLMN
OPQRSTUVWXYZ
1234567890
(.,;:?$-×){äöüàêçñ}

18/18 pt

A decorative font suitable for publicity purposes, of limited use for large formats to attract the attention of the readers. The font's legibility is not its main concern, as it is not very appropriate for running text. It is reminiscent of the old Commodore 64, an 8-bit home computer launched by Commodore International in 1982. This computer would subsequently provide inspiration for a great many musicians and programmers, becoming the most significant 8-bit cult computer on a par with the Spectrum. The Destroy variant offers an incorrect display of the font, probably generated by an error in the computer system.

Police décorative appropriée pour les publicités, en limitant les grands formats afin d'attirer l'attention des lecteurs. Sa fonction principale n'est pas d'être lisible, pour cela elle ne convient pas pour des textes. Elle fait penser à la police de l'ancien Commodore 64, ordinateur personnel de 8 bits construit par Commodore International en 1982. Par la suite, cet ordinateur a inspiré de nombreux musiciens et programmateurs, devenant l'ordinateur de 8 bits le plus important avec le Spectrum. La version Destroy offre une vision erronée de la police, probablement produite par une erreur du système de l'ordinateur.

Fuente decorativa adecuada para temas de publicidad, de uso limitado para tamaños grandes, con el fin de captar la atención de los lectores. Su legibilidad no es la función principal, por lo que resulta poco apropiada para texto corrido. Recuerda la fuente de la antigua Commodore 64, la computadora doméstica de 8 bits lanzada por Commodore International en 1982. Posteriormente, este ordenador inspiraría a muchos músicos y programadores y se convertiría en el ordenador de 8 bits de culto más importante junto al Spectrum. La variante Destroy representa una visualización incorrecta de la fuente, probablemente generada por un error en el sistema de la computadora.

Korner Deli NF

Nick's Fonts | www.nicksfonts.com

ABCDEFGHIJKLMNOPQRSTUVWXYZ[ÄÖÜSSÅØÆŒÇÑ]
ABCDEFGHIJKLMNOPQRSTUVWXYZ
1234567890[.,;:?¿$¢£€¥&-*]{ÄÖÜÅØÆŒÇÑ}

8/10 pt

ABCDEFGHIJKLMNOPQRSTUVWXYZ[ÄÖÜSSÅØÆŒÇÑ]
ABCDEFGHIJKLMNOPQRSTUVWXYZ
1234567890[.,;:?¿$¢£€¥&-*]{ÄÖÜÅØÆŒÇÑ}

10/12 pt

ABCDEFGHIJKLMN
OPQRSTUVWXYZ[ÄÖÜSSÅØÆŒÇÑ]
ABCDEFGHIJKLMNOPQRSTUVWXYZ
1234567890
[.,;:?¿$¢£€¥&-*]{ÄÖÜÅØÆŒÇÑ}

18/18 pt

ABCDEFGHIJKLMN
OPQRSTUVWXYZ
[ÄÖÜSSÅØÆŒÇÑ]
ABCDEFGHIJKLMN
OPQRSTUVWXYZ
1234567890
[.,;:?¿$¢£€¥&-*]
{ÄÖÜÅØÆŒÇÑ}

24/24 pt

Scialo Brothers Bakery is a legendary bakery founded in 1916 in Providence, USA. The design of the sign for the business was created using a combination of paint and neon lighting. This sign, which aged and eroded over the years, provided a source of inspiration for designing this flamboyant typeface clearly rooted in ArtDeco, which incorporates just the right amount of flair from the Big Apple. The font offers the grave and acute accents, circumflex and dieresis for vowels and consonants, and the tilde for the Ã and Õ, along with a large variety of symbols and punctuation marks.

Scialo Brothers Bakery est une boulangerie légendaire fondée en 1916 dans la ville de Providence aux États-Unis. Le design de l'enseigne de la boutique a été créé en associant l'effet de la lumière d'un néon à la peinture. Vieilli et érodé par le temps qui passe, il est la source d'inspiration de cette typographie extravagante de style Art Déco, qui intègre la dose exacte du style de la Grosse Pomme. Cette police propose des accents graves, aigus, circonflexes, des trémas pour les voyelles et les consonnes, des tildes sur le « Ã » et le « Õ », ainsi qu'une grande variété de symboles et de signes de ponctuation.

Scialo Brothers Bakery es una legendaria panadería fundada en 1916 en Providence (Estados Unidos). El diseño del rótulo del comercio es una combinación de pintura y luz de neón. Envejecido y erosionado por el paso del tiempo, el rótulo ha sido la fuente de inspiración para el diseño de esta estrafalaria tipografía de estilo claramente Art decó, que incorpora el toque justo de estilo de La Gran Manzana. Ofrece acentos grave, agudo, circunflejo y diéresis para vocales y consonantes, tilde de la Ã y Õ, una gran variedad de símbolos y signos de puntuación.

Lakeshore Drive NF

Nick's Fonts | www.nicksfonts.com

abcdefghijklmnopqrstuvwxyz[äöüßåøœæçñ]
ABCDEFGHIJKLMNOPQRSTUVWXYZ
1234567890(.,::?¿$¢£€¥&-*){ ÅÖÜÅØÆ ŒÇÑ}

8/10 pt

abcdefghijklmnopqrstuvwxyz[äöüßåøœæçñ]
ABCDEFGHIJKLMNOPQRSTUVWXYZ
1234567890(.,::?¿$¢£€¥&-*){ ÅÖÜÅØÆ ŒÇÑ}

10/12 pt

abcdefghijklmn
opqrstuvwxyz
[äöüßåøœæçñ]
ABCDEFGHIJKLMNOPQRSTUVWXYZ
1234567890
(.,::?¿$¢£€¥&-*){ ÅÖÜÅØÆ ŒÇÑ}

18/18 pt

abcdefghijklmn
opqrstuvwxyz
[äöüßåøœæçñ]
ABCDEFGHIJKLMN
OPQRSTUVWXYZ
1234567890
(.,::?¿$¢£€¥&-*)
{ ÅÖÜÅØÆ ŒÇÑ}

24/24 pt

A ride along the road running along the shore of Lake Michigan in Chicago, USA, provided the source of inspiration for the name of this font. Its form and construction were inspired by Bangalore: a thick pixel bitmap font, designed by Yuji Adachi in 1998. In this version, the pixels have been replaced by soft curves resulting in a semicalligraphic writing style that is very slick, with lavish amounts of style and class. It is a sans serif font with joined up lowercase characters. The font uses continuous construction and has a smooth outline with exaggerated contrast, a vertical axis and abrupt transition.

Une balade sur les rives du lac Michigan à Chicago, aux États-Unis, a été la source d'inspiration du nom de cette police, alors que sa forme et sa construction proviennent de Bangalore : une police de caractères bitmap pixélisée et épaisse, conçue par Yuji Adachi en 1998. Pour cette version les pixels ont été remplacés par des courbes souples dont le résultat est une écriture à moitié calligraphique très aérodynamique, avec du style et de la classe. Il s'agit d'une police sans serif dont les caractères bas de casse sont reliés entre eux. Avec une construction homogène et un profil net, elle présente un contraste exagéré par son axe vertical et sa transition brusque.

Un paseo por una carretera que recorre la orilla del lago Michigan en Chicago, Estados Unidos, ha inspirado el nombre de esta fuente, mientras que su forma y construcción se basan en la Bangalore: una fuente bitmap pixelada y gruesa, diseñada por Yuji Adachi en 1998. En esta versión, los píxeles se han substituido por suaves curvas y el resultado es una escritura semicaligráfica muy aerodinámica, con mucho estilo y clase. Se trata de una fuente de palo seco con unión entre los caracteres de caja baja. De construcción continua y perfil liso, muestra un contraste exagerado, con eje vertical y transición abrupta.

Mailart

K-Type/Keith Bates | www.k-type.com

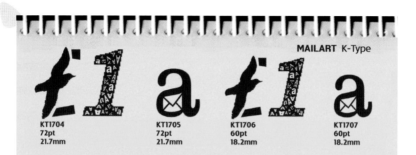

K-Type Freebies are free for personal use from www.k-type.com

abcdefghijklmnopqrstuvwxyz[äöüßåøÆœçñ]
ABCDEFGHIJ︎KLMNOPQRSTUVWXYZ
1234567890[.,:;?¿$¢€¥℃-*]{ÁÖÜÅØŒÇÑ}

8/10 pt

abcdefghijklmnopqrstuvwxyz[äöüßåøÆœçñ]
ABCDEFGHIJKLMNOPQRSTUVWXYZ
1234567890[.,:;?¿$¢€¥℃-*]{ÁÖÜÅØŒÇÑ}

10/12 pt

abcdefghijklmn
opqrstuvwxyz[äöüßåøÆœçñ]
ABCDEFGHIJKLMNOPQRSTUVWXYZ
1234567890
[.,:;?¿$¢€¥℃-*]{ÁÖÜÅØŒÇÑ}

18/18 pt

abcdefghijklmno
pqrstuvwxyz[äöüßåøÆœçñ]
ABCDEFGHIJKLMN
OPQRSTUVWXYZ
1234567890
[.,:;?¿$¢€¥℃-*]
{ÁÖÜÅØŒÇÑ}

24/24 pt

Mail Art is a global movement for exchange and communication through the medium of mail. Historically, it emerged hand in hand with the creation of the postal service. However, it would reach the real heyday of its artistic expression much later, through the Fluxus group or the neo-Dadaists. This font was created using letters, numbers, punctuation marks and symbols sent to Keith Bates by at least 130 mailartists from all over the world. Mailart is a decorative pictographic font that simulates printing errors, and draws its inspiration from rubberstamped envelopes and artworks.

Le Mail art est un mouvement international d'échange et de communication en utilisant la correspondance postale. Historiquement, elle naît avec l'apparition du service postal, puisque celui-ci est son moyen de diffusion. Cependant, son essor apparaît plus tard, avec le Fluxus et les néo-dadaïstes. Cette police de caractères a été créée à partir des lettres, chiffres, signes de ponctuation et symboles qu'au moins 130 mail artistes des quatre coins du monde ont envoyé à Keith Bates. Mailart est une police décorative qui relève de la pictographie et imite les erreurs d'impression, en s'inspirant des enveloppes et des œuvres d'art apposées par des tampons en caoutchouc.

El *mail art* es un movimiento planetario de intercambio y comunicación a través del medio postal. Aunque históricamente nace con la aparición del servicio postal, el auge de esta manifestación artística llegará más tarde, con el grupo Fluxus o los neo-dadaístas. Esta fuente se ha creado a través de letras, números, signos de puntuación y símbolos enviados a Keith Bates por al menos 130 *mailartists* de todas partes del mundo. Mailart es una fuente decorativa pictográfica que simula errores de imprenta, inspirada en los sobres y obras de arte estampadas con sellos de caucho.

Maria Square

Elasticbrand, Arjen Noordeman & Christie Wright | www.elasticbrand.net

ABCDEFGHIJKLMNOPQRSTUVWXYZ
1234567800.,;:?$₤€¥-*

8/10 pt

ABCDEFGHIJKLMNOPQRSTUVWXYZ
1234567800.,;:?$₤€¥-*

10/12 pt

ABCDEFGHIJKLMN
OPQRSTUVWXYZ
1234567800
.,;:?$₤€¥-*

18/18 pt

ABCDEFGHIJKLMN
OPQRSTUVWXYZ
1234567800
.,;:?$₤€¥-*

24/24 pt

The font was designed especially to display the title of the exhibition "Everything is Separated by Water". This was a retrospective exhibition on the work of Maria Magdalena Campos-Pons at the Indianapolis Museum of Art, USA. The design is based on the wood and planks floating in the sea, drifting from country to country. The idea was taken from there and stylized to convert all the bars on the characters into real pieces of wood that are sometimes connected and sometimes not, evoking the concept of the fragility of life and chance encounters. A complete typeface was developed following on from this work.

Cette police a été créée spécialement pour le titre de l'exposition « Everything is Separated by Water ». Une exposition-rétrospective de Maria Magdalena Campos-Pons à l'Indianapolis Museum of Art aux États-Unis. Le design s'inspire des morceaux de bois et des planches qui flottent sur l'eau, vont à la dérive et voyagent de pays en pays. À partir de là, l'idée s'affine au point de transformer toutes les barres des caractères en véritables morceaux de bois qui parfois se touchent entre eux et parfois non, évoquant ainsi le concept de la fragilité de la vie et des rencontres périlleuses. Suite à ce travail, une typographie complète a été élaborée.

La fuente ha sido concebida especialmente para el título de la exposición «Everything is Separated by Water». Se trata de la exposición retrospectiva de María Magdalena Campos-Pons en el Indianapolis Museum of Art de Estados Unidos. El diseño se inspira en las maderas y tablas que flotan en el mar a la deriva y que viajan de país a país. A partir de aquí, la idea se estiliza hasta convertir todas las barras de los caracteres en auténticas piezas de madera que algunas veces se tocan y otras no, evocando el concepto de fragilidad de la vida y los encuentros azarosos. Posteriormente a este trabajo se ha creado una tipografía completa.

Misproject

ABCDEFGHIJKLMNOPQRSTUVWXYZ
1234567890(,.:?¿$¢£¥₦-*)[ÄÖÜSSÅØÆŒÇÑ]

8/10 pt

ABCDEFGHIJKLMNOPQRSTUVWXYZ
1234567890(,.:?¿$¢£¥₦-*)[ÄÖÜSSÅØÆŒÇÑ]

10/12 pt

ABCDEFGHIJKLMNOPQRSTUVWXYZ
1234567890(,.:?¿$¢£¥₦-*)[ÄÖÜSSÅØÆŒÇÑ]

18/18 pt

ABCDEFGHIJKLMNOPQRSTUVWXYZ
1234567890(,.:?¿$¢£¥₦-*)[ÄÖÜSSÅØÆŒÇÑ]

24/24 pt

ABCDEFGHIJKLMNOPQRSTUVWXYZ
1234567890(,.:?¿$¢£¥₦-*)
[ÄÖÜSSÅØÆŒÇÑ]

32/34 pt

Street signs provide the inspiration for this font with two variants for uppercase characters. The font is generally used for alternative, experimental or grunge-style projects on account of its neglected appearance. It is a sans serif font, constructed continuously with squarish curves and no modulation. The stems have parallel edges and the bars occupy a central position. Key characters include: the A with a straight apex; the G without a spur for one variant and a vertical spur for another; and the Q with a tail cutting through the bowl.

Les panneaux de signalisation dans la rue sont la source d'inspiration de cette police de caractères qui proposent deux versions différentes de majuscules. Caractérisée par son aspect sale, elle est le plus souvent utilisée pour des projets grunges, alternatifs ou expérimentaux. Cette police sans serif a une forme homogène avec un aspect des courbes légèrement carré, sans modulation. Les hampes verticales ont les bords parallèles et les traverses sont placées au milieu de la lettre. Les caractères clés sont : le « A » avec une pointe droite, le « G » sans empattement dans une des versions et avec un empattement vertical dans l'autre, puis le « Q » avec la queue qui coupe la panse.

Los rótulos y señales de la calle inspiran esta fuente con dos variantes para caracteres de caja alta. Caracterizada por su aspecto sucio, se suele utilizar para proyectos de estilo *grunge*, alternativo y experimental. Esta fuente de palo seco presenta una construcción continua con un aspecto de las curvas ligeramente cuadrado, sin modulación. Las astas verticales tienen bordes paralelos y las astas transversales se colocan en el centro. Entre los caracteres clave destacados se encuentran la A con el vértice recto, la G sin espuela para una variante y con espuela vertical para la otra y la Q con cola que corta el anillo.

Motion

Anton Studer | www.bubentraum.com

abcdefghijklmnopqrstuvwxyzäöüañ
ABCDEFGHIJKLMNOPQRSTUVWXYZ
123456789(.,;:-*)ÄÖUAÑ

8/10 pt

abcdefghijklmnopqrstuvwxyzäöüañ
ABCDEFGHIJKLMNOPQRSTUVWXYZ
123456789(.,;:-*)ÄÖUAÑ

10/12 pt

abcdefghijklmnopqrstuvwxyzäöüañ
ABCDEFGHIJKLMN
OPQRSTUVWXYZ
123456789(.,;:-*)ÄÖUAÑ

18/18 pt

abcdefghijklmn
opqrstuvwxyzäöüañ
ABCDEFGHIJKLMN
OPQRSTUVWXYZ
123456789(.,;:-*)ÄÖUAÑ

24/24 pt

This decorative font generates movement. Motion is more or less transparent, and can therefore be used to write on designed surfaces without hiding or obscuring any graphics, colors or images. The characters were designed using the same shaping component: fragments of a spring with a constant width for stems, terminals and tails. This sans serif font features continuous curves with a round albeit squarish appearance and no contrast. Key characters include: the lowercase G with its loop and ear; the uppercase G without a spur; and the uppercase R with a straight tail.

Police décorative qui produit du mouvement. Motion est plus ou moins transparente, ce qui permet de l'utiliser sur des superficies dessinées sans cacher ni assombrir les éventuels motifs, couleurs ou images. Les caractères sont conçus avec le même élément : les fragments d'un ressort dont la largeur est la même pour les hampes, les finitions et les queues. Cette police sans serif présente des courbes régulières avec un aspect rond, voire légèrement carré, sans contraste. Les caractères clés qui se distinguent sont : le « G » bas de casse avec boucle et oreille, le « G » haut de casse sans empattement, le « R » haut de casse avec une queue droite.

Fuente decorativa que genera movimiento. Motion es más o menos transparente, de modo que se puede utilizar para escribir sobre superficies diseñadas sin ocultar ni oscurecer los posibles motivos gráficos, colores o imágenes. Los caracteres se han diseñado empleando el mismo elemento formal: fragmentos de un muelle de anchura constante para astas, terminales y colas. Esta fuente de palo seco muestra unas curvas continuas de aspecto redondo, ligeramente cuadrado, sin contraste. Entre los caracteres calve destacan la G de caja baja con ojal y oreja, la G de caja alta sin espuela y la R de caja alta con cola recta.

Mud

Boris Kahl | www.volcano-type.de

riften, Fo tlabels & Design</title><meta http-e quiv="Content- pe" conte
rset =utf-8" /><linkrel="EditURI" type="applica ion/ rsd+xml" title ="RSD" hre
w. ante d e/blo api/ rsd" /> nk rel="alterna e" type= ppli tion/rss+x l"
nm nts" hre f="http://www.slan d.d /crs " /><ink rel= "alternate" type 'appl
+xml" title ="Slanted - Typo Weblog und Magazin RSS" href="http:/www. lante
li nk rel="s ortcut icon" hre f="/file s lanted_favic on.ico" type ="image/x-ico
e=" ext/ja ascript"><!--var az_cha nnel = „sla /node,type_authenticated_ ser
akte r,url_ node"; var az_u = .ads.slanted.de/ elivery/";var az_ s = „ ads .sl
iv ry/";var az_js = „ajs.p p";--></script>/><style ty pe="text/cs s" m dia="
il s css/1 48b1762 4e1c8 5218699 12d 4a c0bf d.css" ;</style>< scrip ty pe=
cript" src="/misc/ query.j "></scri pt><script ype="t ext/javascript" src="/
.j" </scrip ><script ty pe="text/ javascrip t" src="/m isc/collapse js"></ crip
e=" ext/ja ascript" rc="/sites/ all/ modu les/openads/mmm.js"></ scrip styl
" dia="p rint">Bim port„/th mes /slanted/print.css"; </style><!-- (if IE) sty
" m dia="a l">Bimpo rt „/th mes/slanted/fix-ie.css"; </style><!(e dif)--> scr
e=" ext/ja ascript src="/ them es/slanted/j email.js"></script><script type
ip" src=" /themes/ lanted/j sw fobject.js"></ script> script src= "htt //ww
ic .co m/urc in.js" pe="tex javascript"></ ript></ ead><body> <div id=" hea
v cl ss="si deboxitem block"> d v id="bannerD en"><sc ript language ="Ja aS cri
e=" ext/ja ascript"><!--// (CDATA(az_adj 5,'roo' ;//)> --></sc ipt></
v cl ss="si deboxitem lock"> iv id="logo">< mg src= "/files/site /slant ed .j
="Sl anted L ogo" title ="Slant ed" width="731" height=" 158" usem ap="# he der
ne headerM ap" id="h eaderM ap"><area shape ="rect" co ords="0,0 350, 70" h
v. lanted.de" alt="Sl anted Home age" /><area s ape="r ect" coords ="37 0,72
f=" / eint ag/slanted-06-sig s-symbols-ornamen ts#ka f_mich" alt ="Or der Sla

abcdefghijklmnopqrstuvwxyz
ABCDEFGHIJKLMNOPQRSTUVWXYZ
.,Ö

8/10 pt

abcdefghijklmnopqrstuvwxyz
ABCDEFGHIJKLMNOPQRSTUVWXYZ
.,Ö

10/12 pt

abcdefghijklmnopqrstuvwxyz
ABCDEFGHIJKLMNOPQRSTUVWXYZ
.,Ö

18/18 pt

abcdefghijklmnopqrstuvwxyz
ABCDEFGHIJKLMNOPQRSTUVWXYZ
.,Ö

24/24 pt

abcdefghijklmn
opqrstuvwxyz
ABCDEFGHIJKLMN
OPQRSTUVWXYZ

32/34 pt

This font is based on a strict pattern that has subsequently been soiled to achieve a more irregular structure. This enables the font to maintain its pixelated character while displaying an appearance of neglect. The result is a sharp sans serif font, with medium thick strokes and a hollow outline. The stems are of medium thickness with parallel edges. This decorative font is ideal for use in an informal environment, in headlines, posters and exhibition work. Despite the inclusion of upper and lowercase characters, it is too thick for small formats and is therefore not recommended for running text.

Cette police de caractères s'inspire d'un modèle qui a été antérieurement sali dans le but d'obtenir une structure davantage irrégulière. De cette manière, la police conserve son caractère pixélisé tout en transmettant un aspect négligé. Le résultat est une police sans serif bien dessinée, avec des traits d'une taille moyenne et un profil creux. Les hampes sont d'une épaisseur moyenne et les bords sont parallèles. Cette police décorative convient parfaitement à une situation informelle, des titres, des affiches et des expositions. Bien qu'elle comporte des caractères haut et bas de casse, elle est trop grasse pour des petits formats et n'est pas recommandée pour rédiger des textes.

Esta fuente se basa en un patrón estricto que posteriormente se ha ensuciado con el fin de alcanzar una estructura más irregular. De este modo, la fuente conserva su carácter pixelado a la vez que transmite un aspecto descuidado. Es una fuente de palo seco perfilada, con trazos de espesor medio y perfil hueco. Las astas son de grosor medio y de bordes paralelos. Esta fuente decorativa resulta muy apropiada en contextos informales, para titulares, carteles o como material de muestra. A pesar de incluir caracteres de caja alta y de caja baja, resulta demasiado gruesa para tamaños pequeños, por lo que no se recomienda para texto corrido.

Musicals

Brain Eaters Font Company (BEFCo) | www.braineaters.com

Hi-Fi

ABCDEFGHIJKLMNOPQRSTUVWXYZ[]
1234567890(.,;:?$¢&-*)(✦)

8/10 pt

ABCDEFGHIJKLMNOPQRSTUVWXYZ[]
1234567890(.,;:?$¢&-*)(✦)

10/12 pt

ABCDEFGHIJKLMNOPQRSTUVWXYZ[]
1234567890(.,;:?$¢&-*)(✦)

18/18 pt

ABCDEFGHIJKLMN
OPQRSTUVWXYZ[]
1234567890(.,;:?$¢&-*)(✦)

24/24 pt

ABCDEFGHIJKLMN
OPQRSTUVWXYZ[]
1234567890
(.,;:?$¢&-*)(✦)

32/34 pt

With its attractive, wavy appearance, it takes the poster designed by Bill Gold for the film *The Music Man* as its starting point. Directed by Morton DaCosta in 1962, this movie was one of the largest boxoffice hits of the year and since 2005 it has formed part of the U.S. National Film Registry. Robust and fun, this font is more suited to headlines, decorative and fanciful projects. The letters did not look very elegant when the whole alphabet was drawn out, but the typographer wanted to keep the flamboyant style of the original design, a handwritten feel that reflects times gone by.

Avec son apparence ondulée et séduisante, cette police s'est inspirée de l'affiche de la comédie musicale *The Music Man*, conçue par Bill Gold. Dirigé par Morton DaCosta en 1962, ce film a été un des plus grands succès de l'année et depuis 2005 elle fait partie du registre national du film américain. Solide et amusante, elles convient aux titres, aux projets fantaisistes et décoratifs. Les lettres semblaient peu élégantes en dessinant l'alphabet en entier, cependant le typographe a voulu conserver le style extravagant du concept original, c'est-à-dire la sensation d'un dessin fait à la main qui rappelle la vieille époque.

Atractiva y ondulante, esta tipografía está inspirada en el cartel diseñado por Bill Gold para la película *Vivir de ilusión* (1962), basada en el musical de Broadway *The Music Man*. Dirigida por Morton DaCosta, esta película fue uno de los mayores éxitos del año, y desde 2005 forma parte del Registro Nacional de Películas de los Estados Unidos. La tipografía, robusta y divertida, resulta más apropiada para titulares, proyectos caprichosos y decorativos. Las letras pueden parecer poco elegantes al dibujar el alfabeto entero, pero el tipógrafo quiso mantener el estrafalario estilo del concepto original, una sensación de diseño hecho a mano que refleja los viejos tiempos.

Nightfever Normal/Wide/Italic

Donald Beekman, DBXL | www.dbxl.nl

abcdefghijklmnopqrstuvwxyz[aöüßåøçñ]
ABCDEFGHIJKLMNOPQRSTUVWXYZ
1234567890[.,::?$£¥&-*]ÄÖÜÅØÇÑ

8/10 pt

abcdefghijklmnopqrstuvwxyz[aöüßåøçñ]
ABCDEFGHIJKLMNOPQRSTUVWXYZ
1234567890[.,::?$£¥&-*]ÄÖÜÅØÇÑ

8/10 pt

abcdefghijklmnopqrstuvwxyz[aöüßåøçñ]
ABCDEFGHIJKLMNOPQRSTUVWXYZ
1234567890[.,::?$£¥&-*]ÄÖÜÅØÇÑ

8/10 pt

abcdefghijklmn
opqrstuvwxyz[aöüßåøçñ]
ABCDEFGHIJKLMNOPQRSTUVWXYZ
1234567890[.,::?$£¥&-*]ÄÖÜÅØÇÑ

18/18 pt

abcdefghijklmn
opqrstuvwxyz[ööüßåøçñ]
ABCDEFGHIJKLMNOPQRSTUVWXYZ
1234567890[.,::?$£¥&-*]ÄÖÜÅØÇÑ

18/18 pt

abcdefghijklmnopqrstuvwxyz[aöüßåøçñ]
ABCDEFGHIJKLMNOPQRSTUVWXYZ
1234567890[.,::?¿$£¥&-*]ÄÖÜÅØÇÑ

18/18 pt

Nightfever was originally designed as a font for the disco/house record label going by the same name, a subsidiary of the Dutch company United Recordings. Six variants would later be added with a greater thickness to enhance the font's flexibility. The fonts were also adapted and the kerning (the process of adjusting the spacing between pairs of letters) and punctuation were made more precise. Following the disappearance of the record label, the Nightfever font continued to be used for other DBXL projects. The font was made available online in 2008 for free downloads.

La police de caractères Nightfever a été originalement conçue pour le label discographique disco/house du même nom, une filiale de la société hollandaise United Recordings. Par la suite, six autres versions plus grasses ont été créées afin de lui donner une plus grande flexibilité. Les polices ont également été adaptées, l'interlettrage (ou *kerning*, processus qui ajuste l'espace entre les lettres d'un mot), l'espacement et la ponctuation ont été ajustés avec précision. Plus tard avec la disparition du label discographique, la police Nightfever a continué d'être utilisée pour d'autres projets de DBXL. Cette police a été mise sur Internet en 2008 en téléchargement libre.

Nightfever fue originalmente diseñada como fuente para la discográfica de música disco/house con el mismo nombre, un sello subsidiario de la empresa holandesa United Recordings. Más tarde se añadirían seis variantes de más espesor para proporcionar más flexibilidad. Las fuentes también se adaptaron y el *kerning* (el espaciado entre pares de letras) y la puntuación fueron ajustados con precisión. Posteriormente a la desaparición del sello discográfico, la fuente Nightfever siguió utilizándose para otros proyectos de DBXL. La fuente se colgó en la red en 2008 para descargarse gratuitamente.

Ninamasina

Aleksandra Nina Knezevic | www.ninadesign.co.ba

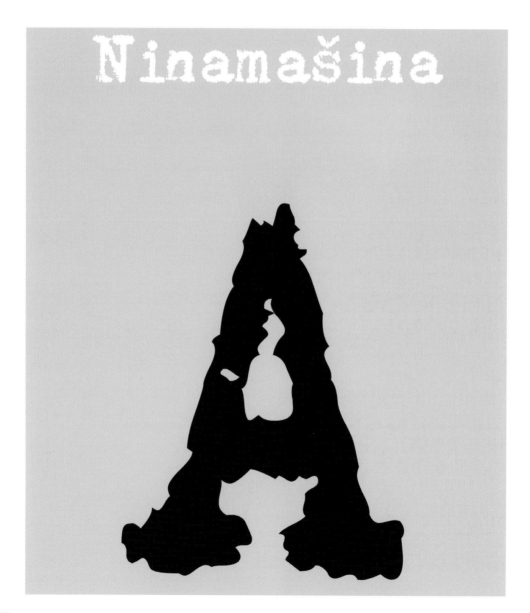

abcdefghijklmnopqrstuvwxyz
ABCDEFGHIJKLMNOPQRSTUVWXYZ
1234567890(.,;:?&)

8/10 pt

abcdefghijklmnopqrstuvwxyz
ABCDEFGHIJKLMNOPQRSTUVWXYZ
1234567890(.,;:?&)

10/12 pt

abcdefghijklmn
opqrstuvwxyz
ABCDEFGHIJKLMN
OPQRSTUVWXYZ
1234567890(.,;:?&)

18/18 pt

abcdefghijklmn
opqrstuvwxyz
ABCDEFGHIJKLMN
OPQRSTUVWXYZ
1234567890(.,;:?&)

24/24 pt

The font's design was based on the printed letters produced by the old typewriter belonging to the designer's father, who used it for years to write his own poems. The result is a Roman font with serifs. The outlines of each design are discontinuous to copy the effect of a manual typewriter. The feet of the characters are all the same and the terminals at the head and base are symmetrical and leaning. Key characters include: the double-storied lowercase a; the lowercase g with a short link, loop and ear; the uppercase G without a spur; and the uppercase R with a curved tail.

Cette police a été conçue en scannant les lettres imprimées par l'ancienne machine à écrire du père de la créatrice. Celui-ci l'avait utilisée pendant des années pour écrire ses poèmes. Le résultat est une police romaine à empattement. Le contour de chaque caractère est discontinu ce qui rappelle l'effet de la machine à écrire manuelle. Les pieds sont uniformes, le trait final de la tête et de la base est symétrique et incliné. Les caractères qui se distinguent sont : le « a » bas de casse en script, le « g » bas de casse avec un petit délié de jonction, boucle et oreille, le « G » haut de casse sans empattement et le « R » haut de casse avec une queue courbée.

La fuente se ha diseñado a partir del escaneo de las letras impresas realizadas con la antigua máquina de escribir del padre de la diseñadora, que la utilizó durante años para escribir sus poemas. El resultado es una fuente romana con remate. Los contornos de cada diseño son discontinuos, para simular el efecto de máquina de escribir manual. Los pies son uniformes y los trazos terminales de la cabeza y de la base son simétricos e inclinados. Los caracteres clave que destacan son la a de caja baja de dos pisos, la g de caja baja de ligadura corta con ojal y oreja, la G de caja alta sin espuela y la R de caja alta con cola curva.

Objects

Lars Harmsen | www.volcano-type.de

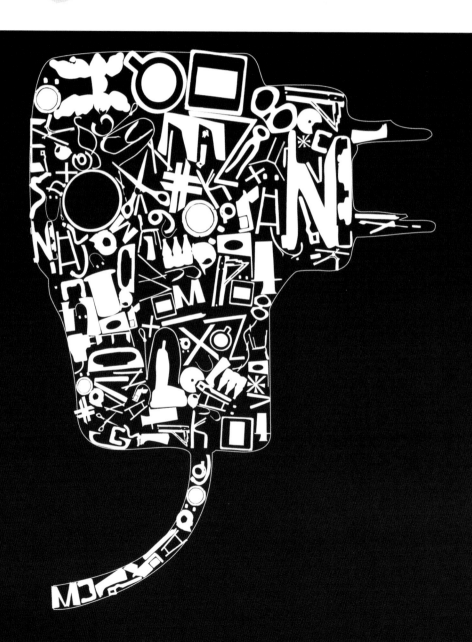

abcdeRghijklmnopqrstuvwxyz[äöüßç]
A8CDEFGHIJKLMN◻P◖IST⋃∨WXYZ
1234567890○(,;.?ſ–*)ÄⒺⓤ

8/10 pt

abcdeRghijklmnopqrstuvwxyz[äöüßç]
A8CDEFGHIJKLMN◻P◖IST⋃∨WXYZ
1234567890○(,;.?ſ–*)ÄⒺⓤ

10/12 pt

abcdeRghijklmnopqrstuvwxyz[äöüßç]
A8CDEFGHIJKLMN◻P◖IST⋃∨WXYZ
1234567890○(,;.?ſ–*)ÄⒺⓤ

18/18 pt

abcdeRghijklmn
opqrstuvwxyz[äöüßç]
A8CDEFGHIJKLMN
◻P◖IST⋃∨WXYZ
1234567890○(,;.?ſ–*)ÄⒺⓤ

24/24 pt

The purpose of this font was to broaden the spectrum of strokes generally used in typographic design. The letters here are not based on the designs drafted on paper, but have been formed physically using everyday objects. First of all, each letter-physical object has been meticulously photographed for subsequent digitilization. Finally, once they have been converted into a digital format, the designs are vectorized to shape the outline and obtain the required form. Objects such as ladders, ovens, cups, pliers, scissors, and bottles are noted while they also contribute to forming each character.

Cette police est née de l'intention d'élargir le spectre des traits qui sont le plus souvent utilisés dans le design de la typographie. Les lettres ne proviennent pas de dessins réalisés sur papier, mais elles prennent les formes physiques d'objets du quotidien. Dans un premier temps, chaque lettre-objet a été méticuleusement photographiée puis numérisée. Ensuite, une fois qu'elles ont été passées au format numérique, les images ont été vectorisées en affinant les contours afin d'obtenir la forme voulue. Les caractères sont formés à partir d'objets comme les escaliers, les fours, les tasses, les pinces, les ciseaux ou les bouteilles.

Nace con la intención de ampliar el espectro de los trazos generalmente utilizados en el diseño de tipografía. Aquí, las letras no parten de los diseños plasmados sobre el papel, sino que se han formado físicamente a partir de objetos cotidianos. En primer lugar, cada letra-objeto físico se ha fotografiado meticulosamente para su posterior digitalización. Finalmente, una vez convertidos en formato digital, los diseños se han vectorizado para perfilar el contorno hasta obtener la forma deseada. Objetos como escaleras, hornos, tazas, alicates, tijeras, botellas se distinguen al mismo tiempo que construyen cada uno de los caracteres.

On Procession

Elasticbrand, Arjen Noordeman & Christie Wright | www.elasticbrand.net

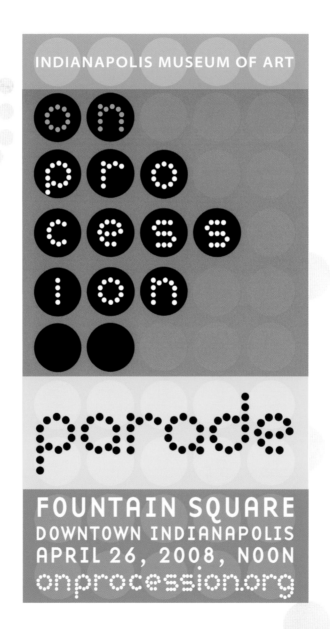

abcdefghijklmnopqrstuvwxyz[]
ABCDEFGHIJKLMNOPQRSTUVWXYZ
1234567890(,:;?$£€¥—*)

8/10 pt

abcdefghijklmnopqrstuvwxyz[]
ABCDEFGHIJKLMNOPQRSTUVWXYZ
1234567890(,:;?$£€¥—*)

10/12 pt

abcdefghijklmnopqrstuvwxyz[]
ABCDEFGHIJKLMNOPQRSTUVWXYZ
1234567890(,:;?$£€¥—*)

18/18 pt

abcdefghijklmn
opqrstuvwxyz[]
ABCDEFGHIJKLMN
OPQRSTUVWXYZ
1234567890(,:;?$£€¥—*)

24/24 pt

This font was created to design the poster for an exhibition entitled On Procession for the Indianapolis Museum of Art, USA. The font emerged as the stylization of the circular shape of the confetti used in parades and processions. This exhibition celebrates artwork that uses the medium of public parades as a creative resource. Using the framework of the artistic display, a real art parade has also been scheduled to take place in the center of Indianapolis. Elasticbrand has since created a wide range of promotional materials, along with a catalog, and has designed several names for exhibitions using this font.

Conçue pour orner l'affiche d'une exposition à l'Indianapolis Museum of Art aux États-Unis, On Procession provient de la stylisation de la forme circulaire du confetti utilisé dans les défilés. Cette exposition célèbre l'art qui utilise les défilés publics comme un support créatif. Dans le cadre de l'exposition, un défilé artistique qui a lieu dans le centre d'Indianapolis a été organisé. Par la suite, Elasticbrand a créé une grande variété de matériaux promotionnels, un catalogue et il a réalisé plusieurs titres pour des expositions en utilisant cette même police.

Creada para el cartel de la exposición titulada On Procession en el Indianapolis Museum of Art de Estados Unidos, esta fuente surge de la estilización de la forma circular del confeti que se lanza en los desfiles. La exposición estaba dedicada al arte que utiliza el medio de los desfiles públicos como soporte creativo. En el marco de la muestra artística, también se programó un desfile, que se celebró en el centro de Indianápolis. Posteriormente, Elasticbrand diseñó una gran variedad de materiales promocionales, un catálogo, y también ha diseñado varios títulos de exposiciones aplicando esta misma fuente.

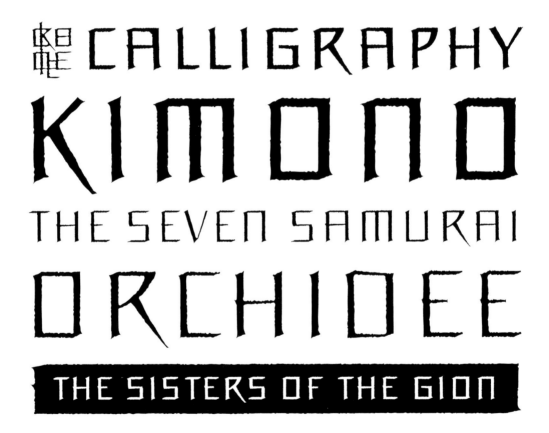

CALLIGRAPHY

KIMONO

THE SEVEN SAMURAI

ORCHIDEE

THE SISTERS OF THE GION

ABCDEFGHIJKLMNOPQRSTUVWXYZ
ÄÖÜ

8/10 pt

ABCDEFGHIJKLMNOPQRSTUVWXYZ
ÄÖÜ

8/10 pt

ABCDEFGHIJKLMNOPQRSTUVWXYZ
ÄÖÜ

10/12 pt

ABCDEFGHIJKLMNOPQRSTUVWXYZ
ÄÖÜ

10/12 pt

ABCDEFGHIJKLMN
OPQRSTUVWXYZ
ÄÖÜ

18/18 pt

ABCDEFGHIJKLMN
OPQRSTUVWXYZ
ÄÖÜ

18/18 pt

The font was created as part of the stationery for the Orchidee Restaurant located inside the luxury Hotel Quellenhof in Aachen, Germany. The restaurant specializes in transcultural Eurasian cuisine. For this reason, the designer has blended some elements taken from traditional Asian typography with European typography. The letters have been designed using Freehand with the repetition of just a few basic elements. To create a rougher outline, the designer has used a Xerox machine to enable him to insert a number of chaotic elements to give the font a handwritten feel.

Cette police de caractères a été conçue pour la documentation du restaurant Orchidée situé dans l'hôtel de luxe Quellenhof à Aachen, en Allemagne. Ce restaurant est spécialisé dans la cuisine européenne et asiatique. Pour cette raison, le graphiste a associé les éléments de la typographie traditionnelle asiatique à la typographie européenne. Les lettres ont été dessinées avec freehand en répétant seulement quelques éléments de base. Afin de créer un contour plus rugueux, le graphiste a utilisé une photocopieuse Xerox ce qui lui a permis d'introduire certains éléments chaotiques pour donner un côté « fait main » à cette police.

La fuente se creó como parte de la papelería para el restaurante Orchidee, situado en el hotel de lujo Quellenhof, en la ciudad alemana de Aquisgrán. El restaurante está especializado en cocina asiática y europea. Por este motivo, el diseñador ha combinado elementos de las tipografías tradicionales de ambas culturas. Las letras se han diseñado con Freehand a través de la repetición de tan sólo unos pocos elementos básicos. Para crear un contorno más rugoso, el diseñador ha utilizado una fotocopiadora Xerox con la intención de introducir algunos elementos caóticos que proporcionan a la fuente un aspecto de «hecho a mano».

Pagra

Font-o-Rama | www.font-o-rama.com

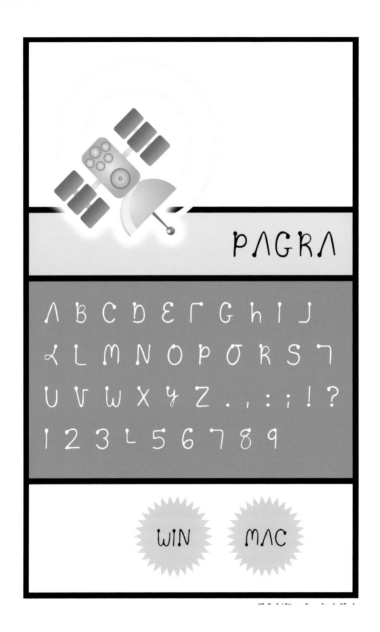

ΛBCΔΕΓGhIJ✕LMNOPΟRSꓶUⅤⱲXⵀΖ
123L567890..;;?−

8/10 pt

ΛBCΔΕΓGhIJ✕LMNOPΟRSꓶUⅤⱲXⵀΖ
123L567890..;;?−

10/12 pt

ΛBCΔΕΓGhIJ✕LMNOPΟRSꓶUⅤⱲXⵀΖ
123L567890..;;?−

18/18 pt

ΛBCΔΕΓGhIJ✕LMN
OPΟRSꓶUⅤⱲXⵀΖ
123L567890..;;?−

24/24 pt

ΛBCΔΕΓGhIJ✕LMN
OPΟRSꓶUⅤⱲXⵀΖ
123L567890..;;?−

32/34 pt

This apparently handwritten font is constructed continuously to produce the appearance of oval curves. The corners are rounded and the stems are very thin and have parallel edges. This is a sans serif font, with one of the stem terminals in each letter being adorned with a circular flourish or swash. The peculiarity of this font lies in the absence of any formal elements such as: the crossbar of the uppercase A; the cross on the uppercase F; the stem of the uppercase K; the absence of a tail on the uppercase Q; and the right arm of the terminal on the uppercase T.

Ressemblant à une écriture manuscrite, cette police a une forme continue avec des courbes ovales. Les extrémités sont arrondies et les fûts très fins avec des bords parallèles. Il s'agit d'une police sans serif, dont l'extrémité d'une des hampes de chaque lettre est ornée d'un motif circulaire. La particularité de cette police réside dans l'absence de certains éléments comme : la traverse du « A » haut de casse et du « F » haut de casse, la hampe du « K » bas de casse, la queue du « Q » bas de casse ainsi que la partie droite de la hampe verticale du « T » haut de casse.

Con aspecto de escritura a mano, esta fuente es de construcción continua con aspecto de las curvas ovalado. Las esquinas son redondeadas y las astas verticales son muy finas y de bordes paralelos. Se trata de una fuente de palo seco, donde el extremo de una de las astas de cada letra queda embellecido con un motivo en forma de mancha circular. La peculiaridad de esta fuente recae en la ausencia de algunos elementos formales, como el asta horizontal de la A de caja alta, la cruz de la F de caja alta, el asta vertical de la K de caja alta, la ausencia de la cola en la Q de caja alta y el brazo derecho en el terminal de la T de caja alta.

Porcelain

Misprinted Type | www.misprintedtype.com

abcdefghijklmnopqrstuvwxyzäöüåçñ
ABCDEFGHIJKLMNOPQRSTUVWXYZ
1234567890(.,;:?¡§&~·*)¡ÀÖÜ ÅÇÑ

8/10 pt

abcdefghijklmnopqrstuvwxyzäöüåçñ
ABCDEFGHIJKLMNOPQRSTUVWXYZ
1234567890(.,;:?¡§&~·*)¡ÀÖÜ ÅÇÑ

10/12 pt

abcdefghijklmnopqrstuvwxyzäöüåçñ
ABCDEFGHIJKLMN
OPQRSTUVWXYZ
1234567890(.,;:?¡§&~·*)¡ÀÖÜ ÅÇÑ

18/18 pt

abcdefghijklmnopqrstuvwxyzäöüåçñ
ABCDEFGHIJKLMN
OPQRSTUVWXYZ
1234567890(.,;:?¡§&~·*)¡ÀÖÜ ÅÇÑ

24/24 pt

From the outset, the style of this font has been classified as grunge. The stroke suggests the design tool is a nib used to convey the sense of being clean but unfinished. It is a calligraphic style devoid of any serifs with the characters joined up. The stem terminals of the uppercase characters are prolonged in all directions by means of a mass of strokes to the point where they all become intertwined. The font is delicate and attractive while also being very dynamic. This elegant handwritten lettering is generally used for experimental grunge projects.

Dès son apparition, cette police a été classée dans le style *grunge*. Le tracé des lettres donne l'impression que la plume a été l'outil de travail, pour transmettre la sensation qu'elles sont nettes mais inachevées. Il s'agit d'un style calligraphique sans serif avec des lettres liées entre elles. Les extrémités des hampes des caractères haut de casse se prolongent dans tous les sens par de nombreux traits qui s'entremêlent. Cette police est belle, délicate et en même temps très dynamique. Cette lettre manuscrite élégante s'utilise le plus souvent pour des projets expérimentaux grunge, alternatif.

Desde su inicio, ha sido siempre catalogada como una fuente de estilo *grunge*. El trazo hace referencia a la plumilla como herramienta de diseño para transmitir una sensación nítida e inacabada. Se trata de una fuente caligráfica sin remates que presenta unión entre los caracteres. Los extremos de las astas de los caracteres de caja alta se prolongan en todas direcciones a través de multitud de trazos, hasta enrocarse entre sí. La fuente resulta bonita, delicada y al mismo tiempo muy dinámica. Esta elegante letra manuscrita se utiliza generalmente para proyectos de estilo experimental, *grunge* o alternativo.

Proto Uncertain

etrus, Linus, Anacletus, Clemens, Evaristus, Alexander, Xystus, Telesphorus, Hyginus, Pius,
Pius, Soterius, Eleutherius, Victor, Zephyrinus, Callistus, Urbanus, Pontianus, Anterus,
nus, Cornelius, Lucius, Dionysius, Felix, Eutychianus, Caius, Marcellinus, Marcellus,
Eusebius, M... des, Silv... Proto Uncertain erius, Damasus, Siricius, Anastasius,
nnocent... Zos... Boni... Cel... ... ... ertius, Leo Magnus, Hilarius, Simplicius,
elix Tertius(Secundus), Gelasius, Anastasius Secundus, Symmachus, Hormisdus, Ioannes, Felix
Quartus(Tertius), Bonifacius Secundus, Ioannes Secundus, Agapetus, Silverius, Vigilius, Pelagius,
oannes Tertius, Benedictus, Pelagius Secundus, Gregorius Magnus, Sabinianus, Bonifacius
Tertius, Bonifacius Quartus, Adeodatus, Bonifacius Quintus, Honorius, Severinus, Ioannes
Quartus, Theodorus, Martinus, Eugenius, Vitalianus, Adeodatus Secundus, Donus, Agatho,
Leo Secundus, Benedictus Secundus, Ioannes Quintus, Conon, Sergius, Ioannes Sextus, Ioannes
Septimus, Sisinnius, Constantinus, Gregorius Secundus, Gregorius Tertius, Zacharias,
Stephanus, Stephanus Secundus, Paulus, Stephanus Tertius, Hadrianus, Leo Tertius,
Stephanus Quartus, Paschalis, Eugenius Secundus, Valentinus, Gregorius Quartus, Sergius
Secundus, Leo Quartus, Benedictus Tertius, Nicolaus Magnus, Hadrianus Secundus, Ioannes
Octavus, Marinus, Hadrianus Tertius, Stephanus Quintus, Formosus, Bonifacius Sextus,
Stephanus Sextus, Romanus, Theodorus Secundus, Ioannes Nonus, Benedictus Quartus, Leo
Quintus, Sergius Tertius, Anastasius Tertius, Lando, Ioannes Decimus, Leo Sextus, Ioannes
Undecimus, Leo Septimus, Stephanus Octavus, Marinus Secundus, Stephanus Septimus,
Agapetus Secundus, Ioannes Duodecimus, Benedictus Quintus, Leo Octavus, Ioannes Tertius
Decimus, Benedictus Sextus, Benedictus Septimus, Ioannes Quartus Decimus, Ioannes Quintus
Decimus, Gregorius Quintus, Silvester Secundus, Ioannes Septimus Decimus, Ioannes
Duodevicesimus, Sergius Quartus, Benedictus Octavus, Ioannes Undevicesimus, Benedictus Nonus,
Silvester Tertius, Benedictus Nonus, Gregorius Sextus, Clemens Secundus, Benedictus Nonus
Damasus Secundus, Leo Nonus, Victor Secundus, Stephanus Nonus, Nicolaus Secundus
Alexander Secundus, Gregorius Septimus, Victor Tertius, Urbanus Secundus, Paschalis
Secundus, Gelasius Secundus, Callistus Secundus, Honorius Secundus, Innocentius Secundus,
Coelestinus Secundus, Lucius Secundus, Eugenius Tertius, Anastasius Quartus, Hadrianus
Quartus, Alexander Tertius, Lucius Tertius, Urbanus Tertius, Gregorius Octavus, Clemens
Tertius, Coelestinus Tertius, Innocentius Tertius, Honorius Tertius, Gregorius Nonus, Coelestinus
Quartus, Innocentius Quartus, Alexander Quartus, Urbanus Quartus, Clemens Quartus,
Gregorius Decimus, Innocentius Quintus, Hadrianus Quintus, Ioannes Vicesimus Primus, Nicolaus
Tertius, Martinus Quartus, Honorius Quartus, Nicolaus Quartus, Coelestinus Quintus,
Bonifacius Octavus, Benedictus Undecimus, Clemens Quintus, Ioannes Vicesimus Secundus,
Benedictus Duodecimus, Clemens Sextus, Innocentius Sextus, Urbanus Quintus, Gregorius
Undecimus, Urbanus Sextus, Bonifacius Nonus, Innocentius Septimus, Gregorius Duodecimus,
Martinus Quintus, Eugenius Quartus, Nicolaus Quintus, Callistus Tertius, Pius Secundus,
Paulus Secundus, Xystus Quartus, Innocentius Octavus, Alexander Sextus, Pius Tertius, Iulius
Secundus, Leo Decimus, Hadrianus Sextus, Clemens Septimus, Paulus Tertius, Iulius Tertius,
Marcellus Secundus, Paulus Quartus, Pius Quartus, Pius Quintus, Gregorius Tertius Decimus,
Xystus Quintus, Urbanus Septimus, Gregorius Quartus Decimus, Innocentius Nonus, Clemens
Octavus, Leo Undecimus, Paulus Quintus, Gregorius Quintus Decimus, Urbanus Octavus,
Innocentius Decimus, Alexander Septimus, Clemens Nonus, Clemens Decimus, Innocentius Undecimus,
Alexander Octavus, Innocentius Duodecimus, Clemens Undecimus, Innocentius Tertius Decimus,
Benedictus Tertius Decimus, Clemens Duodecimus, Benedictus Quartus Decimus, Clemens Tertius
Decimus, Clemens Quartus Decimus, Pius Sextus, Pius Septimus, Leo Duodecimus, Pius Octavus,
Gregorius Sextus Decimus, Pius Nonus, Leo Tertius Decimus, Pius Decimus, Benedictus Quintus
Decimus, Pius Undecimus, Pius Duodecimus, Ioannes Vicesimus Tertius, Paulus Sextus, Ioannes
Paulus Primus, Ioannes Paulus Secundus, Benedictus Sextus Decimus

abcdef ghijklmnopq rstuvwx yz[äöüßåøœoeçñ]
ABCDEFGHIJKLMNOPQRSTUVWXYZ
1234567890(.,;:?¿$¢£€¥∅-*){ÄÖÜÅØÆŒÇÑ}

8/10 pt

abcdef ghijklmnopq rstuvwx yz[äöüßåøœoeçñ]
ABCDEFGHIJKLMNOPQRSTUVWXYZ
1234567890(.,;:?¿$¢£€¥∅-*){ÄÖÜÅØÆŒÇÑ}

10/12 pt

abcdef ghijklmnopq rstuvwx yz[äöüßåøœoeçñ]
ABCDEFGHIJKLMNOPQRSTUVWXYZ
1234567890
(.,;:?¿$¢£€¥∅-*){ÄÖÜÅØÆŒÇÑ}

18/18 pt

abcdef ghijklmnopq rstuvwx yz
[äöüßåøœoeçñ]
ABCDEFGHIJKLMNO
PQRSTUVWXYZ
1234567890
(.,;:?¿$¢£€¥∅-*){ÄÖÜÅØÆŒÇÑ}

24/24 pt

This typographer has managed to transform his own handwriting into a font. He has written out each character very meticulously and conscientiously for subsequent digitalization, keeping to the original form as much as possible. The result is a font that it is faintly reminiscent of automatic writing. However, contrary to what this typographer proposes or the creative process advocated by the surrealist movement, he simply adopts a normal state of consciousness and then starts to write. The set is fairly complete, with upper and lowercase characters, accents, punctuation marks and symbols.

Le typographe a réussi à transformer son écriture personnelle en une police de caractères. Il a écrit de façon consciencieuse et méticuleuse tous les caractères puis il les a numérisés en essayant de conserver le plus possible leur forme originale. Le résultat est une police donnant légèrement l'impression d'une écriture automatique. Toutefois, contrairement à ce que propose cette technique ou le procédé créatif défendu par le mouvement surréaliste, le typographe a simplement adopté un état de conscience normal pour ensuite se mettre à écrire. L'ensemble est assez complet, avec des caractères haut de casse et bas de casse, des accents, des signes de ponctuation et des symboles.

El tipógrafo ha logrado transformar su escritura personal en una fuente. Ha escrito cada carácter de forma meticulosa y consciente para después digitalizarlos, conservando en todo lo posible la forma original. El resultado es una fuente que posee un toque de escritura automática. Sin embargo, al contrario de lo que propone este proceso creativo defendido por el movimiento surrealista, el tipógrafo simplemente ha adoptado un estado de consciencia usual y luego se ha dispuesto a escribir sobre papel. El set es bastante completo, con caracteres de caja alta y baja, acentos, signos de puntuación y símbolos.

Raw Macro

Popdog Fonts | popdog_fonts.tripod.com

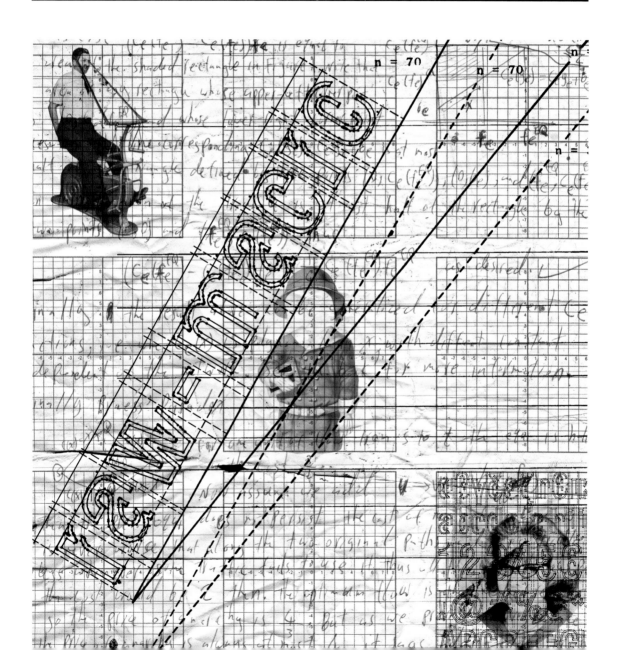

8/10 pt

10/12 pt

18/18 pt

24/24 pt

This book is the first time that Raw Macro is being published in a free font version. Each character appears to be sketched simulating the metric grid of the window for drawing outlines in a CAD software program. The guidelines show the kerning adjustment, the baseline and the nodes. The right side of each character in this serifless font seems to be partly unfinished. The construction of the characters is discontinuous with the appearance of oval curves, devoid of any contrast. Key characters include: the uppercase A with its straight apex; the uppercase G with a vertical spur; and the uppercase Q with its tail cutting through the bowl.

Raw Macro est accessible au public pour la première fois en version gratuite grâce à ce livre. Cette police ressemble à une ébauche de chaque caractère, simulant la métrique du dessin dans un logiciel de design. Les repères signalent l'ajustement de l'interlettrage, la ligne de base et les jonctions. Dans cette police sans serif la partie droite de chaque caractère semble partiellement inachevée. La forme est discontinue avec des courbes ovales, sans contraste. Les caractères emblématiques sont : le « A » haut de casse avec une pointe droite, le « G » haut de casse avec empattement vertical, le « Q » haut de casse dont la queue coupe la panse.

Raw Macro se hace pública por primera vez en versión Free Font con este libro. Cada carácter aparece esbozado simulando la retícula métrica de la ventana de dibujo de contornos en un software de diseño. Las guías muestran el ajuste del *kerning*, la línea base y los nodos. En esta fuente de palo seco, el lado derecho de cada carácter aparece parcialmente inacabado. La construcción es discontinua y con aspecto de la curva ovalado, sin contraste. Los caracteres clave destacados son la A de caja alta con vértice recto, la G de caja alta con espuela vertical y la Q de caja alta con cola que corta el anillo.

Record

Font-o-Rama | www.font-o-rama.com

```
ABCDEFGHIJKLMNOPQRSTUVWXYZ
1234567890(.,;:?¿$¢&-×)(ÄÖÜÁÔÇÑ)
```

8/10 pt

```
ABCDEFGHIJKLMNOPQRSTUVWXYZ
1234567890
(.,;:?¿$¢&-×)(ÄÖÜÁÔÇÑ)
```

10/12 pt

```
ABCDEFGHIJKLMN
OPQRSTUVWXYZ
1234567890
(.,;:?¿$¢&-×)
(ÄÖÜÁÔÇÑ)
```

18/18 pt

```
ABCDEFGHIJKLM
NOPQRSTUVWXYZ
1234567890
(.,;:?¿$¢&-×)
(ÄÖÜÁÔÇÑ)
```

24/24 pt

A font originally designed for 3D animation using a Sony camcorder. It belongs to the LCD font family, which simulate liquid crystal displays. It has a very technological appearance and is therefore very appropriate for this type of design. However, with the development of new technologies it is beginning to look a bit retro. Optimized for use with low-resolution devices, it is not meant for paper but rather to be shown on screen. This type of font is designed taking the pixel grid into account to make it more readable. The result is a sans serif pixel font with monospaced characters.

Cette police était à l'origine conçue pour une animation en 3D d'un caméscope Sony. Elle appartient à la famille typographique LCD qui imite les écrans à cristaux liquides. D'apparence technologique, elle convient pour ce genre de dessins mais en raison de l'avancée des nouvelles technologies elle a un côté plutôt rétro. Optimisée pour être montrée en diapositives de faible résolution, elle n'est pas destinée au papier mais à l'écran. Ce genre de polices est conçu en tenant compte des pixels afin d'être lisible. Le résultat est une police pixélisée, sans serif avec des caractères à chasse fixe.

Fuente originalmente diseñada para una animación de 3D de una videocámara Sony. Pertenece al grupo de tipografías LCD, que son aquellas que simulan las pantallas de cristal líquido. Su apariencia es muy tecnológica, por lo que resulta muy apropiada para ese tipo de diseños aunque, debido al avance de las nuevas tecnologías, adquiere un carácter más retro. Optimizada para ser mostrada en dispositivos de baja resolución, su destino no es el papel sino la pantalla. Este tipo de fuentes están diseñadas teniendo en cuenta la retícula de píxeles para facilitar su legibilidad. El resultado es una fuente pixelada, de palo seco y caracteres monoespaciados.

Risco Rabisco

Ana Paula Putka | www.anaputka.carbonmade.com

abcdefghijklmnopqrstuvwxyzç
ABCDEFGHIJKLMNOPQRSTUVWXYZ

8/10 pt

abcdefghijklmnopqrstuvwxyzç
ABCDEFGHIJKLMNOPQRSTUVWXYZ

10/12 pt

abcdefghijklmnopqrstuvwxyzç
ABCDEFGHIJKLMNOPQRSTUVWXYZ

18/18 pt

abcdefghijklmnopqrstuvwxyzç
ABCDEFGHIJKLMN
OPQRSTUVWXYZ

24/24 pt

This font, based on the texture of chalk, is appealing on account of its primary strokes, which express spontaneity and are full of connotations alluding to childhood. The stroke made with chalk is easily detected at the ends of the stems, which look uneven and poorly defined. This typeface is ideal for contemporary designs or in supplements to graphic artwork with related themes. The curves are continuous with a round, slightly squarish appearance. The strokes are completely uneven and the stems are not parallel. This is a sans-serif font without any contrast.

Fondée sur la texture de l'écriture à la craie, cette police incite à représenter les traits primaires, qui expriment la spontanéité avec de nombreuses connotations enfantines. Le trait tracé à la craie est facilement repérable aux extrémités des hampes qui semblent indéfinies et irrégulières. Elle est appropriée pour des créations contemporaines et pour compléter des ensembles graphiques avec des thèmes qui ont un rapport. Les courbes sont continues, d'aspect circulaire légèrement carré. Les traits sont totalement irréguliers et les hampes verticales ne sont pas parallèles. Cette police sans serif n'a pas de contraste.

Basada en la textura de la escritura con tiza, esta fuente invita a representar los trazos primarios, que expresan espontaneidad un carácter infantil. El trazo producido con la tiza se detecta fácilmente en los extremos de las astas, que son indefinidos e irregulares. Resulta muy adecuada para aplicar en diseños contemporáneos o en complementos de piezas gráficas con temas relacionados. Las curvas son continuas con aspecto redondo y ligeramente cuadrado. Los trazos son totalmente irregulares y las astas verticales no son paralelas. Esta fuente de palo seco no muestra contraste.

Roadway

K-Type/Keith Bates | www.k-type.com/

ABCDEFGHIJKLMNOPQRSTUVWXYZ[ÄÖÜßÅØÆŒÇÑ]
ABCDEFGHIJKLMNOPQRSTUVWXYZ
1234567890(.,:·?¿$ᶜ£€¥&-*)(ÄÖÜÅØÆŒÇÑ}

8/10 pt

ABCDEFGHIJKLMNOPQRSTUVWXYZ[ÄÖÜßÅØÆŒÇÑ]
ABCDEFGHIJKLMNOPQRSTUVWXYZ
1234567890(.,:·?¿$ᶜ£€¥&-*)(ÄÖÜÅØÆŒÇÑ}

10/12 pt

ABCDEFGHIJKLMNOPQRSTUVWXYZ[ÄÖÜßÅØÆŒÇÑ]
ABCDEFGHIJKLMNOPQRSTUVWXYZ
1234567890(.,:·?¿$ᶜ£€¥&-*)(ÄÖÜÅØÆŒÇÑ}

18/18 pt

ABCDEFGHIJKLMNOPQRSTUVWXYZ[ÄÖÜßÅØÆŒÇÑ]
ABCDEFGHIJKLMNOPQRSTUVWXYZ
1234567890
(.,:·?¿$ᶜ£€¥&-*)(ÄÖÜÅØÆŒÇÑ}

24/24 pt

This font is based on the typeface used for signposts on U.S. freeways and also applied to traffic signs in the streets of New York. The freeway signs usually incorporate two different thicknesses of typeface. For this reason, the typographer has designed this font of uppercase characters in two styles: a condensed form for key words and half this size for subscripts. This set includes the acute and grave accent, circumflex, dieresis and tilde for the Ã, Ñ and Õ, plus the numbers and a large variety of punctuation marks and symbols.

Cette police s'inspire de la typographie utilisée pour les panneaux de signalisation des autoroutes américaines, également appliquée aux signalisations des rues de New-York. Les panneaux routiers sont généralement composés de deux grosseurs de police différentes. Pour cela, le typographe a conçu cette police haut de casse de deux manières différentes : une forme condensée pour les mots principaux et un format réduit de moitié pour les autres. Cette police propose des accents graves, aigus, circonflexes, des trémas, des tildes sur le « Ã », le « Ñ » et le « Õ », ainsi qu'une grande variété de signes de ponctuation et de symboles.

Está basada en la tipografía utilizada en la señalización de las autopistas de Estados Unidos y también en las señales de tráfico de las calles de Nueva York. Estos rótulos acostumbran a incorporar en la misma señal dos espesores de fuente diferentes. De la misma manera, el tipógrafo ha diseñado esta fuente de caracteres de caja alta con dos estilos: de forma condensada para las palabras principales y de un tamaño reducido a la mitad para los subíndices. Este set incluye acentos agudo, grave, circunflejo, diéresis y tilde de la Ã, Ñ y Õ, así como números y una gran variedad de signos de puntuación y símbolos.

Rondi

Ewen Prigent | www.laboitegraphique.fr

abcdefghijklmnopqrstuvwxyz
1234567890(.,;:?€&-"-)(äöüåøææçñ)

8/10 pt

abcdefghijklmnopqrstuvwxyz
1234567890(.,;:?€&-"-)(äöüåøææçñ)

10/12 pt

abcdefghijklmnopqrstuvwxyz
1234567890(.,;:?€&-"-)(äöüåøææçñ)

18/18 pt

abcdefghijklmnopqrstuvwxyz
1234567890(.,;:?€&-"-)(äöüåøææçñ)

24/24 pt

abcdefghijklmn
opqrstuvwxyz
1234567890
(.,;:?€&-"-)(äöüåøææçñ)

32/34 pt

Rondi is a soft and sober typeface created in May 2009. This font conveys a sense of gentleness by adopting a playful aspect on account of its roundness and lack of angles. The letters are constructed continuously and are composed of loose, individual elements that come together. The curves appear to be fractured and the arcs are almost closed. The ends of the stems and terminals in this sans serif font have rounded angles. The characters K, R and S appear as small caps and the rest in lowercase letters. Key characters include: the single-storied a and g; the oblique bar on the e.

Rondi est une typographie agréable et sobre créée en mai 2009. Cette police de caractères provoque une sensation de douceur tout en ayant un aspect ludique par sa rondeur et l'absence d'angles. De forme homogène, les lettres sont composées d'éléments individuels qui parviennent à se toucher. Les courbes sont fracturées et les cercles presque fermés. Les extrémités des hampes de cette police sans serif sont arrondies. Les lettres K, R, et S sont en petites capitales tandis que les autres sont en bas de casse. Les caractères clés sont : le « a » et le « g » sur un niveau et le « e » avec une traverse oblique.

Rondi es una escritura amable y sobria creada en mayo de 2009. Su redondez y ausencia de ángulos le otorgan una sensación de dulzura y un carácter lúdico. De construcción continua, las letras están compuestas por elementos individuales sueltos que se llegan a tocar. Las curvas aparecen fracturadas y los arcos son casi cerrados. Esta fuente de palo seco muestra los extremos de las astas y los terminales con ángulos redondeados. Los caracteres K, R y S aparecen en versalitas y el resto en caja baja. Entre los caracteres clave se encuentran la a y la g de un piso y e con barra oblicua.

Saltpeter N Fungus

Galdino Otten | galdinoottenbr.blogspot.com

abcdefghijklmnopqrstuvWxyz[]
ABCDEᴚᴛGHIJKLMNOPQRSTUVWXYZ
1234567890[.,::?$&-}{çñ}

8/10 pt

abcdefghijklmnopqrstuvWxyz[]
ABCDEᴚᴛGHIJKLMNOPQRSTUVWXYZ
1234567890[.,::?$&-}{çñ}

10/12 pt

abcdefghijklmnopqrstuvWxyz[]
ABCDEᴚᴛGHIJKLMN
OPQRSTUVWXYZ
1234567890[.,::?$&-}{çñ}

18/18 pt

abcdefghijklmn
opqrstuvWxyz[]
ABCDEᴚᴛGHIJKLMN
OPQRSTUVWXYZ
1234567890
[.,::?$&-}{çñ}

24/24 pt

This font represents the opposition to the consumer discourse advocated by the mainstream media, selling a world that has been perfected and is totally unreal. It reminds us of how the lack of permanence is a concept that forms an inherent part of life, and more specifically, the impermanence of matter: people grow old and things wear out. Everything is finite and ephemeral or, seen from another perspective, everything is in a constant state of flux. The result is a sans serif font that is decorative and has a somewhat eroded appearance, along with certain characters with flourishes, which are extremely irregular in shape. It combines thickly drawn stems with others that are much thinner. The curves are continuous and have a circular appearance without any contrast.

Cette police représente l'opposition au discours consommateur des grands médias qui vendent un monde parfait et irréel. Elle nous rappelle le concept d'impermanence inhérent à la vie et à la matière : les gens vieillissent et les choses s'usent. Tout est éphémère et finit ou, en d'autres termes, tout change en permanence. Le résultat obtenu est une police à tige sèche, combinant quelques caractères avec empattement, décorative et érodée, dont les caractères sont excessivement irréguliers. Elle associe des hampes à trait épais avec des hampes plus fines. Les courbes sont continues, d'aspect circulaire sans contraste.

Representa la oposición al discurso consumista de los medios de comunicación, y su mundo perfecto e irreal. Esta fuente nos recuerda el concepto de temporalidad inherente a la vida y de la materia: la gente envejece y las cosas se desgastan. Todo es efímero y finito o, visto de otra manera, todo cambia constantemente. El resultado es una fuente de palo seco decorativa y erosionada, con algunos remates y caracteres muy irregulares. Combina astas de trazo grueso con astas más finas. Las curvas son continuas, de aspecto circular y sin contraste.

Sans Culottes

K-Type/Keith Bates | www.k-type.com

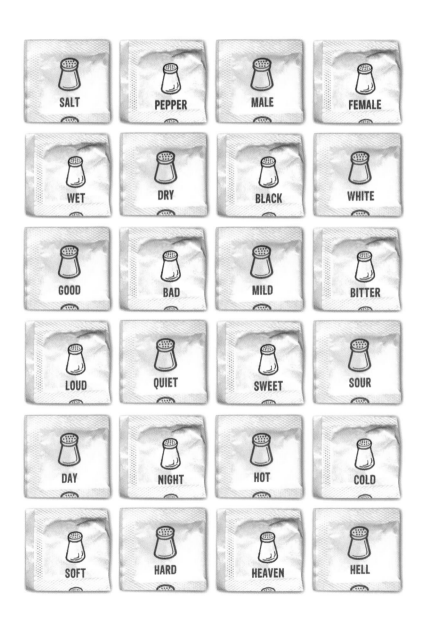

abcdefghijklmnopqrstuvwxyz[äöüßåøœæçñ]
ABCDEFGHIJKLMNOPQRSTUVWXYZ
1234567890(.,;:?¿$¢£€¥&-*){ÄÖÜÅØÆŒÇÑ}

8/10 pt

abcdefghijklmnopqrstuvwxyz[äöüßåøœæçñ]
ABCDEFGHIJKLMNOPQRSTUVWXYZ
1234567890(.,;:?¿$¢£€¥&-*){ÄÖÜÅØÆŒÇÑ}

10/12 pt

abcdefghijklmnopqrstuvwxyz
[äöüßåøœæçñ]
ABCDEFGHIJKLMNOPQRSTUVWXYZ
1234567890
(.,;:?¿$¢£€¥&-*){ÄÖÜÅØÆŒÇÑ}

18/18 pt

abcdefghijklmn
opqrstuvwxyz[äöüßåøœæçñ]
ABCDEFGHIJKLMN
OPQRSTUVWXYZ
1234567890
(.,;:?¿$¢£€¥&-*)
{ÄÖÜÅØÆŒÇÑ}

24/24 pt

The font 4990810 created by Phillip Cavette in 1999 is the source of inspiration for the design of Sans Culottes. The typographer's intentions was to achieve something similar to the original design. Thus, taking the existing font as a starting point, the outlines were redrawn and more auxiliary marks were added, for the purposes of generating a cleaner look without any unevenness in the baseline. Unlike the original font, Sans Culottes is a complete font, which includes both upper and lowercase characters with a large variety of accents, numbers, punctuation marks and symbols.

La police 4990810 créée par Philip Cavette en 1999 a inspiré le design de Sans Culottes. L'intention du typographe était de réaliser une police se rapprochant du design originel. De cette façon, à partir de la police qui existait déjà, les contours ont été redessinés et davantage de marques auxiliaires ont été ajoutées, dans le but de lui donner un aspect plus net et sans irrégularité au niveau de la ligne de base. Contrairement à la police originelle, Sans Culottes est une police d'écriture complète qui inclut des caractères bas et haut de casse, une grande variété d'accents, de chiffres, de signes de ponctuation et de symboles.

La fuente 4990810 creada por Phillip Cavette en 1999 es el motivo de inspiración para el diseño de la Sans Culottes. La intención del tipógrafo ha sido realizar una aproximación al diseño original. De este modo, a partir de la fuente ya existente, redibujó los contornos y añadió más marcas auxiliares, con el fin de lograr un aspecto más nítido y sin irregularidades en la línea base. A diferencia de la original, la Sans Culottes es una fuente completa que incluye caracteres de caja alta y baja con una gran variedad de acentos, números, signos de puntuación y símbolos.

Shambam

Jeroen Klaver & Bobby Pola / ShamFonts / Shamrock Int. |
www.shamrocking.com | www.shamfonts.com | www.shamsterdam.com

ABCDEFGHIJHLMNOPQRSTUVWXYZ
..¨

8/10 pt

ABCDEFGHIJHLMNOPQRSTUVWXYZ
..¨

10/12 pt

ABCDEFGHIJHLMNOPQRSTUVWXYZ
•,¨

18/18 pt

ABCDEFGHIJHLMN
OPQRSTUVWXYZ
•,¨

24/24 pt

ABCDEFGHIJHLMN
OPQRSTUVWXYZ
•,¨

32/34 pt

An informal handwritten font reminiscent of a fine felt-tip pen used as the design tool. The same set includes a double alphabet with similar features but variations in the design of each letter. The font alternates hollow characters with others with positive values by means of insistent strokes used haphazardly. The characters do not rest on the baseline and differ greatly in size. This is a sans serif uppercase font that includes basic punctuation marks. The letters appear to be sketched in an unfinished manner and the stems have rough edges.

Police informelle d'écriture manuscrite dont l'outil de conception semble être un feutre à pointe fine. Cette police propose deux variantes de l'alphabet avec des caractéristiques similaires mais un design différent pour chaque lettre. Elle alterne entre des caractères dont seul le contour se découpe sur le fond et d'autres en négatif avec un trait insistant pour un usage aléatoire. Les caractères ne reposent pas sur la ligne de base et ont des dimensions très irrégulières. Il s'agit d'une police sans serif, haut de casse, qui inclut des signes de ponctuation de base. Les lettres ressemblent à des ébauches, avec un aspect inachevé. Les bords des hampes sont irréguliers.

Fuente informal de escritura a mano que hace referencia al rotulador de punta fina como herramienta de diseño. El mismo set incluye un doble abecedario con características similares pero variando el diseño de cada letra. Alterna caracteres simplemente perfilados con otros rellenos a base de un trazo insistente para un uso aleatorio. Los caracteres no se apoyan en la línea base y tienen dimensiones muy irregulares. Se trata de una tipografía de palo seco y de caja alta que incluye los signos de puntuación básicos. Las letras parecen esbozadas, con un aspecto inacabado. Las astas tienen bordes irregulares.

Shambiel

Jeroen Klaver & Bobby Pola / ShamFonts / Shamrock Int. |
www.shamrocking.com | www.shamfonts.com | www.shamsterdam.com

ABCdEFGHijklmNoPQRStuvwXYZ
ABCdEFGHijklmNoPQRStuvwXYZ

8/10 pt

ABCdEFGHijklmNoPQRStuvwXYZ
ABCdEFGHijklmNoPQRStuvwXYZ

10/12 pt

ABCdEFGHijklmNoPQRStuvwXYZ
ABCdEFGHijklmNoPQRStuvwXYZ

18/18 pt

ABCdEFGHijklmN
oPQRStuvwXYZ
ABCdEFGHijklmN
oPQRStuvwXYZ

24/24 pt

ABCdEFGHijklmN
oPQRStuvwXYZ
ABCdEFGHijklmN
oPQRStuvwXYZ

32/34 pt

The appearance of this font suggests the use of a nib as a design tool. The insistent stroke gives the letters greater thickness, both in the stems and bars, the ends of which are somewhat ill-defined. Every so often, the vigorous movement of a firm, rapid stroke creates a few thinner strokes that protrude from the characters. The letters do not rest on the baseline and the height of the caps and ascenders is uneven. The end result conjures up a sense of movement and chaos. The font's shapeless construction includes some key characters that are given standard treatment such as: the A with its straight apex; and the g with a loop.

Par son aspect, cette police semble avoir été conçue avec une plume. L'insistance du trait amplifie la grosseur aussi bien des hampes que des traverses dont les extrémités ne sont pas définies. Parfois, le tracé ferme et rapide, réalisé par un geste énergique, produit des traits plus fins qui ressortent des caractères. Les lettres ne reposent pas sur la ligne de base, la hauteur des majuscules et des hampes ascendantes n'est pas régulière. Le résultat final provoque une sensation mouvementée et chaotique. Cette police de construction informe propose certains caractères avec des éléments standards comme : le « A » avec une pointe droite et le « g » avec une boucle.

El aspecto de esta fuente hace referencia a la plumilla como herramienta de diseño. El trazo insistente provoca un mayor grosor tanto en las astas como en las barras, cuyos extremos quedan indefinidos. De vez en cuando, el gesto enérgico de trazo firme y rápido genera unos trazos más finos que sobresalen de los caracteres. Las letras no se apoyan en la línea base y la altura de las mayúsculas y de los ascendentes son desiguales. El resultado final crea una sensación de movimiento y caos. Su construcción amorfa incluye algunos caracteres clave con tratamiento estándar, como la A con vértice recto y la g con ojal.

Shears

sugargliderz | www.supermundane.com

abcdefghijklmnopqrstuvwxyz[äöüßåøæœçñ]
ABCDEFGHIJKLMNOPQRSTUVWXYZ
1234567890(.,;¿?¡£$¢£€¥&–*)(ÄÖÜÅØÆŒÇÑ)

8/10 pt

abcdefghijklmnopqrstuvwxyz[äöüßåøæœçñ]
ABCDEFGHIJKLMNOPQRSTUVWXYZ
1234567890(.,;¿?¡£$¢£€¥&–*)(ÄÖÜÅØÆŒÇÑ)

10/12 pt

abcdefghijklmnopqrstuvwxyz[äöüßåøæœçñ]
ABCDEFGHIJKLMNOPQRSTUVWXYZ
1234567890(.,;?¿$¢£€¥&–*)(ÄÖÜÅØÆŒÇÑ)

18/18 pt

abcdefghijklmn
opqrstuvwxyz[äöüßåøæœçñ]
ABCDEFGHIJKLMNOPQRSTUVWXYZ
1234567890
(.,;?¿$¢£€¥&–*)(ÄÖÜÅØÆŒÇÑ)

24/24 pt

Shears is based on the *kirie* technique of papercut art traditional of China and Japan. *Kirie* consists of cutting a single sheet of black paper to obtain a continuous design, with all its parts fully connected, and then mounting it on white paper to create a monochromatic design. This font was designed using a similar technique, by taking the Japanese kirie artist Jiro Takidaira (1921-2009) as a source of inspiration. His *kirie* works use an irreverent tone to convey their message and this font aims to achieve the same tone. Although it is more effective in large formats, the designer proposes that it should be used without any constraint.

Shears s'inspire du *kirie*, une technique traditionnelle développée en Chine et au Japon. Elle consiste à découper une seule feuille de papier noir en obtenant une forme continue, dont toutes les parties sont reliées, puis de la poser sur une feuille blanche afin de créer un dessin monochromatique. Cette police a été conçue à partir d'une technique similaire, en s'inspirant du peintre japonais de kirie Jiro Takidaira (1921-2009). Ses *kiries* utilisent un ton incorrect pour transmettre un message. La police Shears essaie d'atteindre ce ton-là. Bien que le résultat soit meilleur en grand format, le graphiste laisse carte blanche.

Shears se inspira en la técnica *kirie*, tradicional de China y Japón. Consiste en recortar una sola hoja de papel negro logrando un diseño continuo, enteramente conectado en todas sus partes y que luego se monta sobre papel blanco para crear un diseño monocromático. Esta fuente se ha diseñado con una técnica similar, tomando como fuente de inspiración el pintor japonés de *kirie* Jiro Takidaira (1921-2009). Si sus *kirie* se sirven de un tono descortés para transmitir un mensaje, esta fuente pretende lograr el mismo objetivo. A pesar de que resulta más efectiva en tamaños grandes, el diseñador propone una utilización libre.

Slang King

Popdog Fonts | popdog_fonts.tripod.com

abcdefghijklmnopqrstuvwxyz[δφóíεψznp]
ABCDEFGHIJKLMNOPQRSTUVWXYZ
1234567890(.,:?Ω$A&~*){ΔΦάΕΨZΗΡ}

8/10 pt

abcdefghijklmnopqrstuvwxyz[δφóíεψznp]
ABCDEFGHIJKLMNOPQRSTUVWXYZ
1234567890(.,:?Ω$A&~*){ΔΦάΕΨZΗΡ}

10/12 pt

abcdefghijklmn
opqrstuvwxyz[δφóíεψznp]
ABCDEFGHIJKLMNOPQRSTUVWXYZ
1234567890(.,:?Ω$A&~*){ΔΦάΕΨZΗΡ}

18/18 pt

abcdefghijklmn
opqrstuvwxyz[δφóíεψznp]
ABCDEFGHIJKLMN
OPQRSTUVWXYZ
1234567890
(.,:?Ω$A&~*){ΔΦάΕΨZΗΡ}

24/24 pt

This font is more appropriate for titles or headlines than for running text. The strokes have been formed from a web of vertical and diagonal lines. In this way, the font manages to capture our attention, particularly when printed in large letters. Despite the peculiarity of the stroke, the font follows a traditional format with its continuous curves, and stems and arms with parallel edges. The basic set of key characters includes: the double-storied lowercase a; the lowercase f resting on the baseline; the uppercase A with its straight apex; and the uppercase G with its vertical spur. This sans serif font includes both Latin and Greek characters.

Elle est davantage appropriée pour les titres ou les en-têtes que pour les textes. Les traits ont été formés à partir de lignes verticales et de diagonales. De cette manière, la police réussit à capter l'attention, particulièrement pour les grands formats. Malgré la particularité du tracé, la forme des caractères est traditionnelle, avec des courbes continues, avec les hampes et des traverses aux bords parallèles. La sélection de base des caractères les plus frappants inclut : un « a » bas de casse en script, un « f » bas de casse qui s'appuie sur la ligne de base, un « A » haut de casse dont la pointe est droite, un « G » haut de casse à empattement vertical. Cette typographie sans serif existe en caractères latins et grecs.

Es una fuente más apropiada para títulos o encabezamientos que para texto corrido. Los trazos se han formado a partir de una trama de líneas verticales y diagonales. Así, la fuente logra captar la atención, especialmente en tamaños grandes. A pesar de la peculiaridad en el trazo, obedece a una forma tradicional, de curvas continuas con astas y brazos de bordes paralelos. La selección básica de caracteres claves incluye la a de caja baja de dos pisos, la f de caja baja que se apoya en la línea base, la A de caja alta con vértice recto, la G de caja alta con espuela vertical. Esta fuente de palo seco incluye caracteres latinos y griegos.

Soda / Soda Light

Ronan le Guevellou | www.ministryofcandy.com

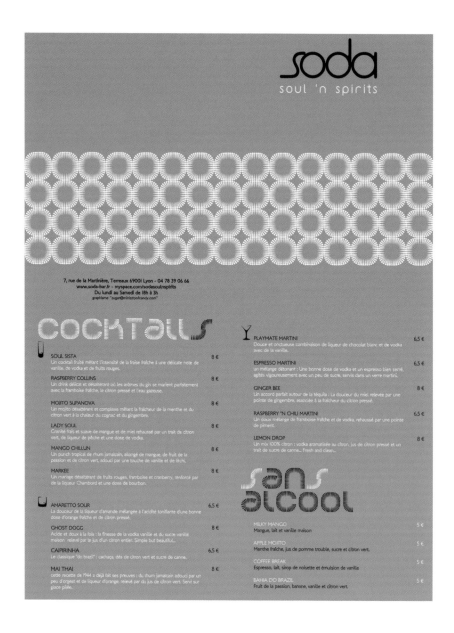

abcdefGHiJKlmnOPQrsTUVWXYZ

8/10 pt

abcdefGHiJKlmnOPQrsTUVWXYZ

8/10 pt

abcdefGHiJKlmnOPQrsTUVWXYZ

10/12 pt

abcdefGHiJKlmnOPQrsTUVWXYZ

10/12 pt

abcdefGHiJKlmnOPQrsTUVWXYZ

18/18 pt

abcdefGHiJKlmnOPQrsTUVWXYZ

18/18 pt

abcdefGHiJKlmn
OPQrsTUVWXYZ

24/24 pt

abcdefGHiJKlmn
OPQrsTUVWXYZ

24/24 pt

This font was originally created to be used in the headings of a bar menu. The design is an adaptation of the decorative motifs used in the business's visual identity. The main element features a circle designed like a disco ball to give a more dynamic, modern effect. This decorative font with its shadowy appearance does not have any flourishes. It displays continuous curves with a squarish appearance; the arcs are almost closed; and there is no contrast. The typeface has two variants: Soda and Soda Light with identical formal attributes but one is the negative design of the other.

À l'origine cette police était conçue pour les titres du menu d'un bar. Le design est une adaptation des motifs décoratifs utilisés pour l'identité visuelle de l'établissement. L'élément central est un cercle conçu comme la boule d'une discothèque pour un effet plus dynamique et actuel. Cette police décorative plutôt sombre n'a pas d'empattement. Elle présente des courbes continues sans contraste mais qui semblent légèrement carrées et des arches presque fermées. La typographie propose plusieurs variantes : Soda et Soda Light avec des attributs formels identiques sauf que l'une est en négatif et l'autre en positif.

Originariamente esta fuente se creó para su aplicación en los títulos de la carta de un bar. El diseño es el resultado de la adaptación de los motivos decorativos utilizados en la identidad visual del establecimiento. El elemento central consiste en un círculo diseñado a la manera de una bola de discoteca, para un efecto más dinámico y actual. Esta fuente decorativa de aspecto sombreado no tiene remates. Muestra unas curvas continuas de aspecto cuadrado sin contraste y los arcos son casi cerrados. La tipografía ofrece dos variantes: Soda y Soda Light, con idénticos atributos formales pero una es el negativo de la otra.

Spacearella

Brain Eaters Font Company (BEFCo) | www.braineaters.com

abcdefghijklmnopqrstuvwxyz[ß]
ABCDEFGHIJKLMNOPQRSTUVWXYZ
1234567890(.,;:?$c£¥&–*){}

8/10 pt

abcdefghijklmnopqrstuvwxyz[ß]
ABCDEFGHIJKLMNOPQRSTUVWXYZ
1234567890(.,;:?$c£¥&–*){}

10/12 pt

abcdefghijklmnopqrstuvwxyz[ß]
ABCDEFGHIJKLMN
OPQRSTUVWXYZ
1234567890(.,;:?$c£¥&–*){}

18/18 pt

abcdefghijklmn
opqrstuvwxyz[ß]
ABCDEFGHIJKLMN
OPQRSTUVWXYZ
1234567890(.,;:?$c£¥&–*){}

24/24 pt

Spacearella is a decorative font based on the typefaces of the nineteen sixties. The name comes from the movie *Barbarella*, a French science-fiction comic book created by Jean-Claude Forest, whose main character became one of the most famous heroines of adult comics, which had their heyday in the sixties and seventies. It is a decorative font with a touch of fantasy, without actually looking like a cartoon. It has exaggerated contrast, a tilted axis and instant transition, along with huge serifs and disproportionate terminals. It is not really appropriate for running text, although it is ideal for medium-sized formats and giant-sized headlines.

Spacearella est une police décorative qui s'inspire de la typographie des années 60. Son nom provient du film *Barbarella*, une bande dessinée de science-fiction créée par Jean-Claude Forest, dont l'actrice principale est devenue une des héroïnes du genre fantastique érotique qui atteint son apogée dans les années 60 et 70. Il s'agit d'une police décorative du genre de la fiction, sans pour autant ressembler au dessin animé. Avec des contrastes exagérés, un axe incliné et une transition instantanée, cette police possède des finitions et des traits démesurés. Elle n'est pas appropriée pour des textes longs mais convient parfaitement aux formats moyens et en-têtes exagérés.

Spacearella es una fuente decorativa que se inspira en la tipografía de la década de 1960. El nombre proviene de la película *Barbarella*, una historieta de ciencia ficción francesa creada por Jean-Claude Forest, cuya protagonista se convirtió en una de las más destacadas heroínas del género fantaerótico, que tuvo su esplendor en los 60 y 70. Es una fuente de fantasía, que no llega al aspecto de dibujo animado. De contraste exagerado, con eje inclinado y transición instantánea, tiene remates y trazos terminales desmesurados. No es apropiada para texto corrido, pero sí para tamaños medios y encabezamientos exagerados.

Harold's Fonts | www.haroldsfonts.com

AS MY WISH WAS TO SERVE AN OPPRESSED PEOPLE, AND ASSIST IN A JUST AND GOOD CAUSE, I CONCEIVED THAT THE HONOR OF IT WOULD BE PROMOTED BY MY DECLINING TO MAKE EVEN THE USUAL PROFITS OF AN AUTHOR.

ABCDEFGHIJKLMNOPQRSTUVWXYZ[ÄÖÜSSÅØÆŒÇÑ]
ABCDEFGHIJKLMNOPQRSTUVWXYZ
1234567890(.,;:?¿$¢£€¥&-☆){ÀÖÜÅØ-ŒÇÑ}

8/10 pt

ABCDEFGHIJKLMNOPQRSTUVWXYZ[ÄÖÜSSÅØÆŒÇÑ]
ABCDEFGHIJKLMNOPQRSTUVWXYZ
1234567890(.,;:?¿$¢£€¥&-☆){ÀÖÜÅØ-ŒÇÑ}

8/10 pt

18/18 pt

18/18 pt

The design is derived from a toy rubberstamp kit from the nineteen seventies. The set includes the Regular and Jumbled variants, which can be combined for a more haphazard effect. Both variants share the same formal attributes and alternate forked serifs and cuneiform wedges on the feet. The Jumbled variant, unlike its Regular counterpart, consists of characters that are combined in a random and confusing manner and do not rest on the baseline. The font is constructed in a continuous fashion, with the curve giving it its circular appearance. There is a high degree of contrast, with a vertical axis and instant transition.

La forme provient d'un jeu de kit de tampons des années 1970. La police se compose des versions Regular et Jumbled, qui peuvent être combinées pour un effet plus aléatoire. Ces deux versions ont les mêmes caractéristiques et alternent entre empattements fourchus et bases cunéiformes. La version Jumbled, contrairement à la Regular, se compose de caractères mélangés de manière confuse et désordonnée qui ne s'appuient pas sur la ligne de base. Il s'agit d'une police de forme continue, avec un aspect carré de la courbe. Cela met en avant un contraste prononcé avec un axe vertical et une transition instantanée.

El diseño deriva de un kit de sellos de caucho de juguete de alrededor de los años 1970. El set incluye las variantes Regular y Jumbled, que resultan combinables entre sí para lograr un efecto más aleatorio. Ambas comparten los mismos atributos formales y alternan los remates bifurcados y cuneiformes en los pies. La variante Jumbled, al contrario de la Regular, consiste en caracteres mezclados de manera confusa y desordenados, que no se apoyan en la línea base. Se trata de una fuente de construcción continua con aspecto de la curva circular. Se observa un contraste alto con eje vertical y transición instantánea.

Stencil Gothic BE

Brain Eaters Font Company (BEFCo) | www.braineaters.com

abc:defghijklmnopqrstuvwxyz
ABCDEFGHIJKLMNOPQRSTUVWXYZ
1234567890(.,;:?$&-*)

8/10 pt

abc:defghijklmnopqrstuvwxyz
ABCDEFGHIJKLMNOPQRSTUVWXYZ
1234567890(.,;:?$&-*)

10/12 pt

abc:defghijklmnopqrstuvwxyz
ABCDEFGHIJKLMNOPQRSTUVWXYZ
1234567890(.,;:?$&-*)

18/18 pt

abc:defghijklmn
opqrstuvwxyz
ABCDEFGHIJKLMN
OPQRSTUVWXYZ
1234567890(.,;:?$&-*)

24/24 pt

This font, designed by Jeff Levine and digitalized by Brain Eaters, is an attractive and practical stencil-like typeface, characterized by its letters divided into several parts to create templates for reproduction on another surface. Jeff has designed a large number of fonts of varying styles, but his designs usually express his passion for stencil fonts. It is intended for use with large formats such as headings or exhibition work, in which it can make a solid, forceful contribution. The typographer cannot think of any better use than marking the words "DANGER EXPLOSIVE!" on wooden crates full of dynamite.

Conçue par Jeff Levine et numérisée par Brain Eaters, cette police est attirante et propose une typographie du style Stencil. Elle se caractérise par les lettres divisées en plusieurs morceaux qui permettent de créer des modèles et de les reproduire sur différentes superficies. Jeff a conçu un grand nombre de polices de différents style, mais ces créations transmettent le plus souvent sa passion pour les typographies Stencil. Elle est conçue pour être utilisée sur des grands formats, pour des titres ou des expositions, donnant un caractère solide et convaincant. Le typographe ne trouve pas d'autre utilité que de marquer sur des caisses remplies de dynamite les mots « DANGER EXPLOSIVE ! ».

Diseñada por Jeff Levine y digitalizada por Brain Eaters, se trata de una atractiva y práctica tipografía de estilo stencil, caracterizada por sus letras divididas en varias partes para crear plantillas y reproducirlas en otras superficies. Jeff es el creador de numerosas fuentes de estilos variados, pero sus diseños en general transmiten su pasión por las tipografías stencil. Está pensada para usarse en tamaños grandes, como titulares o material de muestra, donde aporta un carácter sólido y contundente. Al tipógrafo no se le ocurre mejor utilidad que su uso para marcar cajas de madera llenas de dinamita con las palabras «DANGER EXPLOSIVE!».

ABCDEFGHIJKLMNOPQRSTUVWXYZ[ÄÖÜßÄÖFECÇŃ]
ABCDEFGHIJKLMNOPQRSTUVWXYZ
1234567890(.,:?¿.$¢£€¥¢-+)(ÄÖÜÄÖFECÇŃ)

8/10 pt

ABCDEFGHIJKLMNOPQRSTUVWXYZ[ÄÖÜßÄÖFECÇŃ]
ABCDEFGHIJKLMNOPQRSTUVWXYZ
1234567890(.,:?¿.$¢£€¥¢-+)(ÄÖÜÄÖFECÇŃ)

8/10 pt

ABCDEFGHIJKLMNOPQRSTUVWXYZ[ÄÖÜßÄÖFECÇŃ]
ABCDEFGHIJKLMNOPQRSTUVWXYZ
1234567890(.,:?¿.$¢£€¥¢-+)(ÄÖÜÄÖFECÇŃ)

10/12 pt

ABCDEFGHIJKLMNOPQRSTUVWXYZ[ÄÖÜßÄÖFECÇŃ]
ABCDEFGHIJKLMNOPQRSTUVWXYZ
1234567890(.,:?¿.$¢£€¥¢-+)(ÄÖÜÄÖFECÇŃ)

10/12 pt

ABCDEFGHIJKLMN
OPQRSTUVWXYZ[ÄÖÜßÄÖFECÇŃ]
ABCDEFGHIJKLMNOPQRSTUVWXYZ
1234567890(.,:?¿.$¢£€¥¢-+)(ÄÖÜÄÖFECÇŃ)

18/18 pt

ABCDEFGHIJKLMNO
PQRSTUVWXYZ[ÄÖÜßÄÖFECÇŃ]
ABCDEFGHIJKLMNOPQRSTUVWXYZ
1234567890(.,:?¿.$¢£€¥¢-+)(ÄÖÜÄÖFECÇŃ)

18/18 pt

This font has been spawned by lengthy experience in the field of graffiti together with an interest in the skateboarding culture. Stencil or Die has been designed to reduce the number of angles and details to an absolute minimum in order to facilitate the creation of templates. As in the case of all stencil-like fonts, here too discontinued construction can be observed with the characters being formed by loose elements. It is a sans serif font with a dripping effect on all the feet. This means that it does not need to be inserted manually in the final work. The set includes the Regular and Italic variants with numbers in each case.

Cette police provient de la longue expérience dans le domaine du graffiti et d'un intérêt pour la culture du skateboard. Stencil or Die a été conçue dans l'intention de réduire les angles et les détails afin de faciliter la création de pochoirs. À l'image de toutes les polices Stencil, celle-ci propose une construction irrégulière composée d'éléments isolés. Cette police est sans serif avec un effet dégoulinant au niveau de la traverse inférieure. Cela évite de devoir l'ajouter à la main sur le travail final. La police propose les versions Regular et Italic avec des chiffres dans les deux cas.

Surge de la larga experiencia del tipógrafo en el campo del grafiti junto con el interés por la cultura del *skateboarding*. Stencil or Die se ha diseñado de manera que haya el mínimo de ángulos y detalles posibles, para facilitar así la creación de las plantillas. Como en todas las fuentes de tipo stencil, en ésta también se aprecia una construcción discontinua compuesta por elementos sueltos. Se trata de una fuente de palo seco con efecto chorreante en todos los pies. De este modo ya no hace falta introducir manualmente este efecto en el trabajo final. El set incluye las variantes Regular e Italic, con números en cada caso.

Stretched Signature

Galdino Otten | galdinoottenbr.blogspot.com

abcdefghijklmnopqrstuvwxyz[]
ABCDEFGHIJKLMNOPQRSTUVWXYZ
1234567890(.,:;?¶¢-*)

8/10 pt

abcdefghijklmnopqrstuvwxyz[]
ABCDEFGHIJKLMNOPQRSTUVWXYZ
1234567890(.,:;?¶¢-*)

8/10 pt

abcdefghijklmnopqrstuvwxyz[]
ABCDEFGHIJKLMNOPQRSTUVWXYZ
1234567890(.,:;?$&-*)

8/10 pt

abcdefghijklmnopqrstuvwxyz[]
ABCDEFGHIJKLMN
opqrstuvwxyz
1234567890(.,:;?¶¢-*)

18/18 pt

abcdefghijklmn
opqrstuvwxyz[]
ABCDEFGHIJKLMN
opqrstuvwxyz
1234567890(.,:;?¶¢-*)

18/18 pt

abcdefghijklmn
opqrstuvwxyz[]
ABCDEFGHIJKLMN
opqrstuvwxyz
1234567890(.,:;?$&-*)

18/18 pt

The design originates from the style used by the designer in his own signature. This is easy to see throughout his work, in his blog, and also in his tags as a manifestation of street art. This typeface can be used in several lines and styles of art. It can be applied in work ranging from the simplest of content to the most sophisticated. The key feature is the flexibility of its connections: when it comes to joining up characters it is infinitely flexible, being capable of going beyond the limits of any particular space. The set offers the variants Best, Ext Bold and Flex.

Le designer a créé cette police à partir du style de sa signature. Il est possible de l'apercevoir dans l'ensemble de son travail, sur son blog et sur ses tags, en tant que manifestation de l'art urbain. Cette typographie peut être utilisée pour plusieurs lignes et styles d'art. Elle peut s'appliquer à un travail dont le contenu peut être simple ou sophistiqué. Sa principale caractéristique est la flexibilité de ses connections, de telle sorte que lier les caractères devient extrêmement flexible, pouvant même dépasser les limites de n'importe quel espace. Il existe des variantes telles que Best, Ext Bold et Flex.

El diseño surge del estilo utilizado por el diseñador en su propia firma. Éste resulta apreciable en todo su trabajo, tanto en su blog como en sus Tag, como manifestación de arte callejero. Esta tipografía permite ser utilizada en diversas líneas y estilos de arte. Se puede aplicar tanto en un trabajo de contenido más simple como en uno más sofisticado. Su característica principal es la flexibilidad de sus enlaces, de modo que para unir los caracteres se vuelve infinitamente flexible, siendo capaz de traspasar los limites de cualquier espacio. El set ofrece las variantes Best, Ext Bold y Flex.

Sustainable Amazon

Galdino Otten | galdinoottenbr.blogspot.com

abcdefghijklmnopqrstuvwxyz[¢]
ABCDEFGHIJKLMNOPQRSTUVWXYZ
1234567890(.,;:?$&-*)(ç)

8/10 pt

abcdefghijklmnopqrstuvwxyz[¢]
ABCDEFGHIJKLMNOPQRSTUVWXYZ
1234567890(.,;:?$&-*)(ç)

10/12 pt

abcdefghijklmnopqrstuvwxyz[¢]
ABCDEFGHIJKLMNO
PQRSTUVWXYZ
1234567890(.,;:?$&-*)(ç)

18/18 pt

abcdefghijklmno
pqrstuvwxyz[¢]
ABCDEFGHIJKLMN
OPQRSTUVWXYZ
1234567890(.,;:?$&-*)(ç)

24/24 pt

This font was the designer's contribution to the planet. His intention was to change peoples' mentalities and to invoke an environmental conscience. It is for this reason that the font is Free. It is a decorative font with an animated style that creates irregular characters, with non-parallel stems and positive counters. It is a sans serif font with characters that do not rest on the baseline. It includes both upper and lower case character, with accents, punctuation marks and basic symbols.

Avec cette police le créateur apporte sa contribution à la planète. Il souhaite changer les mentalités et réveiller la conscience écologique des gens. Pour cette raison, il s'agit d'une police Free. Le résultat est une police décorative de style animé qui produit des caractères irréguliers, avec des hampes non parallèles et des contrepoinçons pleins. Il s'agit d'une police sans serif dont les caractères ne reposent pas sur la ligne de base. Elle inclut des caractères haut et bas de casse avec des accents, des signes de ponctuation et des symboles.

El diseñador realiza su contribución al planeta a través de esta fuente. Su intención es transformar la mentalidad de las personas y despertar una conciencia medioambiental. Por ese motivo se trata de una fuente Free. El resultado es una fuente decorativa de estilo animado que genera caracteres irregulares, con astas no paralelas y ojales rellenos. Se trata de una fuente de palo seco cuyos caracteres no se apoyan en la línea base. El set incluye caracteres de caja alta y baja con acentos, signos de puntuación y símbolos básicos.

Sylar Stencil

The Northern Block |www.thenorthernblock.co.uk

Sylar Stencil   **250 Characters**

abcdefghijklmnopqrstuvwxyz

ABCDEFGHIJKLMNOPQRSTUVWXYZ

1234567890#©®@™$¢£¤€&%¶*+

.,:;…!|?¿„""""»«•-–— _=[]{}/,'"^˘¯"»º

àáâãäåæçèéêëìíîïñòóôõöùúûüÿ

ÀÁÂÃÄÅÆÇÈÉÊËÌÍÎÏÑÒÓÔÕÖØŒÙÚÛÜŸ

Give me a pen & pencil. I'll produce accurate
information. Computer unnecessary.

Available As A Free Download
http://www.thenorthernblock.co.uk

abcdefghijklmnopqrstuvwxyz[äöüßåøæœgń]
ABCDEFGHIJKLMNOPQRSTUVWXYZ
1234567890(.,:;?¿$¢£€¥&-*){ÄÖÜÅØŒÇŃ}

8/10 pt

abcdefghijklmnopqrstuvwxyz[äöüßåøæœgń]
ABCDEFGHIJKLMNOPQRSTUVWXYZ
1234567890(.,:;?¿$¢£€¥&-*){ÄÖÜÅØŒÇŃ}

10/12 pt

abcdefghijklmn
opqrstuvwxyz[äöüßåøæœgń]
ABCDEFGHIJKLMNOPQRSTUVWXYZ
1234567890
(.,:;?¿$¢£€¥&-*){ÄÖÜÅØŒÇŃ}

18/18 pt

abcdefghijklmn
opqrstuvwxyz
[äöüßåøæœgń]
ABCDEFGHIJKLMN
OPQRSTUVWXYZ
1234567890
(.,:;?¿$¢£€¥&-*)
{ÄÖÜÅØŒÇŃ}

24/24 pt

The stencil style characterizes this font. The template-like characters follow a modular form consisting of individual elements. This sans serif font has broad proportions, with a small x-height and parallel edge stems. It lacks contrast and is of medium thickness. Key characters include: the uppercase A with a curve on lines that are normally straight and the single-story lowercase a. The features are also to be noted of the single-story lowercase g with an open tail and no link; and the uppercase J resting on the baseline while the lowercase j hangs below it.

Le style Stencil caractérise cette police. Ces caractères de style pochoir ont une forme modulaire composée d'éléments individuels. Sylar Stencil est une police sans serif, de chasse large, avec une petite hauteur d'œil et des hampes verticales aux bords parallèles. Elle ne présente pas de contraste et a un corps moyen. Les caractères clés sont : le « A » haut de casse dont les lignes, en principe droites, sont ici courbées et le « a » bas de casse en script. Il convient également de citer les caractéristiques du : « g » bas de casse d'un seul niveau avec une queue ouvert et sans ligature et le « J » haut de casse aligné sur la ligne de base alors que le « j » bas de casse dépasse la ligne.

El estilo stencil caracteriza a esta fuente. Los caracteres de estilo plantilla obedecen a una forma modular compuesta por elementos individuales. Esta fuente de palo seco es de proporciones anchas, con altura de la x pequeña y astas verticales de bordes paralelos. No muestra contraste y tiene un espesor medio. Entre los caracteres clave se encuentran la A de caja alta, con curvado de líneas normalmente rectas, y la a de caja baja de un piso. También destacan las características de la g de caja baja, de un piso, con cola abierta y sin cuello, y la J de caja alta que se apoya en la línea base, mientras que la j de caja baja sobresale de ella.

The Folded

Anton Studer | www.bubentraum.com

ABCDEFGHIJKLMNOPQRSTUVWXYZ
ABCDEFGHIJKLMNOPQRSTUVWXYZ
1234567890 . , :

8/10 pt

ABCDEFGHIJKLMNOPQRSTUVWXYZ
ABCDEFGHIJKLMNOPQRSTUVWXYZ
1234567890 . , :

10/12 pt

ABCDEFGHIJKLMN
OPQRSTUVWXYZ
ABCDEFGHIJKLMN
OPQRSTUVWXYZ
1234567890 . , :

18/18 pt

ABCDEFGHIJKLMN
OPQRSTUVWXYZ
ABCDEFGHIJKLMN
OPQRSTUVWXYZ
1234567890 . , :

24/24 pt

This involves the process of a typographic experiment involving the creation of a decorative font by making previously determined folds in a sheet of paper. Folded paper planes provided the inspiration for this project. All the letters were created from the folds made in the sheets of DIN A4 paper, with cuts being added in some cases so as to maintain the original size of the paper. The font is available in uppercase characters, with both normal and slanting variants. It also includes a set of numbers and basic punctuation marks such as: the period, comma and colon.

Il s'agit d'un processus d'une expérience typographique qui consiste à créer une police décorative à partir de pliages, étudiés à l'avance, d'une feuille en papier. Les avions en papier sont la source d'inspiration de ce projet. Toutes les lettres ont été créées à partir de pliages de feuilles DIN A4. Dans certains cas, certaines découpes ont été ajoutées afin de conserver la taille de la feuille d'origine. La police offre des caractères haut de casse, avec deux variantes : police romaine et italique. Elle inclut également des chiffres et des signes de ponctuation simples comme : le point, la virgule et les deux points.

Se trata de un experimento tipográfico que consiste en crear una fuente decorativa a partir de la realización de pliegues, previamente estudiados, en una hoja de papel. Los aviones de papel son la fuente de inspiración del proyecto. Todas las letras de esta tipografía han sido creadas a partir de pliegues en hojas de proporciones DIN A4, y en algunos casos se han añadido unos cortes para lograr conservar el tamaño original de la hoja. La fuente ofrece caracteres de caja alta, con variantes de tipo normal e inclinadas. También incluye el set de números y los signos de puntuación básicos como el punto, la coma y los dos puntos.

Tom Violence

Popdog Fonts | popdog_fonts.tripod.com

bcdefghijklmnopqrstuvwxyzabc
ΒΓΔΕΖΗΘΙΚΛΜΝΞΟΠΡΣΤΥΦΧΨΩΑΒΓΔ
βγδεζηθικλμνξοπρστυφχψω/;άëήίóώ,.+-=
234567897!@#$%^&*(?)123456789/!@#$
BCDEFGHIJKLMNOPQRSTUVWXYZABCD
bcdefghijklmnopqrstuvwxyzabcde
ΒΓΔΕΖΗ ΘΙΚΛΜΝΞΟΠΡΣΤΥ
βγδεζηθ κλμνξοπρστυφχψ
234567 897!@#$%^
BCDEF GHIJKLM
bcdefg hijklmn

tom violence
type-face

abcdefghijklmnopqrstuvwxyz✳δφóíεΨζηρ✳
ABCDEFGHIJKLMNOPQRSTUVWXYZ
1234567890(.,:;?$&-*)ΔΦáEΨZHP

8/10 pt

abcdefghijklmnopqrstuvwxyz✳δφóíεΨζηρ✳
ABCDEFGHIJKLMNOPQRSTUVWXYZ
1234567890(.,:;?$&-*)ΔΦáEΨZHP

10/12 pt

abcdefghijklmn
opqrstuvwxyz✳δφóíεΨζηρ✳
ABCDEFGHIJKLMNOPQRSTUVWXYZ
1234567890(.,:;?$&-*)ΔΦáEΨZHP

18/18 pt

abcdefghijklmn
opqrstuvwxyz
✳δφóíεΨζηρ✳
ABCDEFGHIJKLMN
OPQRSTUVWXYZ
1234567890
(.,:;?$&-*)ΔΦáEΨZHP

24/24 pt

This font is a constant reminder of the follies committed during Tom Violence's youth, owing to a lack of caution, while going through a chronic problem with baselines. The result is reminiscent of a photocopy or printed fax with serious errors in the baseline. Despite being covered in stains, it is surprisingly easy to read even in the smallest formats. It is a decorative sans serif font with a neglected appearance and strokes of even thickness. The stems and arms have parallel edges and there is no contrast or modulation. The set includes both Latin and Greek characters.

Il s'agit du souvenir permanent des folies que le personnage Tom Violence a commises pendant sa jeunesse, qui souffre en même temps d'un problème chronique avec les lignes de base. Cela fait penser à une photocopie ou un fax imprimé avec de gros problèmes au niveau de la ligne de base. Bien qu'elle soit complètement tachée, Tom Violence est une police étonnamment lisible même pour les tailles de police les plus petites. Il s'agit d'une police décorative sans serif, d'apparence plutôt sale, d'une grosseur régulière. Les hampes et les traverses ont des bords parallèles et il n'existe ni contraste ni modulation. La police inclut des caractères latins et grecs.

Esta fuente es un constante recordatorio de las locuras cometidas por las imprudencias en la juventud del personaje Tom Violence, que sufre a la vez un problema crónico con las líneas base. Recuerda a una fotocopia o a un fax impreso con graves errores en la línea base. A pesar de estar plagada de manchas, resulta sorprendentemente legible incluso en los tamaños más pequeños. Se trata de una fuente decorativa de palo seco y de aspecto ensuciado, con un grosor de trazo uniforme. Las astas y los brazos son de bordes paralelos y no existe contraste ni modulación. El set incluye caracteres latinos y griegos.

Trouble Regular/Italique/Closebold

Ewen Prigent | www.laboitegraphique.fr

ABCDEFGHIJKLMNOPQRSTUVWXYZ[]
1234567890(.,::?$¢€¥&-*){ÄÖÜÀÁÆŒÇÑ}

8/10 pt

ABCDEFGHIJKLMNOPQRSTUVWXYZ[]
1234567890(.,::?$¢€¥&-*){ÄÖÜÀÁÆŒÇÑ}

8/10 pt

ABCDEFGHIJKLMNOPQRSTUVWXYZ[]
1234567890(.,::?$¢€¥&-*){ÄÖÜÀÁÆŒÇÑ}

8/10 pt

ABCDEFGHIJKLMNOPQRSTUVWXYZ[]
1234567890(.,::?$¢€¥&-*){ÄÖÜÀÁÆŒÇÑ}

10/12 pt

ABCDEFGHIJKLMNOPQRSTUVWXYZ[]
1234567890(.,::?$¢€¥&-*){ÄÖÜÀÁÆŒÇÑ}

10/12 pt

ABCDEFGHIJKLMNOPQRSTUVWXYZ[]
1234567890(.,::?$¢€¥&-*){ÄÖÜÀÁÆŒÇÑ}

10/12 pt

ABCDEFGHIJKLMNOPQRSTUVWXYZ[]
1234567890(.,::?$¢€¥&-*){ÄÖÜÀÁÆŒÇÑ}

18/18 pt

ABCDEFGHIJKLMNOPQRSTUVWXYZ[]
1234567890(.,::?$¢€¥&-*){ÄÖÜÀÁÆŒÇÑ}

18/18 pt

ABCDEFGHIJKLMNOPQRSTUVWXYZ[]
1234567890(.,::?$¢€¥&-*){ÄÖÜÀÁÆŒÇÑ}

18/18 pt

This font is reminiscent of handwriting in that it is coarse and imprecise – very suitable for conveying personal expression with a warm touch. It is a sans serif font with stems and arms whose edges are not parallel but uneven, with a slightly jagged outline. This font is continuously constructed but also shapeless as all the strokes display uneven shapes and thicknesses. This is a very complete font family, despite the fact that it does not include lowercase characters, since it offers the following three basic variants: Regular, bold and italic. It also incorporates all types of accents and punctuation marks, along with a large variety of symbols.

Cette police ressemble à une écriture manuscrite, grasse et non précise, tout à fait appropriée pour transmettre une expression personnelle avec un caractère chaud. Il s'agit d'une police sans serif dont les hampes et les traverses ne sont pas parallèles mais irrégulières, avec un contour légèrement rugueux. Cette police a à la fois une structure homogène et sans forme puisque tous les traits ont des formes et des tailles irrégulières. C'est une famille très complète, bien qu'elle n'ait pas de caractères bas de casse, car elle offre trois variantes : romain, gras et italique. Elle comporte également tout type d'accents, de signes de ponctuation et une grande variété de symboles.

Recuerda la escritura a mano, gruesa e imprecisa, muy apropiada para la expresividad personal y con una nota cálida. Es una fuente de palo seco cuyos bordes de las astas y brazos no son paralelos, sino irregulares, con el contorno levemente rugoso. Esta fuente de construcción continua es al mismo tiempo amorfa, ya que todos los trazos muestran formas y grosores irregulares. A pesar de no incluir caracteres de caja baja, es una familia muy completa, ya que ofrece las tres variantes básicas: Regular, Bold e Itálica. Además, también se incluyen todo tipo de acentos, signos de puntuación y una gran variedad de símbolos.

Typo3 font

Myriam Huré | mirjam.h.free.fr

ČORBA
DE POISSON

NOTE : si c'est votre plat unique, vous pouvez ajouter une poignée de riz.

ATTENTION, les ouïes du poisson doivent être rouges, en signe de fraîcheur.

INGRÉDIENTS
Pour 5 personnes
- 2 l d'eau
- 500 g de têtes et arêtes de truite
- 6 poivrons (rouges) séchés
- 3 carottes
- laurier
- graines d'aneth
- bouillon cube ou vegeta
- farine
- sel, poivre

PRÉPARATION
1. Laver le poisson. Le mettre dans une casserole d'eau sur le feu.

2. Ajouter les poivrons séchés (sans les graines), 2 feuilles de laurier, des graines d'aneth, les carottes épluchées entières, du sel.

3. Au bout d'une demi-heure de cuisson, filtrer le bouillon, puis le remettre sur le feu.

4. Ajouter un peu de vegeta (ou un bouillon cube), du poivre, un verre d'eau avec deux cuillères de farine diluées dedans; couper les carottes en rondelles, éplucher et broyer les poivrons, détacher les morceaux de chair du poisson, et ajouter le tout au fur et à mesure dans la casserole.

(5. Pour épaissir un peu la soupe, on peut faire frire dans une petite casserole un peu de farine dans de l'huile de colza, et l'ajouter au bouillon.)

6. Encore 10 minutes de cuisson et votre soupe est prête. Verser un peu de jus de citron avant de servir.

Les poivrons séchés :
« C'est l'ingrédient qui donne le plus de goût. »

Olga est originaire de Ohrid en Macédoine, célèbre pour son lac.

À la question « si vous étiez condamné à manger un seul aliment jusqu'à la fin de votre vie, que choisiriez-vous ? » elle répond sans hésiter : « le poivron ».

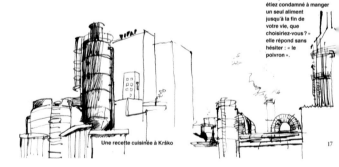

Une recette cuisinée à Krško

16

17

abcdefghijklmnopqrstuvwxyz[äöüœç]
ABCDEFGHIJKLMNOPQRSTUVWXYZ
1234567890(„,?-)

8/10 pt

abcdefghijklmnopqrstuvwxyz[äöüœç]
ABCDEFGHIJKLMNOPQRSTUVWXYZ
1234567890(„,?-)

10/12 pt

abcdefghijklmn
opqrstuvwxyz[äöüœç]
ABCDEFGHIJKLMN
OPQRSTUVWXYZ
1234567890(„,?-)

18/18 pt

abcdefghijklmn
opqrstuvwxyz
[äöüœç]
ABCDEFGHIJKLMN
OPQRSTUVWXYZ
1234567890(„,?-)

24/24 pt

Myriam Huré studied typography at Estienne College in Paris, where she developed her Typo3 font as a class assignment. The font would eventually be applied to the pages of *Cuizine*, a fanzine on graphic and culinary art. The fact that her grandmother thought the cooking recipes were difficult to read motivated her to create a more legible Medium version. The result is an old Roman font. It is characterized by the stems of varying thickness within the same letter. The font has serifs with a sharp, refined shape. Key characters include: the lowercase g with a link, ear and loop; and the uppercase G without a spur.

Myriam Huré a étudié le typographisme à Estienne, où elle a développé le Typo3 font. La police serait appliquée aux pages de *Cuizine*, un fanzine sur l'art graphique et culinaire. Le fait que sa grand-mère considère que les recettes de cuisine étaient difficiles à lire l'a incitée à créer une version Medium plus lisible. Le résultat est une police romaine ancienne. Elle se caractérise par des hampes de tailles différentes au sein d'une même lettre. Les empattements de cette police sont pointus et raffinés. Les caractères clés qui se distinguent sont : le « g » bas de casse avec délié de jonction, queue et empattement, et le « G » haut de casse sans serif.

Myriam Huré estudió diseño tipográfico en l'Ecole Estienne de París, donde desarrolló Typo3 font como trabajo de clase. La fuente acabaría aplicándose en las páginas de *Cuizine*, un fanzine sobre arte gráfico y culinario. A raíz de que su abuela opinara que las recetas de cocina se leían con dificultad, decidió crear una versión Medium más legible. El resultado es una fuente romana antigua. Se caracteriza por las astas de diferente espesor dentro de una misma letra. Esta fuente lleva remates cuya forma es aguda y refinada. Entre los caracteres clave encontramos la g de caja baja con cuello, oreja y ojal y la G de caja alta sin espuela.

uni 05

Craig Kroeger | www.miniml.com

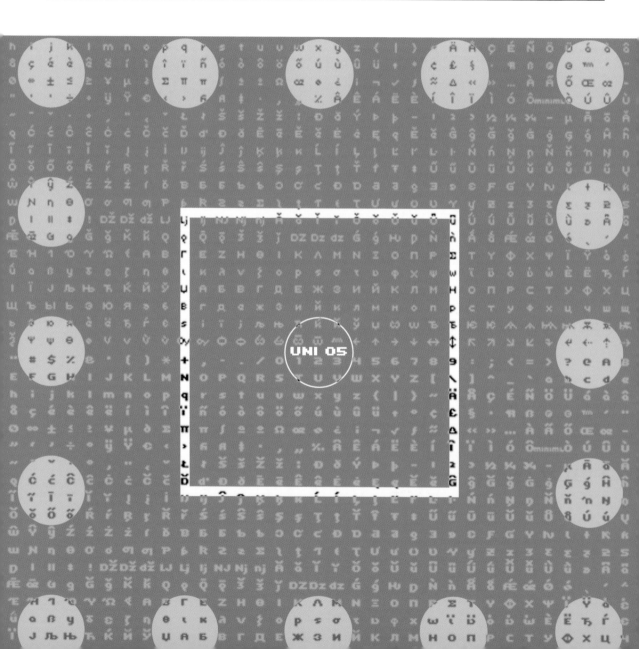

abcdefghijklmnopqrstuvwxyz[áöüßðøœoeçñ]
ABCDEFGHIJKLMNOPQRSTUVWXYZ
1234567890(.,;:?¿$¢£¥&-*){ÁÖÜÅØÆŒÇÑ}

8/10 pt

abcdefghijklmnopqrstuvwxyz[áöüßðøœoeçñ]
ABCDEFGHIJKLMNOPQRSTUVWXYZ
1234567890(.,;:?¿$¢£¥&-*){ÁÖÜÅØÆŒÇÑ}

8/10 pt

abcdefghijklmn
opqrstuvwxyz
[áöüßðøœoeçñ]
ABCDEFGHIJKLMN
OPQRSTUVWXYZ
1234567890
[.,;:?¿$¢£¥&-*]
{ÁÖÜÅØÆŒÇÑ}

18/18 pt

abcdefghijklmn
opqrstuvwxyz
[áöüßðøœoeçñ]
ABCDEFGHIJKLMN
OPQRSTUVWXYZ
1234567890
[.,;:?¿$¢£¥&-*]
{ÁÖÜÅØÆŒÇÑ}

18/18 pt

This font, designed as a small typeface, is compact and very easy to read. With a height of only 5 pixels, it is very suitable for photo captions or footnotes. It can also be used in printed graphics to create a retro computer effect. It is a vector-based pixel font, which is very useful for maintaining the aliasing feature in web applications. The uni 05 font family has four variants: two normal variants with different weights and two monospaced variants with different thicknesses. This family of sans serif fonts includes a set of Latin, Central European and Cyrillic characters.

Conçue comme une police de petite taille, elle est compacte et très lisible. D'une hauteur de seulement 5 pixels, elle convient parfaitement pour des légendes de photo ou des notes de bas de page. Elle peut également être utilisée pour des travaux graphiques afin de donner un effet d'ordinateur rétro. Il s'agit d'une police de type vectoriel et pixélisée, très utile pour conserver le crénelage sur des applications web. Il existe quatre variantes de la famille uni 05 : deux variantes normales de poids différents et deux variantes de chasse fixe et de corps différents. Cette famille sans serif comprend les caractères latins, cyrilliques et d'Europe centrale.

Diseñada como tipografía de tamaño pequeño, es compacta y muy legible. Con tan solo una altura de 5 píxeles, resulta muy adecuada para pies de foto o textos adicionales. También se puede utilizar en trabajos gráficos impresos para generar un efecto de ordenador retro. Se trata de una fuente de tipo vectorial y pixelada, muy útil para conservar el *aliasing* en aplicaciones web. La familia uni 05 se presenta en cuatro variantes: dos variantes normales con pesos diferentes y dos variantes monoespaciadas con diferente grosor. Esta familia de palo seco ofrece el set de caracteres latinos, centro europeos y cirílicos.

Very Damaged

Galdino Otten | galdinoottenbr.blogspot.com

VERY GALDINO OTTEN DAMAGED

ABCDEFGHIJKLM
NOPQRSTUVWXYZ
ABCDEFGHIJKLMNOPQ
RSTUVWXYZ{$?!%@}
1234567890(&#+:)

ABCDEFGHIJKLMNOPQRSTUVWXYZ[ ]
ABCDEFGHIJKLMNOPQRSTUVWXYZ
1234567890(.,:;?$&-){ÇÑ}

8/10 pt

ABCDEFGHIJKLMNOPQRSTUVWXYZ[ ]
ABCDEFGHIJKLMNOPQRSTUVWXYZ
1234567890(.,:;?$&-){ÇÑ}

10/12 pt

ABCDEFGHIJKLMNOPQRSTUVWXYZ[ ]
ABCDEFGHIJKLMNOPQRSTUVWXYZ
1234567890(.,:;?$&-){ÇÑ}

18/18 pt

ABCDEFGHIJKLMNOPQRSTUVWXYZ[ ]
ABCDEFGHIJKLMN
OPQRSTUVWXYZ
1234567890(.,:;?$&-){ÇÑ}

24/24 pt

The design of this font drew its inspiration from posters that had been eroded by sun, wind or human intervention. And also from faded old posters that have yet to be used. The textures of these street posters made such an impression on the designer that they had a huge influence on the shapes designed for this font. A sans serif font that is extravagant and full of fantasy, with a dilapidated look and thickly drawn stems with parallel edges. It falls within the grunge style of fonts and can be applied to several types of work involving graphic design.

L'inspiration pour le design de cette police provient des affiches décolorées par le soleil, le vent et l'intervention humaine, ainsi que de vieux posters qui n'ont pas été utilisés. Les textures présentes dans ces affiches de rue ont tellement impressionné le concepteur que leur grande influence s'apprécie dans le design des formes de cette police. Une police à tige sèche, extravagante et de type fantaisie, qui a un aspect désastreux, avec des hampes à gros trait et des bords parallèles. Il s'agit d'une police de style grunge, applicable à différents types de travaux de design graphique.

La inspiración para el diseño de esta fuente surge de los pósters que se encuentran en las calles, erosionados por el sol, el viento y las intervenciones humanas, o de aquellos carteles envejecidos que no han llegado a utilizarse. Las texturas que presentaban estos pósters impresionaron al diseñador de tal manera que quiso plasmarlas en las formas de esta tipografía. Fuente de palo seco, extravagante y de tipo fantasía, muestra un aspecto dañado, con astas de trazo grueso y bordes paralelos. Se trata de una fuente de estilo *grunge* aplicable para diversos tipos de trabajos de diseño gráfico.

VTKS Easy Way

VTKS | www.vtks.com.br

ABCDEFGHIJKLMNOPQRSTUVWXYZ

8/10 pt

ABCDEFGHIJKLMNOPQRSTUVWXYZ

10/12 pt

ABCDEFGHIJKLMN
OPQRSTUVWXYZ

18/18 pt

ABCDEFGHIJKLMN
OPQRSTUVWXYZ

24/24 pt

ABCDEFGHIJKLMN
OPQRSTUVWXYZ

32/34 pt

Starting with just a ballpoint pen and blank piece of paper on the table, the designer created this font in a fleeting moment of inspiration. The designer values the fact that the font does not have a central point to follow, with each character having different weights. It is a decorative sans serif font that can easily alternate uppercase, lowercase and caps. Its peculiarity resides in the letter G, which is always lowercase with a straight link, open tail and ear. Key characters include: the A with a straight apex; the Q with a long tail; and the R with a straight tail. Numbers, punctuation marks and symbols are not included in the set.

Dans un élan d'inspiration, le graphiste a créé cette police avec uniquement un stylo en main et une page blanche. Le graphiste apprécie le fait que cette police n'ait pas de point central à suivre, chaque caractère a un poids différent. Il s'agit d'une police décorative sans serif qui alterne entre majuscules et minuscules sans aucun problème.
La particularité réside dans la lettre « G » qui est toujours bas de casse avec délié de jonction droit, queue ouverte et empattement. Les caractères clés qui se distinguent sont : le « A » avec une pointe droite, le « Q » avec la queue longue, le « R » avec la queue droite. Elle n'inclut ni chiffres, ni signes de ponctuation, ni symboles.

A partir de tan solo un bolígrafo y una hoja en blanco sobre la mesa, el diseñador creó esta fuente en un fugaz momento de inspiración. El diseñador valora el hecho de que la fuente no tiene un punto central a seguir, sino que cada carácter tiene pesos diferentes. Se trata de una fuente decorativa de palo seco que alterna sin problema las mayúsculas, las minúsculas y las capitales. La peculiaridad se encuentra en la letra G, que siempre es de caja baja con cuello recto, cola abierta y oreja. Entre los caracteres clave destacan la A con vértice recto, la Q con cola larga y la R con cola recta. Los números, signos de puntuación y símbolos no van incluidos en el set.

VTKS News Label

VTKS | www.vtks.com.br

abcdefghijklmnopqrstuvwxyz
ABCDEFGHIJKLMNOPQRSTUVWXYZ

8/10 pt

abcdefghijklmnopqrstuvwxyz
ABCDEFGHIJKLMNOPQRSTUVWXYZ

10/12 pt

abcdefghijklmnopqrstuvwxyz
ABCDEFGHIJKLMNOPQRSTUVWXYZ

18/18 pt

abcdefghijklmn
opqrstuvwxyz
ABCDEFGHIJKLMN
OPQRSTUVWXYZ

24/24 pt

abcdefghijklmn
opqrstuvwxyz
ABCDEFGHIJKLMN
OPQRSTUVWXYZ

32/34 pt

The typographer designed this font to create a bold font with a nostalgic feel to it. The thickness of the stroke is ultra black, flecked with white for a more informal effect. It is a decorative font with flourishes in the form of twisted yarn emerging from the angles on stems, arms, tails, ears, feet and spurs. This sans serif font has continuous curves with a round, slightly squarish appearance. There is a high degree of contrast, with a vertical axis and instant transition. It includes the following key characters: an uppercase A with a straight apex; and a Q with a long tail.

Le design de cette police provient du besoin du typographe de disposer d'une police grasse avec une touche nostalgique. La largeur du trait est très noire et il apparaît tacheté de blanc pour un effet davantage informel. Il s'agit d'une police décorative avec des ornements en forme de fils enroulés qui surgissent des angles présents dans : les hampes, les traverses, les queues, les empattements. Cette police sans serif présente des courbes régulières avec un aspect rond, voire légèrement carré. Cela met en avant un contraste exagéré avec un axe vertical de transition instantanée. Il convient de distinguer les caractères suivants : le « A » haut de casse avec une pointe droite et le « Q » avec une longue queue.

El objetivo del tipógrafo era crear una fuente Bold con aspecto nostálgico. El grosor del trazo es ultranegro y aparece moteado en blanco para un efecto más informal. Es una fuente decorativa, con ornamentos en forma de hilos enroscados que nacen de los ángulos presentes en astas, brazos, colas, orejas, patas y espuelas. Esta fuente de palo seco tiene las curvas continuas con aspecto redondo, ligeramente cuadrado. Muestra un contraste exagerado con eje vertical de transición instantánea. Cabe destacar los siguientes caracteres clave: A de caja alta con vértice recto y Q de cola larga.

VTKS Rock Garage Band

VTKS | www.vtks.com.br

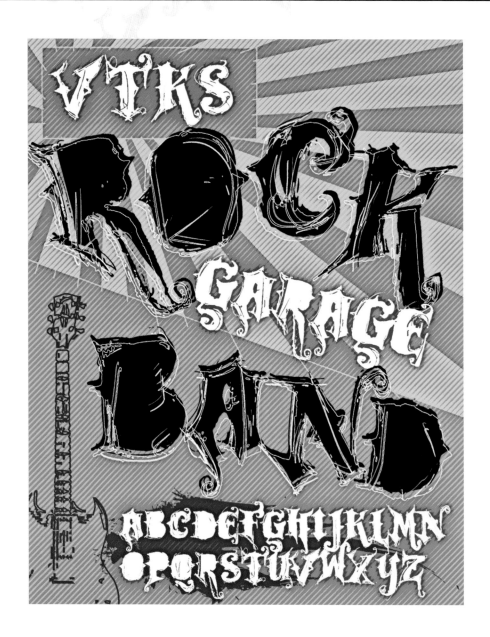

8/10 pt

10/12 pt

18/18 pt

24/24 pt

32/34 pt

Garage rock is a pure form of rock and roll, which was very popular in the United States and Canada during the nineteen sixties. Later on, some rock critics gave it the name of punk rock. The font is intended for print in large formats and low resolution, where errors and irregularities form part of the design. This is one of the most notable characteristics of the punk movement. It is a decorative urban tag font suggesting punch and vigor, appropriate for work with a nasty, informal style such as posters or the field of advertising. With positive counters, it displays exaggerated, ornamental serifs that combine a number of different shapes.

Le *garage rock* est un genre de *rock and roll*, très populaire aux États-Unis et au Canada pendant les années 1960. Par la suite, certains critiques l'ont appelé *punk rock*. Conçu pour des grands formats à faible résolution, où les erreurs et les irrégularités font partie du design (une des caractéristiques les plus marquantes du *punk*). Il s'agit d'une police décorative urbaine qui suggère de l'agressivité, appropriée pour les travaux avec une esthétique sale et informelle comme des panneaux ou des publicités. Avec les boucles coloriées, elle présente des empattements exagérés et des motifs ornementaux avec plusieurs formes.

El *garage rock* es una forma pura del *rock and roll* muy popular en los Estados Unidos y Canadá durante la década de los años 1960. Posteriormente, algunos críticos del *rock* lo etiquetaron como *punk rock*. Está pensada para ser impresa a tamaños grandes y a baja resolución, donde los errores e irregularidades forman parte del diseño, una de las características más notables del estilo *punk*. Se trata de una fuente decorativa rotulada urbana que sugiere agresividad, adecuada para trabajos de cartelería o publicidad con una estética sucia e informal. Con los ojales rellenos, presenta remates exagerados y ornamentales que combinan diversas formas.

VTKS Untitled

VTKS | www.vtks.com.br

ABCDEFGHITKLMNOPORSTUVWXYZ
1234567890 .,?

8/10 pt

ABCDEFGHITKLMNOPORSTUVWXYZ
1234567890 .,?

10/12 pt

ABCDEFGHITKLM
NOPORSTUVWXYZ
1234567890 .,?

18/18 pt

ABCDEFGHITKLMN
OPORSTUVWXYZ
1234567890 .,?

24/24 pt

ABCDEFGHITKLMN
OPORSTUVWXYZ
1234567890 .,?

24/24 pt

The typographer, seeking a slightly retro look, hopes to offer a font that is not only attractive but also strange at the same time. It is a decorative sans serif font, with an eroded appearance and subtly rounded angles. The stems are of varying width and the thickness of the stroke is ultra black. It has continuous construction, and is slightly shapeless with the round curves having a squarish appearance. There is a high degree of contrast, with the vertical axis slightly removed from the center and abrupt transition. Key characters include: the A with a straight apex; the G without a spur; and the Q with a tail cutting through the center of the bowl.

En quête d'un résultat un peu rétro, le typographe souhaite transmettre un aspect à la fois attirant et curieux. Il s'agit d'une police décorative sans serif avec un aspect érodé et des angles subtilement arrondis. La largeur des hampes varie et l'épaisseur des traits est très noire. La construction est homogène, plutôt sans formes avec des courbes arrondies légèrement carrées. On dénote un fort contraste avec l'axe de construction vertical qui n'est pas tout à fait au centre et une transition brusque. Les caractères emblématiques sont : le « A » dont la pointe est droite, le « G » sans empattement et le « Q » dont la queue coupe la panse.

Con un toque un tanto retro, el tipógrafo ha querido crear una fuente de aspecto atractivo y extraño la vez. Se trata de una fuente de palo seco decorativa, con aspecto erosionado y ángulos sutilmente redondeados. La amplitud de las astas es variable y el grosor del trazo es ultranegro. Muestra una construcción continua, algo amorfa con aspecto de la curva redonda ligeramente cuadrada. Se aprecia un contraste exagerado con eje vertical ligeramente desplazado del centro, con transición abrupta. Los caracteres clave destacados son la A con vértice recto, la G sin espuela y la Q con cola que corta el anillo en el centro.

Xilo Galdino

Galdino Otten | galdinoottenbr.blogspot.com

This font was conceived based on the northeast popular couture of Brazil. It can also interact with the Oxent Silibrina font, witch was also conceived by this purpose. I hope the artist that choses it not only be able to denote traces of this couture but also feel free to create new themes aproaching this style. Like in this exemple named:

Dreaming with (Dom) Quixote and (Ariano) Suassuna, 2007.

SONHANDO COM QUIXOTE E SUASSUNA

ABCDEFGHIJKLM
NOPQRSTUVWXYZ
abcdefghijklmnop
rstuvwxyz{$?!%@}
1234567890(&#+:)

abcdefghijklmnopqrstuvwxyz[äöüaçñ]
ABCDEFGHIJKLMNOPQRSTUVWXYZ
1234567890(.,;:?$¥&-*)(ÃÖÜÂÇÑ)

8/10 pt

abcdefghijklmnopqrstuvwxyz[äöüaçñ]
ABCDEFGHIJKLMNOPQRSTUVWXYZ
1234567890(.,;:?$¥&-*)(ÃÖÜÂÇÑ)

10/12 pt

abcdefghijklmn
opqrstuvwxyz[äöüaçñ]
ABCDEFGHIJKLMN
OPQRSTUVWXYZ
1234567890
(.,;:?$¥&-*)(ÃÖÜÂÇÑ)

18/18 pt

abcdefghijklmn
opqrstuvwxyz[äöüaçñ]
ABCDEFGHIJKLMN
OPQRSTUVWXYZ
1234567890
(.,;:?$¥&-*)(ÃÖÜÂÇÑ)

24/24 pt

Its style is reminiscent of xylography in the cordel literature (Portuguese for 'string literature') within the pop culture of northeastern Brazil. This consists of booklets or leaflets hanging from a string in the places where they are sold, in the form of a novel, poem or song with woodcut illustrations on the cover. The strokes of this font are similar to xylography, generating robust shapes but with a certain number of informal details such as asymmetrical serifs, or extremely eloquent strokes and flourishes. Its casual appearance makes it suitable for short texts, advertising, headlines and any other display application.

Son style fait penser à la xylographie dans la littérature de cordel au sein de la culture populaire du Nord-Est du Brésil. Elle se compose de pamphlets et de petits feuillets qui sont suspendus à des ficelles, dans les lieux où ils sont vendus. Il s'agit de nouvelles, de poèmes ou de chansons avec des illustrations de xylographie en couverture. Les traits de cette police ressemblent à la xylographie, produisant des formes robustes et quelques détails informels comme l'asymétrie des empattements ou les traits et les empattements chargés d'expressivité. Par son aspect désinvolte elle convient parfaitement à des textes courts, des publicités, des gros titres ou des expositions.

Por su estilo, recuerda a las xilografías de la literatura de cordel típicas de la cultura popular del noreste de Brasil. Se trata de cuadernillos (con poemas, novelas o canciones) que los vendedores exponen colgados de una cuerda, y que van ilustrados con xilografías en la portada. Los trazos de esta fuente hacen referencia a la xilografía, generando formas robustas pero con ciertos detalles informales como la asimetría de sus serifas o los trazos y remates cargados de expresividad. Su aspecto desenfadado la hace muy apropiada para textos cortos, publicidad, titulares y cualquiera otra aplicación de exhibición.

Yanone Kaffeesatz Regular/Light/Bold

Yanone | www.yanone.de

abcdefghijklmnopqrstuvwxyz[äöüßåøæœçñ]
ABCDEFGHIJKLMNOPQRSTUVWXYZ
1234567890(.,;:?¿$¢€¥&-*)ÄÖÜÅØÆŒÇÑ

8/10 pt

abcdefghijklmnopqrstuvwxyz[äöüßåøæœçñ]
ABCDEFGHIJKLMNOPQRSTUVWXYZ
1234567890(.,;:?¿$¢€¥&-*)ÄÖÜÅØÆŒÇÑ

8/10 pt

abcdefghijklmnopqrstuvwxyz[äöüßåøæœçñ]
ABCDEFGHIJKLMNOPQRSTUVWXYZ
1234567890(.,;:?¿$¢€¥&-*)ÄÖÜÅØÆŒÇÑ

8/10 pt

abcdefghijklmnopqrstuvwxyz[äöüßåøæœçñ]
ABCDEFGHIJKLMNOPQRSTUVWXYZ
1234567890(.,;:?¿$¢€¥&-*)ÄÖÜÅØÆŒÇÑ

18/18 pt

abcdefghijklmnopqrstuvwxyz[äöüßåøæœçñ]
ABCDEFGHIJKLMNOPQRSTUVWXYZ
1234567890(.,;:?¿$¢€¥&-*)ÄÖÜÅØÆŒÇÑ

18/18 pt

abcdefghijklmnopqrstuvwxyz[äöüßåøæœçñ]
ABCDEFGHIJKLMNOPQRSTUVWXYZ
1234567890(.,;:?¿$¢€¥&-*)ÄÖÜÅØÆŒÇÑ

18/18 pt

This was the first complete typeface created by Yanone. Because of his lack of self-confidence and knowledge of the typography scene, he decided to publish his font family for free, achieving unexpected international acclaim. With 100,000 downloads from the Yanone website, Kaffeesatz has been used in German gyms, shopping malls in Dubai and at McDonald's in New Zealand. It was also applied in cafeteria designs all over the world, since the bold variant is reminiscent of the typeface prevalent in the cafés of the twenties. Yanone would subsequently redo a large part of the font and publish it under the name of FF Kava at FontShop's bookshop FontFont.

Voici la première typographie complète de Yanone. Par manque de confiance et de connaissance du monde typographique, il a décidé de publier la famille gratuitement, acquérant une reconnaissante inespérée au niveau international. Avec 100 000 téléchargements depuis la page web de Yanone, la police Kaffeesatz a été utilisée dans des gymnases en Allemagne, des centres commerciaux à Dubaï et un Mc Donald's en Nouvelle Zélande. On la retrouve dans le design de nombreux cafés dans le monde entier, car sa variante bold fait penser à la typographie des cafés des années 1920. Par la suite Yanone a refait une grande partie de la police qui est publiée dans la librairie FontShop's sous le nom de FF Kava.

Fue la primera fuente completa de Yanone. Por falta de confianza en sí mismo y desconocimiento del panorama tipográfico, el diseñador decidió publicar la familia gratuitamente, y logró un inesperado reconocimiento internacional. Con 100.000 descargas, Kaffeesatz se ha aplicado en gimnasios alemanes, centros comerciales en Dubai y en Mc Donald's de Nueva Zelanda. También la utilizan cafeterías de todo el mundo, ya que la variante Bold recuerda la tipografía de estos locales de los años 1920. Posteriormente, Yanone rehizo gran parte de la fuente y la publicó en FontFont Library como FF Kava.

Yard Sale

Harold's Fonts | www.haroldsfonts.com

LOST DOG, BEAGLE/BASSET MIX, ROUGHLY 7 YRS OLD. SHE IS A DEAR MEMBER OF THE FAMILY. A CASH REWARD OF $100 IS OFFERED FOR HER SAFE RETURN, NO QUESTIONS ASKED. SHE WAS LAST SEEN ON 138TH STREET AT 7TH AVE, AROUND 7AM. IF YOU HAVE HER, OR ANY INFO, PLEASE CALL! (210)400-1815 WE ARE EAGERLY AWAITING HER RETURN!

ABCDEFGHIJKLMNOPQRSTUVWXYZ
1234567890(,,::? ¿$¢£€¥¢-*)ÄÖÜÅØ ÆŒÇÑ

8/10 pt

ABCDEFGHIJKLMNOPQRSTUVWXYZ
1234567890(,,::? ¿$¢£€¥¢-*)ÄÖÜÅØ ÆŒÇÑ

10/12 pt

ABCDEFGHIJKLMN
OPQRSTUVWXYZ
1234567890
(,,::? ¿$¢£€¥¢-*)ÄÖÜÅØ ÆŒÇÑ

18/18 pt

ABCDEFGHIJKLMN
OPQRSTUVWXYZ
1234567890
(,,::? ¿$¢£€¥¢-*)
ÄÖÜÅØ ÆŒÇÑ

24/24 pt

A typeface based on the handwritten lettering of small posters crammed full of words, stuck all over the neighborhood by a strange local resident and typography fan. The letters were drawn originally with a thick felt-tip pen and then scanned and adjusted on the computer. The result is a letter with a nice uneven appearance that is fun and entertaining, and very appropriate for casual designs. The personal, spontaneous style is ideal for use in the field of advertising. It is not designed on grids nor do the various characters share any common features. Instead, it is similar to freehand writing.

Cette typographie s'inspire de l'écriture manuscrite qui figure sur des petites affiches où abondent les mots, qu'un voisin particulier, ami du typographe, a collé dans tout le quartier. Les caractères de cette police ont premièrement été dessinés avec un feutre à grosse pointe puis scannés et peaufinés à l'ordinateur. Le résultat est une lettre qui semble irrégulière, agréable, gaie et amusante, particulièrement appropriée pour des créations désinvoltes. Son style personnel et spontané convient parfaitement à la publicité. Les différents caractères n'ont pas été conçus dans un quadrillage et ils n'ont aucun trait commun mais ils imitent une écriture à main levée.

Esta tipografía está basada en la letra manuscrita de unos pequeños anuncios llenos de palabras que un peculiar amigo y vecino del diseñador colgó por todo el barrio. Estas letras fueron dibujadas primero con un rotulador grueso de punta de fieltro para ser posteriormente escaneadas y afinadas en el ordenador. El resultado es una letra de apariencia irregular, amable, alegre y divertida, muy apropiada para diseños desenfadados. Su estilo personal y espontáneo resulta adecuado para publicidad. No está diseñada sobre cuadrículas ni existen rasgos comunes entre distintos caracteres sino que emula la escritura a mano alzada.

Ziperhead

Popdog Fonts | popdog_fonts.tripod.com

ABCDEFGHIJKLMNOPQRSTUVWXYZ⟨ΔΦΕΨZHP⟩
ABCDEFGHIJKLMNOPQRSTUVWXYZ
1234567890(.,;:!€✳_✳)(ΔΦΕΨZHP)

8/10 pt

ABCDEFGHIJKLMNOPQRSTUVWXYZ⟨ΔΦΕΨZHP⟩
ABCDEFGHIJKLMNOPQRSTUVWXYZ
1234567890(.,;:!€✳_✳)(ΔΦΕΨZHP)

10/12 pt

ABCDEFGHIJKLMN
OPQRSTUVWXYZ⟨ΔΦΕΨZHP⟩
ABCDEFGHIJKLMNOPQRSTUVWXYZ
1234567890(.,;:!€✳_✳)(ΔΦΕΨZHP)

18/18 pt

ABCDEFGHIJKLMN
OPQRSTUVWXYZ⟨ΔΦΕΨZHP⟩
ABCDEFGHIJKLMN
OPQRSTUVWXYZ
1234567890
(.,;:!€✳_✳)(ΔΦΕΨZHP)

24/24 pt

This font has been designed for occasional, isolated use as it is not a typeface suitable for running text. It is a handwritten font similar to letters engraved on a wooden tree trunk. This suggests that a gouge has been used as a design tool. In this sans serif font, the terminals of the stems and arms are tapered and imperfect. The treatment of the curves is continuous with a circular appearance and the bowls are closed. Key characters include the A with its tilted apex. The set includes both Latin and Greek characters, bold for uppercase and normal for lowercase.

Cette police a été conçue pour un usage sporadique et isolé car elle n'est pas appropriée pour les textes. Il s'agit d'une police d'écriture à la main qui imite les lettres gravées sur un tronc d'arbre dont l'outil de travail semble avoir été la gouge. Les extrémités des hampes et des traverses de cette police sans serif sont fuselées et imparfaites. Les courbes sont continues et ont un aspect arrondi, les boucles semblent fermées. Parmi les caractères clés, il convient de citer le « A » dont la pointe semble inclinée. La police inclut des caractères latins et grecs, gras pour haut de casse et normaux pour bas de casse.

Esta tipografía ha sido concebida para un uso esporádico y aislado, y no resulta apta para texto corrido. Se trata de una fuente de escritura a mano alzada que simula las letras grabadas en el tronco de un árbol, haciendo referencia a la gubia como elemento de diseño. En esta fuente de palo seco, los extremos de las astas y brazos quedan desfilados e imperfectos. El tratamiento de las curvas es continuo, con aspecto circular, y los anillos aparecen cerrados. Entre los caracteres clave destaca la A, con el vértice inclinado. El set incluye los caracteres latinos y los griegos, Bold para caja alta y normal para caja baja.

Z-Wisdom

Popdog Fonts | popdog_fonts.tripod.com

ετσι την τελειότητα φερώμεθα

perhaps the reason why it is considered a good thing to think about our community motto is because altho it had an obvious application to the little party of children as we were at the beginning — we might think that now there is not the same need for it — that

it has very little
to be only the same
maturity, we
schools in eng
study, a house
up and a new one
of postulants c

immediate ap
but we are n
different stage

z wisdom

abcdefghijklmnopqrstuvwxyz(δφὸίεψζηρ)
ABCDEFGHIJKLMNOPQRSTUVWXYZ
1234567890(.,;:?$&-*)ΛΔΦἀΕΨΖΗΡ

8/10 pt

abcdefghijklmnopqrstuvwxyz(δφὸίεψζηρ)
ABCDEFGHIJKLMNOPQRSTUVWXYZ
1234567890(.,;:?$&-*)ΛΔΦἀΕΨΖΗΡ

10/12 pt

abcdefghijklmn
opqrstuvwxyz(δφὸίεψζηρ)
ABCDEFGHIJKLMN
OPQRSTUVWXYZ
1234567890
(.,;:?$&-*)ΛΔΦἀΕΨΖΗΡ

18/18 pt

abcdefghijklmn
opqrstuvwxyz
(δφὸίεψζηρ)
ABCDEFGHIJKLMN
OPQRSTUVWXYZ
1234567890
(.,;:?$&-*)
ΛΔΦἀΕΨΖΗΡ

24/24 pt

Despite the eroded appearance inside the stroke, this decorative sans serif font has a clean, well-defined outline. It displays a continuous construction with the curve giving it a circular appearance, and no contrast. The stems have parallel edges and the bars occupy a central position. The proportions are wide with a generally even width in the caps and a small x-height. Key characters include: the double-storied lowercase a; the uppercase A with a straight apex; the uppercase G with a vertical spur. The set includes both Latin and Greek characters.

Bien que l'intérieur des caractères semble érodé, les contours de cette police décorative sans serif sont nets et définis. La construction est homogène avec des courbes circulaires, sans contraste. Les hampes verticales ont des bords parallèles et les traverses sont placées au milieu de la lettre. La taille des caractères est grande avec une largeur des capitales régulière et une petite hauteur d'oeil. Les caractères clés sont : un « a » bas de casse en script, un « A » haut de casse dont la pointe est droite, un « G » haut de casse à empattement vertical. La police inclut des caractères latins et grecs.

A pesar del aspecto erosionado en el interior del trazo, esta fuente decorativa de palo seco tiene un contorno limpio y definido. Muestra una construcción continua con aspecto de la curva circular y sin contraste. Las astas verticales son de bordes paralelos y las astas transversales quedan en posición central. Tiene unas proporciones anchas con anchura de las capitales generalmente regular y la altura de la x pequeña. Entre los caracteres clave se encuentran la a de caja baja de dos pisos, la A de caja alta con vértice recto y la G de caja alta con espuela vertical. El set incluye caracteres latinos y griegos.

Leabharlanna Poiblí Chathair Bhaile Átha Cliath
Dublin City Public Libraries

© All the fonts featured in this book and CD are offered free of charge. However, they remain copyrighted material and property of their creators. In case of commercial use, republishing or lucrative purposes please get in touch with the individual designers.
Encourage creativity, respect copyright!
The designers decline all responsibility for errors or deficiencies in the fonts or in the documentation accompanying them, as for any damage that may arise from them.
The accompanying CD is not for sale. The publishers decline all responsibility should the CD be incompatible with your computer system.

© Toutes les polices de caractères présentes dans cet ouvrage et dans ce CD sont offertes à titre gracieux. Cependant, elles constituent un matériel protégé par les droits d'auteur et sont la propriété de leurs créateurs. Pour tout usage commercial, lucratif ou de réédition, veuillez contacter le designer concerné.
Encouragez la créativité, respectez le copyright !
Les designers déclinent toute responsabilité en cas d'erreur ou de carence des polices de caractères ou de la documentation qui les accompagne, ainsi que pour tout dommage qu'elles pourraient occasionner.
Le CD ci-joint n'est pas destiné à la vente. Les éditeurs déclinent toute responsabilité en cas d'incompatibilité entre le CD et votre ordinateur.

© Todas las fuentes que aparecen en el libro y en el CD se ofrecen gratuitamente. No obstante, conservan el copyright y son propiedad de sus creadores. Para usos comerciales, editoriales o lucrativos, póngase en contacto con sus respectivos diseñadores.
Fomenta la creatividad, ¡respeta el copyright!
Los diseñadores no se hacen responsables de cualquier error o deficiencia que pueda haber en las fuentes o en la documentación que las acompaña, así como por los posibles daños que pudieran generarse por estos.
El CD adjunto no está a la venta. Los editores no se hacen responsables en caso de que el CD fuera incompatible con el sistema operativo de su ordenador.